"This compelling multi-voice story explains how Asian America came into being as both a political identity and a place to call home ... *Serve the People* powerfully argues that recovering and remembering the Asian American Movement is not to live in the past, but rather to claim the future that the Asian American Movement envisioned."
—Tracy Lai, *International Examiner*

"This fascinating study is highly recommended for those interested in Asian American history and the civil rights movement."
—Joshua Wallace, *Library Journal*

"With meticulous research and more than a hundred interviews, Karen Ishizuka traces the links between Yellow Power and other radical movements. This engaging book breaks through to new levels of insight into this still-neglected movement of far-reaching influence."
—Helen Zia, author of *Asian American Dreams: The Emergence of an American People*

"Karen Ishizuka deftly captures a generation of activist voices from San Francisco to Los Angeles, Seattle to New York. This thoughtful history chronicles a movement just as significant as the Black and Chicano movements and provides a revelatory insight into what it means to be American."
—Jesús Salvador Treviño, author of *Eyewitness: A Filmmaker's Memoir of the Chicano Movement*

"Karen Ishizuka has opened a window to an ignored but significant part of American history. I love the captivating cartoons, newspaper and arts sections, but what really enlivens her narrative and adds depth to her work is her personal relationship to this history."
—Dale Minami, attorney and cofounder, Asian Law Caucus

"An exceptionally well-researched and engaging book."
—Jonathan Y. Okamura, *The Hawai'i Herald*

D0796986

"Every now and then someone gets pissed enough to poke the model minority myth of Asian American passivity in the eye. Karen Ishizuka's new book does just that."
—Miriam Ching Louie, author of *Sweatshop Warriors: Immigrant Women Workers Take On the Global Factory*

"Thoughtful and readable, *Serve the People* explores how activists of Chinese, Japanese, and Filipino descent forged the identity of 'Asian American' to make sense of grievances uniting Asian-based ethnic groups. In the process, they acted valiantly, if not always effectively, for a more democratic, egalitarian US."
—J.S. Frank, *Choice*

"Peers behind the contemporary narrative of Asian Americans achieving 'visibility,' with an intricate depiction of the movement that originated the Asian American vision … One of the first comprehensive histories of the movement … *Serve the People* sheds a backlight on our hyphenated cultural present—not just in terms of who and what 'Asian American' has come to mean, but also in terms of how any political movement becomes an identity and vice versa."
—Michelle Chen, *CultureStrike*

"With scholarship and verve, Ishizuka traces the creation of what would be called the 'yellow power movement' … From San Francisco to New York to Los Angeles, from students to activists, Ishizuka depicts how the story of Asian America is multi-voiced and variegated."
—Stephanie Bartolome, Greenlight Bookstore, *Brooklyn Paper*

"Fascinating and thorough history … The range and depth covered within these pages makes this tome essential reading for anyone interested in the past, present and future of what it means to be Asian American."
—Mike Sonksen, *Entropy*

"An indispensable narrative archive of Asian-American organizing and insurgency."
—Brandon Shimoda, *The Millions*

# SERVE THE PEOPLE

# SERVE THE PEOPLE

*Making Asian America in the Long Sixties*

Karen L. Ishizuka

VERSO
London • New York

This paperback edition first published by Verso 2018
First published by Verso 2016
© Karen L. Ishizuka 2016, 2018
Foreword © Jeff Chang 2016, 2018

1 3 5 7 9 10 8 6 4 2

**Verso**
UK: 6 Meard Street, London W1F 0EG
US: 20 Jay Street, Suite 1010, Brooklyn, NY 11201
versobooks.com

Verso is the imprint of New Left Books

ISBN-13: 978-1-78168-998-1
ISBN-13: 978-1-78168-863-2 (UK EBK)
ISBN-13: 978-1-78168-864-9 (US EBK)

**British Library Cataloguing in Publication Data**
A catalogue record for this book is available from the British Library

**Library of Congress Cataloging-in-Publication Data**
A catalog record for this book is available from the Library of Congress

Typeset in Adobe Garamond Pro by MJ & N Gavan, Truro, Cornwall
Printed in the US by Maple Press

For

My New York *Onesans*:

Kazu Iijima
Yuri Kochiyama
Michi Weglyn
Aiko Herzig-Yoshinaga

Brothers:

Chris Iijima
Victor Shibata
Louie Green

and

Most of All:

Bob

*Fierce-browed, I cooly defy a thousand fingers*
*Head-bowed, like a willing ox, I serve the*
*children.*

Lu Xun, 1942

# Contents

*Foreword* by Jeff Chang                                      xi

Introduction: Wherefore Asian America?                         1

ACT I: American Chop Suey

  1.  Growing Up Alien in America                    15

  2.  Living in B&W                                   37

ACT II: Once in a Movement

  3.  Yellow Power                                    59

  4.  Spontaneous Arisings                            75

  5.  Gooks                                           97

  6.  To Serve the People                            115

  7.  Arts of Activism                               133

  8.  Other Wars                                     165

## ACT III: Finding Our Truth

9.  Self-Appraisals and Evaluations — 189

10.  Generations to Come — 209

*Acknowledgments* — 227
*Illustration Credits* — 231
*Notes* — 233
*Index* — 257

# Foreword
## by Jeff Chang

Consider the Asian American at the dawn of her history—skipping past the toddling and babbling, leaping straight into loud youthful rebellion. There was a time, Karen Ishizuka reminds us, when the term "Asian American" was not merely a demographic category, but a fight you were picking with the world, an argument you intended to draw out with indifferent or hostile parties. In 1969, "Asian America" was about young people, mostly second-, third-, or even fourth-generation in the United States, waking to their in-betweenness—between Black and white, migrant and citizen, silence and screaming—and finding collective release in a mass upwelling of feeling.

To say that the notion of Asian America was a social construct is to ignore the beautiful, sometimes destructive energies of this great becoming, the passionate ideas, the dazzling creations, and the abject failures of a multitude in motion. *Serve the People* is a history of what it felt like to live in those times—from the intensity and ecstasy of the period of discovery to the terror and betrayal of the spent revolution. It is the story of imaginations afire—a grand and necessarily naive project to enlarge possibility in a time of change.

Asian America was born in an age of countercultural ferment. There is a familiar developmental arc to countercultures, a narrative in three acts. Act One speaks of emergence: the sense of something big, the intoxicating musk of sweaty rooms, the explosion of ideas, the taking to the streets. Act Two is maturation: it's the time of manifestos, standing-room-only meetings, confrontations with authority, the building of institutions, the anticipation of power. Act Three is the period of backlash and/or transfiguration: the revolution is televised, the empire strikes back, the pressure drops, the witch hunts, the factions, the meltdown, the crossover, the spectacle. All this happened.

But Asian America was more than just a counterculture. By the mid 1970s, it was embarrassing to call oneself a "hippie," still is. But "Asian American" has come to symbolize much more and much less—about which more shortly—than its advocates ever intended. We have come to call the moment that Ishizuka captures the Asian American movement because after it we saw ourselves differently. The movement built a national infrastructure that advanced a racial critique of identity, economy, and culture, developed a body of knowledge around those of Asian and Pacific Islander descent in the United States and around the globe, and established a way of approaching questions of identity and justice.

As it did, Asian America became less than what its pioneers had hoped as well. Being Asian American now hardly requires radicality. In an era where pseudo-intellectuals like Michele Malkin can trade on their race and gender to decry feminist and antiracist work, it is no wonder that the hard-thinking, self-sacrificing renegades who made Asian Americans visible through their rigorous activism and art may now feel nostalgic for the old struggle.

But Asian America has always been about being in-between. Liminality is not permanent. Remember the old racist school rhyme about the Chinaman sitting on the fence? Racism always requires making a choice. But in the postmulticultural United States, racial hierarchy, our in-between position—as recipients of racist love almost as perilous as racist hate—is at once comfortable and discomforting. Where do we go from here? The choices we make now will resonate long past the middle of this century, when the United States becomes a "majority minority."

In this regard, the Long Sixties still casts its long shadow. Asian Americans may never find the same certitude the dreamers of then seemed to have about the path toward racial justice. At any rate, Ishizuka also shows the price of that certitude: the cruel self-policing, the horrible omissions, the paths left untaken. It is also true that each generation must deal with the struggles left unresolved by those who came before. While Ishizuka is committed to telling the story of her peers and her time, she is hardly a triumphalist. She is critical where the story demands it. These Asian American dreamers powerfully reshaped our world, but the failure of their revolution—and the subsequent compounding damage of five decades of reactionary backlash—leaves us a half-century later with many of the conditions that shaped their era—resegregation, growing inequality, historical amnesia.

That is the nature of struggle. As Grace Lee Boggs, whose spirit lingers over Ishizuka's book, reminds us, every change produces new conditions, new opportunities, and new battles. Our job is in part to recognize how we win just as precisely as we recognize how we lose, so that we may face the present and future without illusion. Ishizuka's finally hopeful narrative lets us know that those who are concerned with change cannot submit to pessimism. History is not a burden, a blueprint, or an ending; it is a beacon. *Serve the People* may teach us how we might overcome our ache and learn to see and dream big again.

# INTRODUCTION

## Wherefore Asian America?

> *Discovery cannot be purely intellectual but must also involve action; nor can it be limited to mere activism, but must include serious reflection.*
>
> Paulo Freire

U p until the cultural revolution of the "Long Sixties"—the elongated decade that began in the mid 1950s and lasted until the mid 1970s—there were no Asian Americans. Rather, we were Americans of Japanese, Chinese, or Filipino ancestry: the ethnicities that constituted the majority of Asians in the United States at that time. Being non-white in a Eurocentric society, we were subject to the dominance of whiteness and subsequent subordination faced by all Americans of color. Yet not being black in a society that was defined and rendered in black and white rendered us inconsequential, if not invisible. And while we were Americans—by 1970 almost 80 percent of Japanese Americans and roughly 50 percent of Chinese and Filipino Americans were born in the United States[1]—we were not seen as such.

And so, in the late 1960s, pushed by a racist war against people who looked like us and pulled by the promise of a Third World that called for self-determination instead of assimilation, Asians throughout the United States came together to create a home we never had. We called it Asian America.

The prehistory of Asian America began with the large-scale immigration of laborers from China, Japan, and the Philippines to the territory of Hawai'i and the continental United States, beginning in the mid 1800s. Impelled by poverty and political unrest in their home countries, most intended to make their fortune in what the Chinese called the "Gold Mountain" and then return to their homelands. However, as the days became years, finding more hardships than riches, and despite exclusionary laws and discriminatory quotas, these "Birds of Passage," as the Japanese called themselves, ended up staying and making America their home.

In the 1950s, '60s, '70s, and even today, even though many of us have been Americans for generations, being neither white nor black, we are still routinely asked: "What are you?" "Do you speak English?" "Where do you come from?" Just as our forebears were considered "aliens ineligible to citizenship," barred from naturalization, we too felt alien in America. After years of being treated, as Sharon Maeda put it, "like foreign exchange students" in our own country, by the mid 1960s we were chomping at the bit and ready to throw off the rider. Like Steve Louie, who jumped up and cried "Yes!" when he saw African Americans standing up to growling police dogs, water hoses, and fellow Americans on his black and white TV, and like Evelyn Yoshimura, who recognized the kinship of being called "sister" by a black Muslim, Asians in America identified with and were inspired by the civil rights and Black Liberation movements. And when Sharon, Steve, Evelyn, and others of our generation saw people who looked like us being slaughtered in a racist, imperialistic war, we were compelled to enlist in the anti–Vietnam War movement.

By the late 1960s, Chinese, Japanese, and Filipino Americans had formed a movement of our own—an Asian American movement. From the streets, the campuses, and even from middle-aged, middle-class urban enclaves throughout the United States, these self-defined Asian Americans linked destinies to defy white standards of truth and beauty, lay claim to our lost histories, and affirm ourselves as a political force. In light of decades of thinking that we needed to accommodate to an unjust system, the notion of self-determination was groundbreaking and profound. It provided a revolutionary new level of understanding that would anchor, as well as inspire, the development of an alternative epistemology. We burned the state-imposed effigy of "Oriental," raised a collective fist, and in the poetics of Manong Al Robles, shouted "puckyooo sunn-obbaa-bit, muderrpuckkerrrrrrrr!!!"[2]

Looking like the enemy, we brought a new level of racial analysis to the fight against the Vietnam War. Learning about the expendability of Chinese railroad workers, the exploitation of Filipino cannery and farm workers, and the mass incarceration of Japanese Americans during World War II, we deepened and expanded the history of US labor and the scope of civil rights. Spurred by the Black Liberation movement and anticolonial struggles around the world, we claimed our place in the United States as Americans of color and strengthened the multiethnic scaffold of US history and identity. This newfound consciousness and activism led to a political awakening that overhauled how Asians in the United States were viewed—and, more importantly, how we viewed ourselves.

Against the backdrop of the Vietnam War and the revelation of the Third World, the concept of "Asian American" was formed as a political identity developed out of the oppositional consciousness of the Long Sixties in order to be seen and heard. Simone de Beauvoir contended that one was not born but rather became a woman. Similarly, one was not born but rather willfully became an Asian American.

These days, however, the term has been neutralized into a mere adjective, barely more than a census label. As storyteller and musician Charlie Chin reflected,

> Currently when you say Asian American, all it means is that you are of Asian descent. But originally, it was a loaded word, an explosive phrase that defined a position, a very important position: I am not a marginalized person. I don't apologize for being Asian. I start with the premise that we have a long and involved history here of participation and contribution and I have a right to be here.

Charlie's singing partner, Chris Iijima, added: "It was less a marker of what one was and more a marker of what one believed."[3]

## Finding Our Truth

The elongated, contradictory, and complex era that British historian Arthur Marwick branded the "Cultural Revolution of the Long Sixties" for its unprecedented groundswell of social and cultural transformation lasted, he said, from 1958 to 1974.[4] Political theorist Fredric Jameson likewise periodized the Sixties as beginning in the late 1950s with the decolonization of British and French Africa, emphasizing its beginnings in the Third World, and ending in 1974 with the winding-up of the anti-war movement.[5]

Continuing to act as both a touchstone and catalyst, the spirit of the Long Sixties is best summarized by Malcolm X: "We want freedom by any means necessary. We want justice by any means necessary. We want equality by any means necessary." Intervening between the xenophobia of the 1950s and the neoliberalism of the 1980s, the standard laundry list of the civil rights, countercultural, anti-war, liberation, and solidarity movements that challenged the mythical norm hardly conveys the passions, transformations, and new ways of thinking that the political movements of the Sixties engendered. In the social history of the United States, when Flower Power morphed into Black Power, it marked a cultural as well as political turn that retrofitted the country in ways we are still trying to understand. In addition to the abundance of books on the era, in 2008 a group of young scholars founded an academic journal called *The Sixties: A Journal of History, Politics and Culture* in the continuing quest to understand the epoch because, they said, "We were too young to have been fully in the thrall of the Sixties, but just old enough to know that we missed something big."[6]

Despite the considerable literature on social movements of the Sixties, there is glaringly little on the Chicana/o movement or the American Indian movement, and even less on the Asian American movement. In 1989, activist and educator Elizabeth Martínez pointed out, "The most serious neglect is in the treatment of Asian Americans. Not one of the twenty-four books [on the progressive social movements of the 1960s] seriously recognizes Asian American protest."[7] Almost twenty years later, Asian American movement scholar Diane C. Fujino still found that "Asian American activism barely registers on any political radar."[8]

Even given the opportunity of recovering the activism of the 1970s, which is when the Asian American movement was at its peak, anthologies with titles like *The Hidden 1970s: Histories of Radicalism* (2010) fail to address any aspect of Asian American activism.

There have only been a handful of books that specifically address the Asian American movement of the Long Sixties as a whole. The first full-length study was William Wei's *The Asian American Movement* (1993), which characterized it as primarily "a middle-class reform movement." Fred Ho edited the anthology *Legacy to Liberation: Politics and Culture of Revolutionary Asian Pacific America* (2000), which contrastingly claimed that the Asian American movement "was unique in comparison to other US social movements in that it was overwhelmingly radical and revolutionary." The anthology *Asian Americans: The Movement and the Moment* (2001), edited by Steve Louie and Glenn Omatsu, provided a variety of first-person perspectives as well as a rich array of archival images and texts from the era. *The Snake Dance of Asian American Activism: Community, Vision and Power* (2008) by Michael Liu, Kim Geron, and Tracy Lai analyzed the Asian American movement through the lens of social movement theory, interpreting it as persisting until the late 1980s. *Stand Up: An Archive Collection of the Bay Area Asian American Movement, 1968–1974* (2009) by the Asian Community Center Archive Group compiled primary texts and images that would otherwise be hard to access. *Chains of Babylon: The Rise of Asian America* (2009), by Daryl Maeda, focused on the Asian American movement as a cultural movement, following cultural theorist Lisa Lowe's dictum, "Where the political terrain can neither resolve nor suppress inequality, it erupts in culture." Two years later, Maeda wrote *Rethinking the Asian American Movement* (2011), a concise, informative overview.

Both separately and together, these texts broke new ground, uncovering and mining this neglected area of US history, thereby blazing a pathway for this book and the many more that should be written. Like the proverbial blind sages describing different parts of an elephant, these books indicate how the Asian American movement looks from various points of view—which is as much a testament to the movement's broad and inclusive reach as it is reflective of differences in standpoint. Although each of these publications is important and instructive, Diane

Fujino argued that there is still relatively little scholarship on the era in the field of Asian American studies, which, she said, has produced a tension between "acknowledging and erasing" its activist history.[9]

Former Students for a Democratic Society (SDS) member Bernardine Dorhn claimed that the Sixties "began in 1954 and they're not over yet." Dorhn's comrade Tom Hayden added, "If the sixties are not over, it is up to the sixties generation to continue trying to find our truth." In the words of L. Ling Chi Wang, a pioneer in the field of Asian Americans studies, "To me, the genesis of the Asian American movement is the turning point in our history in this country." This book is part of an ongoing effort to find that truth. How did Asian America come into existence? How, once created, did this new consciousness engender new ideas that were epistemological and ontological as well as ways of being that were transformational and liberating? And is the story of the making of Asian America relevant to the present, or is it merely a matter of nostalgia?

### Views from Within

In the history of social movement studies, a preoccupation with the external structures of organization and strategy tended to overshadow internal constructions of meaning and purpose for participants. But social movements are more than demonstrations, demands, political slogans, and ideologies. At their heart are moments of personal awareness that are strengthened through the life-pulse of collective ownership; lead to political, social, and cultural activism; and have resulted in new identities, agencies, and understandings. As social movement scholar James M. Jasper noted, research that focuses exclusively on the organizations of protest "lose sight of the careers of protest, the personalities of protestors and the pleasures of protest."[10] In this book, I have sought to understand those careers, those personalities, those pleasures, knowing that it is lived experiences and impassioned expressions that make a movement a movement and more than just a political campaign.

The process of politicization begins with individual epiphanies— "aha moments" that turn up the volume, demanding to be heard. Many originate in childhood, when life is more visceral than cerebral, and adults do not suspect that you are cognizant but you are. Like when you're minding your own business, and suddenly you're "the Dirty Jap" instead of "Jack Armstrong, All-American Boy"[11] like my husband Bob Nakamura; or when you are kicked off a bus for being a Dirty Jap when you are really Filipino, like Bob Santos; or when you have to wear a pin declaring "I'm Chinese" in order to differentiate yourself from the Dirty Jap, like Paul Louie. Suffered at the moment of impact more as injuries and indignities than as epiphanies, these experiences are filed away in a Pandora's box that you don't even know you are carrying around.

I didn't. It was not until 1969 that the burgeoning Asian American movement created a safe enough space that my Pandora's box could be pried open. Instead of unleashing demons, it showed me the way home. Like so many of us, I awakened to the Asian American movement while I was a student. I found the first issue of *Gidra*—the first and longest-lasting newspaper of the Asian American movement—in April 1969, while attending California State College, Los Angeles. That summer I enrolled in an ad hoc undertaking called the Asian American Experimental College, an early effort to take the campus into the community, taking Alan Nishio's class "Social Conflict and the Process of Change." The impact of fellow travelers was paramount.

In the fall, I moved to San Diego for graduate studies in social work. Working in the area of drug-abuse prevention, I met Victor Shibata and other members of Yellow Brotherhood, as well as Ray Tasaki, Russell Valparaiso, and others from Asian American Hardcore—two self-help groups working with endangered people. They responded to my call to come down from Los Angeles to meet with young people with whom I was working. Being near Camp Pendleton and in the grip of the anti-war effort, I met Pat Sumi, who was at that time organizing with the Movement for a Democratic Military. Meanwhile, researching the mental health effects of the World War II camps on my generation (which was born after the war) for my master's thesis, I campaigned for the repeal of Title II of the Internal Security Act, the so-called concentration camp law that was still on the books, corresponding with Ray Okamura, one of the front-runners of the campaign.

While in Chicago attending a social work conference, I met former

Weatherman Shinya Ono, who was recently released from prison, in a demonstration (in the snow) protesting the hotel in which I was staying for serving grapes during the grape boycott. I attended summer conferences of the San Francisco Center for Japanese American Studies, where I met George and Nancy Araki, Jim and Lane Hirabayashi, Phil Taijitsu Nash, Philip Gotanda, and many others.

In the summer of 1972, I was among a group of mutineers who tried to get a progressive slate elected to the national Japanese American Citizens' League (JACL) at their conference in Washington, DC—an attempted takeover, if you will, of a ready-made national, but middle-of-the-road, Asian American organization. We failed, but not without a vociferous fight, during which nine staff members resigned en masse. That would-be coup was also where I got to know people like Ron Hirano, Jeffrey Matsui, Ron Wakabayashi, and Bob Nakamura, who I would marry six years later.

A turning point came after the conference, when together with Warren Furutani, Victor Shibata, and Alan Ohashi, I took the train up to New York City, where I met four remarkable women who I forever after affectionately called my New York *onesans* ("older sisters")—Kazu Iijima (who cofounded Asian Americans for Action, the first Asian American political group on the East Coast), Yuri Kochiyama (best known for cradling Malcolm X when he died), Aiko Herzig-Yoshinaga (who uncovered key archival evidence regarding the World War II injustice to Japanese Americans), and Michi Weglyn (the first Japanese American to write a major book on the World War II incarceration of Japanese Americans). Not only were they all trailblazers—each became a personal mentor to me in lifelong and multiple ways.

My first visit to the Big Apple, the ever-present din and summer heat of the big city heightened the intensity and dynamism of our East Coast counterparts, making me feel like an outright country cousin as they whisked us off to meetings, meals, and more meetings. Some of us stayed in Washington Heights with Tak and Kazu Iijima; others stayed with Yuri and Bill Kochiyama in Harlem. I met Chris Iijima and his sister Lynne, Audee and Aichi Kochiyama, Bea Hsia, and many others. I answered the phone at the Kochiyama residence and took a message from Kathleen Cleaver. We were there when the murder of

Nguyen Thai Binh, a Vietnamese anti-war activist who would be my future daughter's namesake, elicited one of Yuri's stirring impromptu discourses, this one about why we all must work that much harder. In an exchange that reflected the fast-paced intensity of the times as well as regional differences in how things got done, we SoCal folks expressed our bewilderment about the mysterious subterranean subway system by asking our New York cohorts how they got to more than one meeting a night without a car. Their response was: "We were going to ask you the same thing. How do you get to more than one meeting a night without a subway?"

I was not a leader or organizer, I never got arrested. Rather, I was one of the 99 percent who were caught by what activist and anthropologist Karen Brodkin called a "contagious energy" that drew people to action, even if they had never been active before. It was a sense, she explained, of liberation, of infinite possibility—an explosive energy.[12]

## Theory in the Flesh

The importance of lived experience as the bedrock of theory has been established in particular by Third World feminists. Cherrie Moraga and Gloria Anzaldúa proposed a "theory in the flesh" in which "the physical realities of our lives ... all fuse to create a politic born out of necessity."[13] Barbara Christian claimed that people of color theorize in narrative forms, "in the stories we create ... because dynamic rather than fixed ideas seem more to our liking."[14]

In the words of Brazilian educator and philosopher Paulo Freire, "It is only when the oppressed find the oppressor out and become involved in the organized struggle for their liberation that they begin to believe in themselves."[15] To help me understand the genesis of the Asian American movement, I called upon activists who were among the first to find the oppressor out and transform themselves and others from Orientals into Asian Americans. I attempted to access a broad range of perspectives and experiences encompassing the major ethnicities of Chinese, Japanese, and Filipino (regrettably omitting less populous Asian ethnic groups of the era) from a cohort as various as possible in terms of age,

gender, class, demography, and sexual orientation, within the constraints of time and resources—around 120 people over approximately
eight years. Some of these first responders were movers and shakers;
others were grunts—the proletariat of the movement. All were makers
of history as Marx indicated, or, as anthropologist Barbara Meyerhoff
termed, "authors of ourselves." Architects and construction workers of
Asian America, they are the standard-bearers of Paulo Freire's declaration: "The oppressed must be their own example in the struggle for their
redemption."[16]

I asked them to share personal discoveries and experiences that led to
their intervention in history as contributors to social change, believing
that the makers of history are often the best historians. To this end, they
shared where and how they had grown up, the people and events that
influenced who they had become, and the inner and outer contours of
their activism. Together, their discoveries, activism and reflections are
symbolic of our generation of political cohorts as a whole.[17]

With these three themes, this book paints a broad panorama of Asian
America through untold stories of some of its pioneers, privileging thick
description over thin conclusions. As they spoke, many conflated pro-
nouns, speaking in the plural using "us" and "we" instead of "I" and
"me," reflecting the communal nature of the mission. In retelling their
experiences, which have become our history, I too have adopted the
first-person plural, liberally speaking of a collective "we."

"Act I: American Chop Suey" addresses why and how Asian America
came to be. In the 1950s and 1960s, few in number and being neither
black nor white, Chinese, Japanese, and Filipinos in the United States
grew up as aliens, outside the taxonomy of Americanness—an enigma
to others as well as to ourselves. Navigating the sea of whiteness that
surrounded us, and being used as a model minority in racial relations,
we resolved to determine who we really were.

"Act II: Once in a Movement" invokes the pivotal era of Asian
American activism from 1968 to the mid-to-late 1970s, when social,
political, and cultural issues erupted concurrently, rapidly, and in multiple places. We realized that trying to assimilate not only didn't work, it
was no longer the goal. Fed up with our marginal status, outraged by
an unnecessary war against fellow Asians, and inspired by Third World

movements at home and abroad, we established new organizations, cultural productions, forms of knowledge, and ways of being, creating a political culture that was uniquely ours.

"Act III: Finding Our Truth" reflects on the memory and meaning of the Asian America movement. As Frantz Fanon asserted, "Each generation must, out of relative obscurity, discover its mission, fulfill it, or betray it."[18] Part of that mission is to prevent what Diane Fujino calls "intergenerational discontinuity"—the disruption of information between generations.[19] Yet, even as we pass on the lessons, the continuum shifts, and the context changes. Ultimately, the very least we can do is to pass on our stories and continue to live and fight for the change we sought in our youth, knowing that each generation must find its own mission, make its own mistakes, and experience its own nostalgia.

Not that it was a linear progression between Act I and Act III. Like all social movements, the Asian American movement was like a cosmic Venn diagram of overlapping personal meaning, political activism, and cultural production. While every person I interviewed would maintain that the whole of the Asian American movement was and is greater than their part in making it, without their particular awakenings and activism Asian America would never have come into being. Back in the day, collective action overruled individual performance and that was good—necessary even—in order to put into practice a philosophy of communality. However, as much as the Asian American movement was ultimately a collective grassroots effort, and whereas we once operated in collectivity and anonymity, I believe that we now need to put at least some of the names and faces to the many deeds and ideas, in order to remind ourselves of a kinship and mutuality that would otherwise remain unknown.

In this way this book is more theirs—the activists, artists and workers who shared their experiences and understandings during this unrepeatable moment—than it is mine. It reflects their memories and rich descriptions of the enormous elephant that was the Asian American movement. In the course of the many years it has taken me to write this book, some have called me "courageous" for attempting to corral this mighty creature within the covers of a single volume, no doubt in part referring to the inevitable scrutiny and criticism that would come from those to whom the Asian American movement has meant so much. As one interviewee commented, "Those who were closest to it may have the hardest time seeing the whole picture."

Despite my attempt to check off with everyone whose stories I included for accuracy, and the review of several people who read all or some of this book in its many drafts, it will undoubtedly elicit disputes and disagreements—and so it should. This book is but one endeavor to document our history before too many more of us leave this earth or forget how to tie our shoes. I hope it will encourage—and provoke—others to write about the many aspects of the Asian American movement that need to be told. At the very least, I trust that it will serve as a reminder of what Clive James wrote about cultural amnesia: "If we can't remember it all, we should at least have some idea of what we have forgotten."[20]

# ACT I: AMERICAN CHOP SUEY

*Genuine American Chop Suey Served Here*

Shanghai restaurant sign

## ONE

## Growing Up Alien in America

*For all practical purposes, I am a "white man," whether or not the white world is willing to accept me as one. In fact, I get the shock of my life every morning when I wake up, look in the mirror, and see a Chinese man staring back at me!*

Edward Long

Edward Long, then a student at the University of California, Los Angeles, read an article about the newly formed Asian American Studies Center in the campus newspaper. It unsettled him so much he was compelled to write a letter to the editor in which he questioned why there should be such a program, since "most Orientals are more 'American' than Oriental anyway." His reasoning was: "I wear a shirt and tie, not a Chinese robe. I speak English, not Mandarin. Though I eat Chinese food, I prefer steak and potatoes. I believe in Jesus Christ, not Confucius."[1] His reasoning was circular. Like many others, he apparently thought that the only way to be American was not to be Asian, that being Chinese and being American were mutually exclusive and cognitively dissonant.

I ran into my own macabre mirror in elementary school. I was one of a handful of Asian kids who grew up in a lower-middle-class area of Santa Monica, California. Across the alley from our house lived another Japanese American family with a boy my age. We didn't know each other well; after all, he was a boy at an age when we girls thought they were the ones who were alien. One day, walking home with a few white girl friends, they spotted him and started chanting "Joe, Joe the Eskimo!" over and over again. And I joined in: "Joe, Joe the Eskimo!" in great glee at ganging up on and tormenting the male species, when one of the girls turned to me and said, "But you're an Eskimo too." I was stunned. I was mortified. I thought we were taunting him because he was a boy; besides, it rhymed! I had no idea it was about race. I had no idea I was ridiculing myself.

Although Asians have lived as Americans since the mid 1800s, over the years the media has depicted us as the Yellow Peril, Fu Manchu, the Dragon Lady, Charlie Chan, Suzie Wong, the Dirty Jap, the China Doll, the Kung Fu Wonder, Long Duk Dong, and the Model Minority—but rarely as Americans.

"Where are you from?"
"Los Angeles."
"Where are your parents from?"
"Los Angeles."
"Well then, where were you born?"
"Los Angeles."
"I mean before that!"

Rather than Americans, we were "Orientals"—although, as Edward Long insisted, "most Orientals are more 'American' than Oriental anyway." In addition to being conflated with one another because "all Asians look alike," Chinese, Japanese, and Filipinos were linked by being Orientalized—the term Edward Said gave to a wide range of false assumptions underlying Western attitudes representing Asians as weak and suitable for colonization.[2]

The irony of growing up Asian in the United States in the 1950s and 1960s is that we didn't know we were alien. We thought we were American. It's like the flip side of Americans thinking chop suey is a Chinese dish when it was invented in the United States. Grace Zia Chu, the Julia Child of Chinese cooking, wrote that when she was in Shanghai after World War II she spotted a sign that advertised: "Genuine American

Chop Suey Served Here."[3] Likewise, Asians in the United States were the anthropomorphic version of American chop suey—originated here but served up as "Oriental" in the great "melting pot" of America.

### Cracks in the Melting Pot

In the catechism of Americanism, the "melting pot" was like cleanliness and godliness—a sacrament to American democracy. A metaphor for the diversity of the United States, it really meant the diversity of Europeans in the United States. This homeland homily began in 1782 during an earlier period of revolution, near the close of the American War of Independence, when J. Hector St. John de Crèvecœur proudly wrote that in America, where he was a newly minted citizen, "individuals of all nations are melted into a new race of men." Yet when he rhetorically asked, "Whence came all these people?" he responded, "They are a mixture of English, Scotch, Irish, French, Dutch, Germans, and Swedes."[4] In 1908 the metaphor became public currency with a play called *The Melting Pot*, in which the immigrant protagonist dramatically orated: "America is God's Crucible, the great Melting Pot where all the races of Europe are melting and re-forming!"[5]

Eighty-five years before the Statue of Liberty welcomed the tired, poor, and huddled masses to our shores, the first Naturalization Act of 1790 restricted naturalization to "free white persons," specifying whiteness as a legal prerequisite to national identity. Later, due in large part to the abolition of slavery, a new Naturalization Act in 1870 extended citizenship to aliens of African nativity or descent. As neither white nor black, Asians were "aliens ineligible for citizenship."

The first wave of Asian immigrants were the Chinese in the mid 1800s, enticed to California, called *gam saan* or "Gold Mountain," because of the gold rush, and imported to work the sugar plantations of Hawai'i to meet production demands. Coinciding with the abolition of the African slave trade, Chinese also filled the need for cheap labor to build the transcontinental railroad as well as service the multiplying boomtowns of the Wild West. But as the economic boom went bust and white workers clamored for even the menial work that previously only

Chinese would take, laws such as "An Act to Protect Free White Labor Against Competition with Chinese Coolie Labor, and to Discourage the Immigration of the Chinese into the State of California" (known as the Anti-Coolie Act of 1862) were passed. Despite the small Chinese population—a mere 35,000 nationwide in 1860—trade unions, newspapers, and even pulp novels like Sax Rohmer's popular Fu Manchu series broadly decried the "yellow peril" that would allegedly overrun America. Chinese were mobbed, lynched, and run out of towns throughout the west, causing Mark Twain to comment wryly, "I am not fond of Chinamen, but I am still less fond of seeing them wronged and abused."[6]

In 1882, what had begun as a regional rant against a small minority became federal legislation with the passage of the Chinese Exclusion Act, which effectively ended Chinese immigration, exempting only a handful of diplomats, teachers, students, and merchants. The act remained in effect for over seventy years, until it was repealed in 1943 in order to smooth transnational relations with China, which became an ally during World War II. While the termination of the Chinese Exclusion Act finally enabled Chinese who had been living in the United States to become naturalized citizens, it limited Chinese immigrants to just 105 per year. Unlike European quotas, which were based on country of citizenship, the immigration quota for Chinese was based on ethnicity. It was the first and only time an ethnic group was singled out for exclusion.

After the Chinese were banned, Japanese laborers were contracted—first to Hawai'i and then to the continental United States—as a fresh source of cheap labor. Like the Chinese before them, Japanese immigrants worked in primarily low-status, low-paying jobs; and like the Chinese, they too quickly took center stage as the "yellow peril," especially after Japan's victory in the Russo-Japanese War of 1904–05—the first in which an Asian nation defeated a western nation. That same year labor unions in California formed the Asiatic Exclusion League to push for federal legislation to stop Japanese from immigrating, although there were only about 25,000 Japanese in the entire United States at that time. In 1907, anti-Japanese forces succeeded in pressuring San Francisco to segregate Japanese American schoolchildren, which in turn fostered the acerbically named "Gentlemen's Agreement," which stopped the further immigration of laborers but allowed entry to wives and family members of Japanese already residing in the United States. In 1913, California was the first of fifteen states to pass Alien Land Laws, making it illegal for "aliens ineligible to citizenship" to own land. Meanwhile, anti-miscegenation laws criminalized interracial marriages.

With these incremental anti-Asian laws as stepping stones, the Immigration Act of 1924 was passed. It consisted of two parts. The first was the Asian Exclusion Act that stopped all immigration of "aliens ineligible to citizenship," which targeted the Japanese. The second part was the National Origins Act, which codified preferred immigration from northern and western Europe by allowing a maximum of 2 percent of the total number of people of each nationality counted in the 1890 census when the United States was overwhelmingly European. According to the US Department of State's Office of the Historian, the purpose of this act was "to preserve the ideal of American homogeneity."[7]

In 1898, as part of the spoils of the Spanish-American War, Spain ceded the Philippines to the United States for $20 million. Upon being annexed to the United States, the islands' 7 million inhabitants became "US nationals," meaning that they were suddenly Americans by nationality but without the rights of citizenship. Now exempt from the restrictive immigration laws that excluded Chinese and Japanese laborers, Filipinos were heavily recruited as the third source of cheap Asian labor. While in 1920 there were only 5,000 Filipinos in the United States, by 1930—after the Asian Exclusion Act of 1924 barred Japanese immigration—the Filipino population rose to over 45,000. In 1934 the Tydings-McDuffie Act, which provided eventual independence to the Philippines, immediately changed the official status of Filipinos in the United States from "US nationals" to "aliens ineligible for citizenship," thereby subjecting them to the quota system—specifying, for Filipinos, a quota of a mere 50 per year.

Already famously demonized as being "half-devil and half-child," in Rudyard Kipling's widely circulated 1899 poem, "The White Man's Burden" in the 1930s, Filipinos were accused of being an economic and racial threat to the United States, like the Chinese and Japanese before them. Anti-Filipino riots broke out throughout small cities in central

California where Filipinos worked as farmworkers. Indeed, before World War II, when the number of African Americans in the West was relatively small, it was the other colored folk—Asians, Mexicans, and American Indians—who bore the brunt of American racism on the West Coast and were subject to legal and extralegal discrimination and segregation. In 1946, writer and labor activist Carlos Bulosan wrote in *America Is in the Heart*: "I came to know that the public streets were not free to my people. We were stopped each time ... patrolmen saw us driving a car. We were suspect each time we were seen with a white woman."[8] While Arthur Schlesinger listed the melting pot concept as number five in the United States's top ten contributions to civilization,[9] Nathan Glazer and Daniel Moynihan concluded, "The point about the Melting Pot ... is that it never happened."[10]

In 1952, the Immigration and Nationality Act (also known as the McCarran-Walter Act) abolished existing limitations to naturalization based on race. Japanese residents who had made the United States their home for almost a hundred years, and Filipinos who had been reclassified as "aliens" in 1934, were finally granted the right to become naturalized citizens. At the basis of the Act, however, was the continuation and codification of the National Origins Quota System, which upheld the restrictive 1924 system but revised the quotas to one-sixth of 1 percent of each nationality's population in 1920.[11] The result was the continuation of preferred immigration from northern and western Europe.

The Immigration and Nationality Act of 1965, passed during the Civil Rights era, has been considered by many as the most significant single piece of federal legislation for Americans of Asian descent. By finally abolishing the restrictive national-origins quota system, it dramatically changed the landscape of Asian America. Record numbers of immigrants from Asia—as well as Latin America and other non-western countries—changed the color, complexity, class, and cuisine of the country, finally making good on its declaration as a nation of immigrants. But the long-term social, political and economic ramifications of the Act on the country were vastly underestimated at the time. Passed in large part because of the Civil Rights movement, immigration itself was not a burning public issue. The country's attention was preoccupied with advancing long-overdue racial equality in voting and housing rights, as well as with what was quickly becoming an unpopular war in Vietnam. Belying its far-reaching impact on the United States, the new immigration act was, at the time of its passage, thought to be more symbolic than consequential—an antidote to the country's embarrassment during the Cold War of not being the beacon of democracy it professed to be.

The intent of the 1965 Act was twofold: to reunite families of immigrants already in the United States and to attract professionals with expertise that was in short supply. In a 2006 National Public Radio program on the significance of the 1965 immigration law, sociologist Stephen Klineberg noted:

> Congress was saying in its debates, "We need to open the door for some more British doctors, some more German engineers." It never occurred to anyone, literally, that there were going to be African doctors, Indian engineers, Chinese computer programmers.[12]

The 1965 Immigration Act substantially increased immigration from all Asian countries, with the exception of Japan. Chinese immigration grew from 105 per year in 1943 to 5,000 per year in the early 1960s and to 24,000 per year by 1977 when the immigration reforms were fully realized. Annual Filipino immigration increased from 50 in 1934 to 3,000 in the early 1960s and then to 36,000 by 1977. By 2012, Asians had become the fastest growing racial or ethnic group in the United States, having expanded by over 600 percent since the 1965 immigration act.

### Asians in America

Published in the March 1972 issue of the Asian American movement newspaper *Gidra*, a map titled "Asians Throughout America," based on 1970 US census figures, graphically illustrated the population statistics and national dispersion of the three largest Asian ethnic groups—Japanese, Chinese, and Filipino—during the rise of the Asian American movement.

The demographics of Asian Americans in 1970 reflected the immigration reforms of 1965. Although still concentrated in Hawai'i and

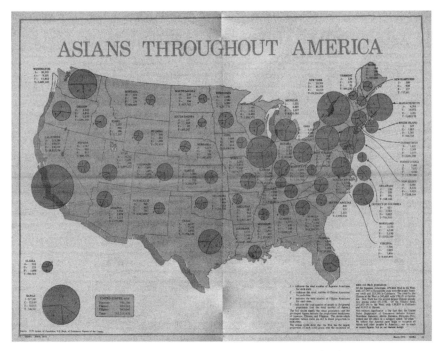

Fig. 1.1: Demographics of Japanese, Chinese and Filipinos in
the US using 1970 census figures, *Gidra* 43 (March 1972)

the West Coast, the map (Fig 1.1) shows that Japanese, Chinese, and
Filipino Americans lived in every state of the nation. Japanese comprised the largest group, with a population of 591,290, constituting 34
percent of all Asian Pacific Islanders (APIs) residing in the United States.
(Chinese numbered 435,062, or 25 percent of US APIs, and Filipinos
totaled 343,060, about 20 percent of US APIs[13]). While California was
the state with the highest number of APIs, they made up just 2.8 percent
of the state's population. In contrast, although numerically Hawai'i had
considerably fewer in absolute terms, APIs made up 57.7 percent of the
state's total population, making Hawai'i the only state in which APIs
comprised the majority.[14]

By 1970, 80 percent of the Japanese and roughly 50 percent of the
Chinese and Filipino populations had been born in the United States.
Nationwide, 90 percent lived in urban areas, of whom almost half were
concentrated in five metropolitan areas: Los Angeles/Long Beach, San
Francisco/Oakland, New York, Chicago, and Honolulu. Since one of

the objectives of the 1965 Act was to increase the numbers of professionals in occupations where there were shortages, the class composition of the Asian immigrant population became increasingly more professional and less working-class.

As distinctive as we were—by ethnicity, geography, class, gender, and sexual orientation—there was one thing we all shared: feeling estranged from the broader society of which we were supposedly a part. Despite our national distribution, APIs comprised less than 1 percent of the US population in 1970.[15] In the aftermath of World War II and in the heat of the Cold War, widespread suburbanization and proliferating xenophobia, inflamed by McCarthyism, fostered conformity to the consumerist and social norms of white middle-class aspirations of beauty and behavior. Although the Civil Rights movement was in full swing, ideas like "multiculturalism" and "identity politics" were not yet in our vocabulary. Whether isolated within the predominantly white society or insulated in ethnic enclaves, in the 1950s and 1960s we were still stewing in the mythical melting pot.

## Isolated

My husband, Bob Nakamura, was five years old when World War II broke out. Fifteen years earlier, in 1926—two years after the Asian Exclusion Act of 1924 effectively barred further immigration from Japan—Bob's father jumped ship in San Francisco. Seeing no respite from his impoverished Kagoshima country life of eating sweet potatoes morning, noon and night, Harukichi Nakamura boarded a ship bound for the United States, despite the immigration ban. When it reached San Francisco, he paid a hefty bond as security against jumping ship and then proceeded to do just that.

He had worked his way down to Los Angeles, married, and built a small but thriving produce business when Pearl Harbor was bombed. Two months later, Mr. and Mrs. Nakamura, with four-year-old Bob—along with 110,000 other Japanese Americans living on the West Coast—were uprooted from their homes and sent to what FDR himself called concentration camps and federal spin doctors later rechristened "relocation centers" and even "pioneer communities." The young Nakamura family lost everything they had worked for except what they could carry—the federally imposed limit on what they were allowed to bring to camp—which included bedding and babies. At so young an age, Bob could not grasp the unconstitutionality of the incarceration or the economic losses it inflicted upon his parents and their whole generation. But in his young mind he realized that "one day you're 'Jack Armstrong, All-American Boy,' and the next day you're a Jap."

When he was in camp, Bob asked his parents, "When are we going back to America?" When they did return, three years later, the country was undergoing an economic boom. However, Mr. Nakamura, stripped of resources to re-establish his produce store, strapped a lawnmower onto a bike and became a gardener, working six days a week, year in and year out, for the next forty years. Young Bob returned to trying to be Jack Armstrong, the all-American boy. But the racism that had landed them in camp followed them out. Although not as blatant as in the South, segregation was part of the fabric of Los Angeles in the 1950s. When his Cub Scout troop went to the public swimming pool, Bob was barred from entering. Even ten years later, he was refused service at a restaurant.

Bob dealt with discrimination like many people of color did and still do: by trying to be better than everyone else. "I played football. I was on the debate team. I did dramatic interpretation. I was in the boy's choir. You name it. Except for a couple of people, I didn't hang out with other Asians, so it even affected my choice of friends." Bob instinctively understood that, in order to get by in the white world, he must wear a Fanonian white mask:

> I was doing everything I thought would make me white, and of course I found out I still wasn't. I wanted to divest myself of all cultural roots, and then I paid for it. I began to feel very isolated because I had no roots, no community, because I did this on purpose.

Since he had tried to become American (which meant white) without success, Bob tried turning Japanese. Intending to emigrate to Japan, he moved to Tokyo in the early 1960s in the hope of finding home. He had even lined up a job. Once there, however, he realized he was

more American (even without being white) than Japanese and deject-
edly returned to Los Angeles.

The United States was no kinder or gentler to Steve Louie, a decade
younger than Bob and a third-generation American. His grandfather
had arrived in 1882, just three months before the Chinese Exclusion Act,
and both Steve's parents were born and raised in the United States. His
father was a Presbyterian minister with a Harvard degree who believed
in racial integration so strongly that he decided to take positions only in
white communities. His mother was PTA president, although she was
relieved of her position when she objected to the purging of *Catcher in
the Rye* from the school library.

Both joined African Americans and other people of color in the 1964
California campaign to defend the Rumford Fair Housing Act, which
prevented discrimination in the renting or selling of property. In the
face of the postwar housing boom stimulated by the GI Bill, residential
segregation was still enforced by restrictive racial covenants that had
come into vogue after World War I, when African Americans migrated
in large numbers from the South.

When the Louies moved to one of the newly developed suburbs of
Los Angeles, they experienced housing discrimination firsthand. Despite
Reverend Louie's position as a man of God and his Ivy League pedigree,
he was forced to live in a hotel room for nine months because nobody
would sell him a house. As Steve recalls, "the La Cañada Presbyterian
Church finally felt so badly about it that one of the members who was a
contractor built my folks a house and sold it to them at cost."

Steve got the Ching Chong Chinaman treatment from children,
which was tacitly approved by their parents who would only laugh.
"I basically fought my way through elementary, junior high and high
school." His father, being a Christian minister, urged him to turn the
other cheek. But Steve told him, "If I turn the other cheek, it's just
gonna get whooped on too and that's not gonna happen." Not that the
scrawny four-eyed minister's kid did not know how to use his words.
"Well fuck you, you asshole, you white piece of shit!" He lost as many
fights as he won. If they were his size or smaller, he would do his best
to "beat the living crap out of them." If they were bigger, he would just
run. As he said, "It was very practical—a survival thing."

The racial taunts were salted by the bigotry of class. "They were all very rich and we were very poor. We were the kind of family that got Thanksgiving and Christmas food from the church members every year for as long as I can remember." He recalled the day he got thrown out of a classmate's house by the butler. "We were doing homework and he literally picked me up by my shirt collar and my belt and tossed me out the front door. At the time my biggest thing was, 'Why the frickin' hell do I have to go through this? And why don't people just accept people as people?'"

Across the nation, on the East Coast, Helen Zia's parents were among the Northern Chinese who fled the Japanese occupation of China, where her father's family had been killed in the massacre of Nanjing. "My father was the Confucian patriarch and my mother the Confucian wife. The daughter obeys the father, the wife obeys the husband, the widow will obey the sons. There was one set of rules for my brothers and one set for me." Like most immigrants, her father worked at whatever he could. He was a Fuller Brush man, a Good Humor man, a cab driver, and worked in an auto factory and then in a dairy farm before settling on a small cottage industry in their house making and selling tchotchkes to flower shops. "We didn't expect or ask for anything; we knew there wasn't any money. We were also aware that going to college was a hardship because we were the labor force. Us kids produced the things my father would sell."

Helen was born in Newark, New Jersey, and grew up in Levittown, one of the first mass housing developments established in the 1950s. Located near Fort Dix, it was geared toward military families and, as segregated housing was the norm throughout America, planned as an all-white community. But it was illegal to discriminate in federally subsidized housing,[16] so Levittown was forced to integrate after an African American officer took his case to the New Jersey Supreme Court. Helen's parents moved in soon after, and she remembers eggs being thrown at their house. "My father was a very outspoken, angry Chinese guy. His favorite response to neighbors who objected to us was, 'You don't like us? Fine. We'll sell the house to a black person.'"

Helen recalls that most of the time the racism was not overt but "all around us, all the time." Much of the town housed military families during the Vietnam War, as nearby Fort Dix and McGuire were staging areas for the war. Helen worked at a dry-cleaning shop during high school and remembers a time when two soldiers came in to pick up their laundered and pressed fatigues. "They took one look at me—I'm the counter girl—and said, 'Oh, they're everywhere, aren't they?' So things like that happened all the time. As they say, 'Death by a thousand paper cuts.'"[17]

Helen felt she had to get out of Levittown, and the only way she knew was to go to college. Without assistance from her high school teachers and counselors or her immigrant parents, she figured out how to apply and was ultimately accepted by many schools. But her father refused to sign admission and scholarship papers, saying that the proper place for an unmarried Asian daughter was at home with her parents. Up to that time Helen had been the obedient Chinese daughter who never talked back to her elders, but "I knew I would drown if I stayed. So he signed the papers and walked out of the room."

Helen was made very aware that she didn't belong in the United States. "That thing about 'Where are you from?' or 'Go back to where you came from,' I heard that so many times. Go back where? New Jersey? I'm here! They wanted me to go back to a place I never came from, so maybe I should be there. Maybe that's where I really belong." So, like Bob Nakamura, Helen did go "back." In 1972, while a student at Princeton, she wrote a proposal to study in China and became one of the first Americans to do so. Once there, however, Helen quickly realized she didn't belong in China either.[18] Genuine American chop suey.

The experiences of Bob, Steve, and Helen reflect themes of segregation and discrimination that imposed a sense of angst and alienation. Although Bob lived in Los Angeles, one of the most diverse cities in the country, people of color were still subjected to the white standards and desires of the 1940s and 1950s. A decade later, in the 1960s, civil rights had not yet reached Steve's Los Angeles suburb, and his race and class were a shared liability, each salting the other's wounds. In New Jersey where there were far fewer Asians than on the West Coast, Helen was told so many times to go back where she came from that when she did, the fiasco made her feel doubly alien. Stories like theirs were common. Whether on the West or East Coast—or in between, where

Asians were fewer and more isolated, like Rocky Chin who grew up in Appalachia, and Mike Yanagita in Michigan—segregation and discrimination enshrouded Asians in cocoons, where they waited to take wing.

### Insulated

Even as some grew up isolated, others were growing up anchored in insular ethnic enclaves that provided them with a built-in comfort zone of security and self-assurance. It was only when they grew older and their world expanded that they realized they were not considered part of the broader society. At the time, however, like people who had grown up poor without knowing it, although their pond may have been small, it was theirs, and they belonged.

Doug Aihara grew up in Little Tokyo, although he lived in East Los Angeles with a variety of Latino, white and Asian friends, reflecting historian Carey McWilliams's 1940 assessment of Los Angeles as the nation's "racial frontier."[19] Doug's Nisei[20] father built one of the first Japanese American insurance agencies and was a stalwart in the Little Tokyo business community. His Nisei mother, having been subjected to the wholesale racism of the World War II incarceration, proactively fortified Doug by instilling in him that being Japanese American was "special"—and he believed her.

This belief was reinforced by his immersion in an all-inclusive Japanese American community that centered around the Koyasan Buddhist Temple in Little Tokyo, of which his grandparents were early members. Founded in 1912, Koyasan is one of the oldest Buddhist temples in North America and was a vibrant center for Japanese Americans throughout Southern California. Growing up, Doug spent almost as much time there as he did in public school. Besides going to Sunday school, Doug was a member of Koyasan's large and active Boy Scout troop; founded in 1931, it is one of the oldest existing Boy Scout troops in California. In addition to becoming an Eagle Scout, part of belonging to the troop was participating in their award-winning drum-and-bugle corps, which required even more time at the temple. "I was involved with scouts and the corps four days during the week and all day Saturdays and Sundays."

He was so deeply absorbed in this parallel Japanese American subculture that he "thought all Japanese Americans were the same—intact families, middle-class, hard-working. I grew up thinking we were the model minority." When I asked him if he ever remembered wanting to be white, he said not really, because "being Japanese American was special."

Peggy Saika grew up in Sacramento's Japantown, before it was overtaken by urban renewal in the late 1950s. By 1910, Sacramento had become home to the fourth-largest Japanese American population in California. Before World War II, Japantown had grown into a mini city created as much by community solidarity as against a racially segregated and hostile external world. During World War II, like all Japanese Americans living on the West Coast, Japantown residents were removed and detained in barbed-wire enclosed camps for the duration of the war. After the war, Japantown struggled to rebuild. Although the area never regained its prewar prominence, even in its diminished state, it once again became the hub of Japanese American community activity for the Sacramento Valley region. It was a tight-knit community where everybody knew each other. Peggy's parents ran the Sakura Fountain in Japantown, where her father had a card room in the back and her mother presided over the soda fountain in the front. She went to the Buddhist church, where even non-Buddhist kids hung out, so that, as she said, her whole world was contained within fifteen blocks. Surrounded by Chinese, Latinos, and low-income white and black families from the housing projects, Peggy did not realize until later that people referred to her neighborhood as "the ghetto."

When Peggy went to high school, "it was like, 'Oh my god, what happened?' The first day of school I'm with my friends from junior high. We're all Asians, and we walk into the assembly hall and all the teachers and everybody you see are white! Everybody!" Nevertheless, Peggy ran for a student body position as she had in junior high school, "where Asians were just so active you did everything; it was no big thing to run for office, or win." When Peggy ran for an office in high school, however, she said, "I knew by the second time I ran that if you weren't white, if you won anything at Sac High, you would be an anomaly." But, with the encouragement of her older sister, she did run again—and again. I asked her what made her continue, and if she didn't get discouraged. "I think it's a personality thing more than any ambition. I'd think, 'Oh this is so sad, nobody wants to vote for me.' But then I would just start thinking, 'Okay, what else can I do?'" The fourth time Peggy ran, she won. She was an anomaly.

Like Doug and Peggy, Qris Yamashita was immersed in an all-encompassing Japanese American universe. She grew up in Gardena, the US city with the largest Japanese American population outside Hawai'i, comprising 20 percent of the city. After the 1906 earthquake in San Francisco, as part of the general movement of Japanese immigrants to the Los Angeles area, many were drawn to the rich soil and mild climate of Gardena. Within the next twenty years, the Japanese Cultural Institute,[21] Japanese Business Association, and Japanese language school were established, in addition to Japanese Baptist and Buddhist churches, a number of restaurants, and a market. She went to Gardena High School, which was at that time predominantly Japanese American. "Let's face it, in those days JA's ran the school—the student government, everything."

Qris also attributes the solidity of her ethnic identity to being brought up by her Kibei mother. Kibei literally means "returning to America." Before World War II, there were an estimated 8,000 Kibei who had been born in the United States, sent to Japan for their education because their parents planned eventually to return, and brought back to the United States when those intentions were not fulfilled.[22] When Qris's mother was twelve she was sent to Kumamoto, where she stayed for ten years—longer than most. Returning as an adult, she found herself more Japanese—in language, culture, and conduct—than her Nisei counterparts who had grown up as red-blooded Americans, and raised her children accordingly.

When Qris went to college, it was the first time she had been outside a Japanese American universe. When she took one of the early Asian American studies classes, she was puzzled. "One of the things they started talking about was identity. Given the way I grew up, I knew I was Japanese American and I couldn't figure out why other people didn't know who they were."

In stark contrast to Bob Nakamura, Steve Louie, and Helen Zia, who grew up feeling isolated, Doug, Peggy, and Qris were nurtured in the palpable reality of an all-embracing subculture. They were surrounded by an ethnic community that provided them with an inner sense of belonging and certainty. As a result, they felt normal, not like an oddity—accepted rather than negated. They were the empirical evidence upon which multiculturalism was based. By instilling in Doug that he was "special," his mother activated an anticolonial stance that honored who and what she knew him to be as his birthright. Doug did not question his mother, just as Peggy heeded the encouragement of her older sister to run for office and Qris did not rebel against spending her Saturdays at Japanese school. Concentric circles of cultural institutions like the Buddhist temple, Japanese American Boy Scout troop and Japanese language school strengthened their ethnically anchored world and created a safe space in which they were never assaulted with accusations that they did not belong. Part of their self-assurance, as Peggy said, was no doubt "a personality thing"; but growing up in holistic Japanese American communities in the 1950s and 1960s offered an early, lived experience that no doubt provided a sense of inner security and confidence that fortified them when later they encountered the larger world.

### *"Why There Are No Asian Americans in Hawaiʻi"*

If small, insular ethnic enclaves in California could buttress those who grew up within them, how much more might they do so when the ethnic region encompassed the city, or even the entire state? Hawaiʻi is no racial paradise. There are serious disparities in socioeconomic status and opportunity that lead to interethnic strife and conflict. However, the biggest difference between growing up Asian in Hawaiʻi and growing up Asian on the continental United States was being part of the majority, instead of being a minority. Unlike growing up on the continental United States, in Hawaiʻi most of the population looked like you, soy sauce was as prevalent as salt, and you could get rice rather than potatoes with your eggs.

In the 1930s and 1940s, Nisei in Hawaiʻi lived under the omnipotence of the "Big Five" oligarchy but never developed the minority mentality that constrained their mainland counterparts. Instead, they were bolstered by other Asian plantation workers in an attitude that would be personified by the postwar International Longshore and Warehouse Union motto: "An injury to one is an injury to all." In 1997, when I interviewed Mike Tokunaga, a member of the segregated 100th Battalion during World War II and a behind-the-scenes dynamo of Hawaiʻi's 1954 Democratic Revolution, he reveled in recalling how the "Hawaiʻi boys" would be quick to respond to acts of discrimination they witnessed in the South, where they went for training. The first time off the island, and having had no previous contact with African Americans, one of his favorite stories was when a bus driver refused to pick up some black workers despite the fact that the bus was almost empty. Mike said a couple of the "boys" charged up to the bus driver and physically threw him out. One jumped behind the wheel and drove the bus back to pick up the workers. Mike added, with a satisfied laugh: "That's the way we were."

Darcie Iki is a Yonsei—a fourth-generation Japanese American—who was born and raised on Oahu. Like the rest of her generation and the generation before her, she never felt like a minority—until she came to the continental United States for college. "It almost felt like a foreign country. I felt like everyone just looked right over me or right past me. It was the first time I questioned who I was and how I fit in." Darcie added that she didn't think discriminatory acts affected her as deeply as they affected her friends who had grown up as "minorities." "While I was angered, my response was more a feeling that something was wrong with them, not me. But when it hit my mainland friends, it reverberated at their core. They got so angry it was hard for them to let go of it."

Jeff Furumura moved to Hawaiʻi in 1990 after having been born and raised in Los Angeles. Growing up in LA, Jeff had developed a low tolerance for racism, whether the perpetrator was white or black:

> I would just flip out and go into berserker mode. For example, I once pulled my knife on a black guy who started yelling at me because I refused to give him money on my way back to my car from the gas station cashier window. He yelled at me, 'You fuckin' Chink asshole … ' but didn't finish because when I got back to my car, I reached into

the glove box, pulled out my knife and—I can't believe I did this—chased him with it! He was pretty fast, luckily for both of us.

When Jeff first arrived in Honolulu, a friend took him to eat in Chinatown, and Jeff asked, "Where's J Town?" The answer: "The whole city is a J Town—maybe the whole state." At that time Japanese comprised 22.3 percent of the population of Hawai'i,[23] with the total API population weighing in at a hefty 61.8 percent. This compared to the meager 9.6 percent of APIs in California in 1990.[24] Jeff's reaction was, "Yes!!"

As ethnic studies professor Jonathan Okamura explained in his 1994 article, "Why There Are No Asian Americans in Hawai'i," being in the majority, there was no political or social need for Asian Americans to establish and affirm a pan-Asian American identity in Hawai'i.[25] Rather than "Asian American," another category of pan-ethnic identity took hold—that of being "local." As defined by Okamura, "local" was an identity born out of the working-class commonality between Native Hawaiians and immigrant plantation groups who shared an oppositional stance to the dominant *haole* (white) rule, as well as an appreciation of and commitment to the Hawaiian values of *aloha kanaka* (love of the people) and *aloha 'aina* (love of the land).[26]

In addition to the positive aspects of life for Americans of Asian descent in Hawai'i, singer/songwriter and law professor Chris Iijima also witnessed the complexities and inequities of interethnic relations on the islands. Japanese Americans had an unearned advantage in Hawai'i by virtue of their sizable population. Although they did not hold the highest occupational status and were especially absent in the corporate arena (which was the real source of power), because of their numbers, Japanese in Hawai'i were a visible political and economic force on the islands. Chris had grown up in New York City and moved to Honolulu from Massachusetts in 1999 with his Caucasian wife Jane, their nine-year-old son Alan, and six-year-old son Christopher. A few years later, his parents, Kazu and Tak, who had grown up in California but lived in New York after being released from camp, came to live with them. One evening while they were sitting around the dinner table in their home in Manoa Valley, Chris asked them if they ever recalled being called a

Chink or Chinaman. "My dad remembered it, of course. I remembered it, and even Alan remembered it. But Christopher, who was six when we moved to Hawai'i, didn't." Chris added that, although it was easier for a Japanese or Chinese American to grow up in Hawai'i, "in a way I'm glad I had the experience of having been discriminated against, because when you're here in Hawai'i, as a Japanese American you don't realize that Filipino kids and Samoan kids are going through what Japanese kids go through on the mainland."

### Alien Americans

"Alien" has been a persistent theme in the history of Asians in America. In the beginning, Asians were "aliens ineligible for citizenship." Alien Land Laws prohibited Asians from owning land. During World War II, Japanese were enemy aliens. Professor Robert G. Lee stressed that, although the terms "alien" and "foreign" are sometimes used interchangeably, they carry different connotations. Aliens are outsiders who are inside: "The alien is always out of place, therefore disturbing and dangerous."[27]

Certainly, there must be Asians who grew up isolated from other Asians who did not feel disaffected or alienated. Likewise, there were no doubt Asians who grew up insulated within ethnic enclaves who did not feel fortified by their racially defined pond. Clearly, all young people go through identity crises. At some point, and to varying degrees, everyone wonders who they are and where they belong. Growing up Asian in America is not just a matter of "us" against "them." It is much more complex. In addition to constraints of race and ethnicity, there are webs of class and gender, interethnic as well as intraethnic conflicts, generational differences, various immigrant states of understanding, situational realities, and infinite individual dispositions. These interconnected conditions and circumstances refract into a myriad of challenges and compromises that each person must negotiate individually. A multitude of factors—known and unknown—influence how one grows up, alien or not.

For people of color in this country, however, color is an inescapable factor—as Cornel West asserted, "race matters." And in a black-and-white society, Asians provided a peculiar conundrum that no one seemed to know what to do with. As "aliens ineligible for citizenship," and then as "Orientals," Asians were, as sociologist Mia Tuan put it, "forever foreign."[28] Firmly outside the hierarchical taxonomy of Americanness, accused of being unassimilable, Asians in America were rendered politically disenfranchised and socially negligible.

On a more personal level, the dilemma was existential. The catch was how to be who you were despite constraints of color, class, and gender. Estrangement and alienation have been conditions of modern society throughout the industrial age, information age, space age, teen age and old age. They are a political disorder endemic to capitalist societies— a social phenomenon of feeling isolated and alone, an existential state of never feeling like a whole person. For people of color, alienation is heightened by the second sight that W. E. B. Du Bois called "double consciousness"—the "sense of always looking at one's self through the eyes of others."[29] Double consciousness is not just a matter of self-reflection, but includes an awareness of a societal double standard, of being judged through the filter of white supremacy compounded by the practice of blaming the victim. The result, as Du Bois stated, was "two warring souls in one dark body ... whose dogged strength alone keeps it from being torn asunder."

When Du Bois pierced the veil of double consciousness, he was addressing the plight of the "American Negro." Yet the sense of feeling one's "two-ness" referred just as aptly to the dichotomy between who we, as Asians in America, were and what others thought us to be. When Du Bois wrote, "He simply wishes to make it possible for a man to be both a Negro and an American without being cursed and spit upon by his fellows," he spoke to young Steve Louie's simple question, "Why the frickin' hell do I have to go through this? And why don't people just accept people as people?"

When political sociologist C. Wright Mills wrote, "Know that many personal troubles cannot be solved merely as troubles, but must be understood in terms of public issues," he addressed Steve's quandary by taking the problem off of him personally, to cast a critical eye on the society that had caused the problem in the first place. There is an indelible link between our private lives and the seemingly separate social world in which we live. The personal is political. Or, as Chris Rock quipped, "Don't hate the player, hate the game."

## TWO

## Living in B&W

*Is yellow black or white?*

Gary Okihiro

Sharon Maeda spent her early childhood in a predominantly black neighborhood in Portland—the only area where her parents could find a house after World War II. Sharon's grandparents had been farmers in Hood River, Oregon. During the war her parents were sent to the Minidoka concentration camp in Idaho. When they were released from camp, they were banned from returning to their homes on the West Coast. Third-generation Japanese Americans like Sharon were thus born in unfamiliar cities in the Midwest like Milwaukee, where they lived for only a short time until their parents were allowed to return to their homes.

In Portland, Sharon's portal into the dream world of high society was through *Ebony* magazine, which she devoured after school with her girl-friends. Later, her father got a job at Boeing and moved his family to a suburb of Seattle, specifically for its good school district. They found a house, but when the owner of the real estate agency discovered they were Japanese, he refused to complete the sale. When the owner of the house found this out, he contacted Sharon's father and sold them the house directly. He notified all his neighbors that a Japanese American family was moving in and that they should be "nice to them" and, Sharon said, they were. Yet, when her parents worked in their front yard, people driving by would stop and ask how much they charged, assuming they were the gardeners.

In school, Sharon and her sister were two of only four students of color. They were considered so different that they were "treated like foreign exchange students." In Portland, her African American Brownie leader taught the girls how to set a formal table "with cocktail forks, and all because she said some day we might have to work for white people." In contrast, in the suburbs of Seattle, her cohorts staged "Coketail parties." "We'd dress up in cocktail dresses and heels. The guys would wear suits and somebody's parents would bring out all their martini glasses, except we'd have 7-Up and Coke in them. They were Coketail parties! Preparing us for society!"

## Navigating Whiteness

A critical part of growing up Asian was coming to terms with whiteness. Whiteness was the gold standard, the mainstream, the norm. It was everywhere—so much so it was invisible. In the northernmost country of North America, Alan Kondo, who would later become one of the pioneering filmmakers of Visual Communications, grew up in an all-Jewish neighborhood of Toronto. When he came home from his first day in kindergarten, his mother asked if there were any other Japanese in his class. He answered that they were all Japanese. In fact, they were all Jewish. It was the last time he was truly color-blind.

In considering how male privilege is denied while protected, feminist Peggy McIntosh realized that, as a white person she had been taught that racism puts others at a disadvantage but not that white privilege put her at an advantage.[1] Whiteness presupposes belonging, being heard and heeded. It bestows a sense of entitlement, a state of dominance: "white" = "right." And its currency is so embedded it is taken for granted, by both whites and non-whites. Among the fifty daily unconscious effects of whiteness McIntosh identified was that, when white people do well, they are not considered a credit to their race—and when they do not do well, neither are they thought to be a disgrace to their race. On the other hand, as Frantz Fanon wrote, "When people like me, they like me 'in spite of my color.' When they dislike me, they point out that it isn't because of my color. Either way, I am locked into the infernal circle."[2]

Political scientist Claire Jean Kim contended that Asian Americans are racialized in relation to and through interaction with whites and blacks. Because of the social capital associated with whiteness, she suggested, "If the black struggle for advancement has historically rested upon appeals to racial equality, the Asian American struggle has at times rested upon appeals to be considered White."[3] In other words, if African Americans contend with the problematic notion of "passing" for white, Asian Americans grapple with the farcical notion of "becoming" white. Former Clinton speechwriter Eric Liu wrote, "I never asked to be white … But like so many other Asian Americans of the second generation, I find myself now the bearer of a strange new status: white by acclamation … To the extent that I have moved away from the periphery and toward the center of American life, I have become white inside."[4]

White standards for non-whites are normalized in White America as well. As Asian American studies professor Elaine Kim wrote:

What seems to infuriate some people the most is the thought of an ungrateful Asian American siding with other people of color, presumably against whites. They want to hold onto their notion of Asian Americans as docile honorary white people whose very existence proves that other people of color are lazy and stupid and that racism does not exist in US society.[5]

Similarly, literary critic David Leiwei Li, also referring to the concept of "honorary white people," made the distinction between whiteness as a birthright and whiteness as an accomplishment conferring social status[6]—"white by acclamation," in Eric Liu's terms. Sociologist Min Zhou posited that since ethnic groups initially considered non-white, such as the Irish and Jews, attained the status of being "white" by acquiring status and wealth, it was not surprising that non-whites would aspire to becoming "white" as a mark of material success.[7]

We have been so schooled in the idea that "white is right" that, in direct contrast to the "black nod"—the nonverbal tilt-of-the-head acknowledgement of one black person to another that signals community membership, that "we're all in this together"[8]—during the late 1950s and early 1960s, Sanseis unconsciously employed what can be called the "Asian aversion," the unconscious practice of averting our gaze when encountering another Asian in public. It was a knee-jerk reaction, something we were never taught or understood, but did. Like waking up in the morning and seeing some Chinese man in the mirror, it seems as if we were so uncomfortable when confronted with our own likeness that we automatically looked away in self-conscious embarrassment.

Historically, disassociation was a strategy of accommodation in the name of survival. During World War II, Chinese Americans and Filipino Americans were required to wear national identification buttons to keep them from being mistaken for the enemy. Bob Santos was in first grade when he went to class one day and found that his Japanese American classmates, who comprised 90 percent of the school, had been sent to camp. In their absence, he and other Filipino kids were harassed so much for being "Japs"—including by adults—that, even as children, they had to wear buttons that claimed: "I am Filipino."

Japanese Americans also dissociated themselves from all things Japanese. Because threats and rumors were rampant—of deportation to Japan, of confinement within reservations like American Indians, even of extermination like Jews in Europe—many Japanese Americans destroyed cultural objects, burned family photographs, resigned from ethnic organizations, and renounced Buddhism in favor of Christianity in a range of futile attempts to prevent backlash.

Anthropologist Karen Brodkin pointed out that social identity in the United States is not only created through abstract constructs like race but is also hammered out concretely within the context of American nationhood. After all, since the founding of the nation, citizenship had been restricted to "free white persons." Brodkin added that, by the 1920s, scientific racism sanctioned the notion that "real Americans were white and that real whites came from northwest Europe."[9] In this racialized framework of nationality, white is not only right—it is the ideal of Americanism. If you speak good English (or, more correctly, speak English well) and are a Christian and a strapping capitalist, you are, to some extent, culturally white, and hence an upstanding American. If, however, you speak nonstandard (meaning substandard) English, are not Christian, and measure success in nonmaterial terms, your status as an American is brought into question.

Even as Cornel West has maintained that whiteness is parasitic on blackness,[10] Edward Said contended, "European culture gained in strength and identity by setting itself off against the Orient as a sort of surrogate and even underground self."[11] Similarly, Stuart Hall noted that "Without the Rest, the West would not have been able to recognize and represent itself as the summit of human history."[12] And Professor of English and African American Studies Helen H. Jun indicated that the Chinese immigrant functioned as the "negative instance of national belonging."[13] Just as there is no white without black, and no West without the Rest, we were the Opposite Other by which Americanism was fully articulated. By embodying the inherently alien and fundamentally heathen, the unassimilability of Asianness served to delineate true Americanness.

### Negotiating Blackness

Before Mike Murase immigrated to Los Angeles from Japan in 1956 at the age of nine, he had been given a book about Abraham Lincoln freeing the slaves. When he landed in San Francisco, he noticed that all the people in uniforms were white and all the people who were hauling the cargo were black. "And I said to myself, 'I thought these people were freed.'" Not long after that, the black-and-white dichotomization of the United States was made clear to Mike by means of his black-and-white television set. Since his family had settled in South Central LA, most of Mike's friends were black and Asian. "Throughout that time I thought white people were on television and black people populated real life."

Notwithstanding the standardization of whiteness, if we started out as Oriental, before we became Asian American we were black. Stuart Hall posited that when the term "black" was coined, it signified the common experience of racism and marginalization regardless of race.[14] Helen Jun argued that Asian Americans and African Americans have been racially defined in relationship to each other since the nineteenth century.[15] American Studies professor Bill V. Mullen claimed that, from the earliest days of the United States, Africans and Asians in the Americas have been linked by a shared tradition of resistance to class and racial exploitation and oppression.[16] More emphatically, in Spike Lee's 1989 film *Do the Right Thing*, when a Korean grocer was held up by young African Americans, he exclaimed: "I black! You, me, same! We same!" Although most people in movie theaters across the United States laughed out loud when they heard this line, many Asian Americans of my generation did not. Rather, they intuitively recognized the sentiment, as ludicrous as it must have sounded to black and white viewers alike.

This racial relationship between Asian and African Americans is not new, nor is it solely symbolic or ideological. While it does not imply equivalence or presuppose a shared kinship of identity—and whether either side recognizes it or not—there has long been a complex social and political connection between Asian Americans and African Americans.

W. E. B. Du Bois, widely known for proclaiming in 1903 that "the problem of the Twentieth Century is the problem of the color line,"[17] knew that the color line was global. Seeing beyond a world rendered in black and white, he was particularly taken with yellow power. According to scholars Bill Mullen and Cathryn Watson, "Du Bois consistently saw Asia as the fraternal twin to African—and African American—struggle for political freedom and cultural self-preservation."[18] When, in 1904, Japan became the first nation of color to defeat a white nation, Du Bois stated: "The Russo-Japanese war has marked an epoch. The magic of the word 'white' is already broken … the awakening of the yellow races is certain. That the awakening of the black races will follow in time, no unprejudiced student of history can doubt."[19]

Langston Hughes also saw the potential in Asia for African American liberation. Hughes went to China in 1933, three years before Du Bois first traveled to China. There he met Madame Sun Yat-sen and the revolutionary Chinese poet Lu Xun, whose poem inspired Mao Zedong's famous "Serve the People" essay. Hughes was likewise inspired and wrote just under twenty anticolonial poems linking his own particular experience to the revolutionary reality of China at the time.[20] In the most well-known of these poems, "Roar China!," he called on China to "Eat bullets, old maker of firecrackers / And spit out freedom in the face of your enemies!" Hughes also exhorted China to "Smash the revolving doors of the Jim Crow Y.M.C.A.s / Crush the enemies of the land of bread and freedom!"[21]

During World War II, black newspapers were among the few that opposed the mass incarceration of Japanese Americans, emphasizing its roots in racial discrimination. The *Northwest Enterprise* in Seattle cautioned its readers, "The same mob spirit which would single them [Japanese Americans] out for slaughter has trailed you through the forest to string you up at some crossroad."[22] The Los Angeles–based *California Eagle* condemned the wholesale incarceration of Japanese Americans as the "greatest disgrace of Democracy since slavery," and encouraged its readers to recognize their common bond with Japanese Americans on racial grounds.[23] Langston Hughes, as a columnist for the African American newspaper the *Chicago Defender*,[24] wrote consistently and loudly against the mass incarceration of Japanese Americans, likening their treatment to that of African Americans. "What has happened lately to the American Japanese and what has happened all along to us, puts American Negroes and American Japanese in the same boat."[25]

In 1955, twenty-nine Asian and African nations came together as the Asian-African Conference in Bandung, Indonesia, in the midst of worldwide decolonization, to articulate a position against a world increasingly polarized between Western democracies and Communist nations. They called for peaceful settlement of international disputes, nonintervention in the internal affairs of nations, and respect for the equality of races. It was an unprecedented international episode that showed the world an undeniable colored force in the face of white, Western supremacy.

In the 1960s, Mao Zedong issued two statements championing the African American liberation struggle. The first, issued on August 8, 1963, was a response to civil rights leader Robert F. Williams. Williams, who was then in exile in Cuba before moving to China, had written to Third World leaders around the world to rally international support for African Americans' struggle against racism.[26] Mao's second statement was issued on April 13, 1968, a few days after the assassination of Martin Luther King, Jr. Both statements called for universal support for African Americans, linking their plight with the larger system of colonialism and imperialism.[27] At the same historical moment in the United States, Black Panthers sold copies of Mao's *Little Red Book* alongside their newspaper the *Black Panther*, and Mao Zedong Thought offered black radicals a non-white, non-Western vision of class struggle and world revolution.[28]

Los Angeles, in particular, has had a long history of black–Japanese American relationships. By 1920 there were some 15,500 African Americans and 21,000 Japanese Americans in the city of Los Angeles. With racial covenants imposing housing segregation, they often inhabited adjacent and overlapping areas, leading historian Daniel Widener to conclude, "where one group was found, the other was likely as well."[29] When Japanese Americans were forced out of their homes and into US concentration camps during World War II, Little Tokyo became Bronzeville. In the 1950s, Nisei jazz musician Paul Togawa played with Lionel Hampton, while Ornette Coleman played the Club Ginza.[30] In 1965, East West Players, the nation's oldest continuing Asian American theatre, grew out of the Inner City Cultural Center—one of the first multicultural theater companies in the country. Linked in this way throughout the city, the Japanese American–African American connection found a nexus in the Crenshaw district of Los Angeles. While it had originally been a white neighborhood shielded by racial covenants, when discriminatory housing restrictions were ruled unconstitutional, the Crenshaw neighborhood became more colorful. Historian Scott Kurashige indicated that, whereas in 1950 there were a total of seventy blacks and Asians in the area, by 1960 the number had multiplied to 8,500—half black and half Japanese American.[31]

In addition to the ethnic and racial culture into which we are born and the values of the Eurocentric society that surrounds us, we also take on the cultural qualities of the immediate neighborhood in which we live. Growing up in the Crenshaw district of Los Angeles, the cultural standard was black, not white. When Mari Matsuda took her husband Chuck Lawrence to her cousin's wedding in the Crenshaw district, Chuck, who is black, asked, "Why are they only playing black music from the '60s and '70s?" Mari answered, "Because it's a Sansei wedding in Los Angeles! Ten thousand and one gold cranes, Cantonese food, James Brown and 'Earth, Wind and Fire.'"[32] When I asked Evelyn Yoshimura, who grew up in the Crenshaw area, if there was a time when she remembered wanting to be white, she replied, "No but I remember wanting to be black." She also recalled that, against the linguistic backdrop of being called "Oriental," "Jap" or "Chink," when a Black Muslim selling copies of *Muhammad Speaks* called her "Asian sister," the first time she had ever heard that phrase, it immediately resonated with her. No doubt Evelyn was among the Asian Americans in the theatre who understood what the Korean grocer meant when he declared, "I black. You, me, same."

If Crenshaw was primarily black and Japanese in the 1960s, Watts was at the time all black. That's where Reverend Masao Kodani grew up. He went to Centennial High School in Compton, where he was one of two non–African Americans, and didn't realize until he went to the University of California, Santa Barbara, that he didn't speak standard English. He thought he spoke and sounded like everyone else—which he did—until, at the predominantly white university, he discovered the language he spoke was Black English. White students would egg him on to talk so they could hear Black English coming from an Asian face, "Say something, go ahead!" they would goad. "Say what!?" he would retort. Mistaking his response for a question, they would reply, "You know, just talk!"

On the other coast, the black–Asian American connection was less pervasive, but epitomized by Yuri Kochiyama. Yuri began her life-long commitment to social justice when she and her family moved to Harlem in 1960. Yuri and her husband Bill joined the Harlem Parents Committee, attended the local Freedom School with their children, went to demonstrations and rallies, and were so involved in the struggle for racial equality that in 1963 they took their six children to Birmingham, Alabama, to take a firsthand look at one of the flash points of the Civil Rights movement. Within a month after their visit, the infamous bombing of the 16th Street Baptist Church, where the Southern Christian Leadership Conference was headquartered, killed four young girls. In her memoir, Yuri wrote, "We did not celebrate Christmas that year: no presents for the kids, not even a Christmas tree. Instead we donated money to the movements in the South."[33]

That same year, Yuri met Malcolm X when he came to support Congress of Racial Equality demonstrators (which included Yuri and her son Billy), who had been arrested for disorderly conduct demonstrating for construction jobs for people of color. Yuri later joined Malcolm's Organization for Afro-American Unity and attended their

Liberation School, where she recalls James Shabazz talking about the linkages between Africans and Asians.[34] Malcolm came to Yuri's house for a meeting with *Hibakusha* (atomic bomb survivors) and sent her eleven postcards from his international travels, writing in one, "I think you are the most beautiful family in Harlem."[35] Yuri and Malcolm even had the same birthday—May 19. Most famously, Yuri and her son Billy were in attendance at the Audubon Ballroom on Sunday, February 21, 1965, when Malcolm X was assassinated:

> Malcolm only got to say a few words beyond 'A Salaam Alikum' … when a ruckus in the middle section of the hall began … Two or three men rose up from the front and they started shooting, and the whole place went into utter chaos … Chairs were crashing to the floor, people were hitting the floor; there was screaming. A brother in front of me ran to the platform, so I followed after him … [Malcolm] was having difficulty breathing, so I put his head in my lap …[36]

A photo in *Life* magazine of Yuri cradling Malcolm as he died finished her sentence.

According to historian Gary Okihiro, "Yellow is emphatically neither white nor black; but insofar as Asians and Africans share a subordinate position to the master class, yellow is a shade of black, and black, a shade of yellow."[37] In the words of Mari Matsuda:

> We Asian Americans landed here and were essentially Black: our lives expendable, and our economic success a threat to White supremacy … We walk through the fire that the color line produced, and we ignore this history at our peril. Thus I do not reject the Black/White paradigm. I claim the cause of Black liberation as my own.[38]

Poet Lawson Inada felt this same kinship:

> The music we most loved and played and used was Negro music. It was something we could share in common, like a "lingua franca" in our "colored" community. And in our distorted reality of aliens and alienation, it even felt like citizenship.[39]

### Neither White Nor Black

Helen Jun relates the story of one Reverend Blakeslee who, in 1877 during the push for Chinese Exclusion, blithely testified before the California State Senate to "the practical superiority of slavery over Chinese immigration." Touting the benefits of the former institution, he declared, "Slavery took the heathens and by force made them into Americans."[40] Denigrating the Chinese as socially impractical, he elevated America's greatest dishonor into a prep school for citizenship. Before the dichotomy between black and white was the opposition between Christians and heathens.[41]

Within this byzantine social milieu, African American attitudes toward Asians were conflicted. Blacks were concentrated in the South, and the small number of Chinese were clustered in the West, so that, while most African Americans never had direct contact with Chinese, the black press picked up the tone of mainstream yellow journalism and expressed no love for the foreigners either. However, when the discriminatory Chinese Exclusion Act arose, the black press opposed the federal legislation, implicitly understanding its racist basis. Individual black leaders also expressed support for the Chinese. Reminding African Americans of the racial consistency of being non-white, Frederick Douglass declared that white southerners "would rather have laborers who will work for nothing; but as they cannot get the Negroes on these terms, they want Chinamen who, they hope, will work for next to nothing. The Chinaman will not long be willing to wear the cast off shoes of the Negro, and if he refuses, there will be trouble again."[42] As scholar Nami Kim pointed out, black political support of Chinese immigration was not based on racial identification but on a common struggle against white supremacist nationalism.[43]

The enigmatic reality of yellow being neither black nor white was manifested in various exasperating ways. In a 1995 interview I conducted with Ron Oba, a member of the US Army's segregated 442nd Regimental Combat Team, Ron recalled being confronted with separate toilet facilities for the first time during basic training in Mississippi.

The "Whites Only" line was usually so long, the Hawai'i boys would use the colored restrooms. After several weeks, the colonel called the companies together and said that the people of Hattiesburg were disturbed that we were using the colored section in the buses and restrooms and that we should use the one marked for whites. When one of the boys asked why, the colonel answered, "Because you're more white than black."[44]

In Los Angeles, when Chris Aihara was in third grade, she was sitting with three other girls—two African American and one white—when one of the African American girls suddenly jumped up with a gleeful discovery. Pointing to each of them in turn, she counted off, "Black, white, black, white!" referring to Chris as white. As if this little girl could only see in B&W, she looked at Chris and saw that, because she wasn't black, she must be white. From Chris's perspective, she knew she wasn't black, but she also knew she wasn't white. She didn't know what to say. Years later, when she was in college, a young African American woman told Chris that, as far as she was concerned, she was "just like a white person." This time Chris knew more about her own history, and told her about how Japanese Americans had been rounded up and put into camps during World War II only because of their race. This time it was her African American cohort who didn't know what to say.

In New Jersey, Helen Zia also had an African American friend who could also only see in B&W. During a civil rights walkout in high school, Helen's friend suddenly turned to her and demanded, "Helen, you've got to decide whether you're black or white." Helen had already put her body on the line by walking out, so it was not a question of what side she was on. It was a rhetorical question of a political order. Helen said, "I was speechless. 'Decide whether I'm black or white? How do I do that? And in my consciousness, it wasn't like I was jumping up and saying 'I'm not either!' Because what was I?"

In Florida, Don Kao knew who he was. Unlike most of us who were born in the United States and assumed we were American, Don stated unequivocally, "The whole time I grew up, it was always 'Chink' or 'Ching Chong' or some kind of racist stereotype, so I never thought of myself as being American," reverberating Langston Hughes's sentiment, "America never was America to me." Even privileges of class did not shield Don or his family from racism. Sent to an elite boarding school, Don recalled, "I was questioning race while embracing my class background, but we were clearly outclassed. While my father had a second-hand Cadillac, my classmates arrived in Mercedeses and Rolls Royces." His father, trained in China as a surgeon, was an exceptionally skilled general practitioner in a small Florida town, where Don recalled hearing kids at school make fun of his father's accent even as they relied on him for their medical needs. Regarding the segregated water fountains and bathrooms that surrounded him, Don sardonically credits the Chinese Exclusion Act of 1882 for his being able to use the ones designated for whites only. "We had been excluded for eighty years, so no one knew what to do with us. Besides, race was black and white. We were foreigners."

### Dual Domination

We lived in a black-and-white world in which we were neither one nor the other. But our lives were not simply a matter of color. Chinese in the United States lived within what L. Ling Chi Wang called a "structure of dual domination."[45] Simply put, this is the notion that, in addition to the United States, China also exerted an oppressive political and cultural force over Chinese Americans, and the two nations worked in tandem to keep Chinese Americans suppressed. On one hand, the ideology of white supremacy manifested itself in exclusionary and discriminatory legal and extralegal activities. At the same time, the Chinese Benevolent Associations (also called the Six Companies)—which had strong ties to the Kuomintang, China's Nationalist Party—controlled the Chinatowns across the country. They stressed loyalty to one's clan, village, and nation-state. This cultural and political mandate reproduced traditional Chinese institutions and events in the community and enforced Chinese values and lifestyle within the family.

Particularly repressive were traditional values of expected behavior for women. As Helen Zia commented, "The daughter obeys the father, the wife obeys the husband, the widow will obey the sons." Fay Chiang grew up in the back of a laundry in Queens, where there was so little space that "everything we had had to fold up: folding beds, folding chairs, folding tables." Later her family moved to Chinatown, which was "like a Chinese village, very restricted, where everyone knew everyone and women had very specified roles." As the eldest of four children of immigrant parents who did not speak English, Fay became the family translator when she was only in second grade—not an uncommon burden for children of immigrants. When Fay turned thirteen, her mother started molding her to be a proper housewife. However, Fay had an early, toxic dose of domestic responsibility. She also wanted to be an artist. She was accepted to many art schools, which offered her partial scholarships; but her parents would not release their income tax returns, which she needed for the applications, because her father had entered the country as a "paper son"—illegally, with false papers. So Fay ended up going to Hunter College, where she joined the Chinese Club in a search for meaningful activity. But, "All they wanted to do was meet guys and get married, which was the last thing I wanted to do because I had already helped raise three younger siblings. I said to myself, 'Is this going to be my life for the rest of my life?!'"

The basic dynamics of dual domination can be applied to Japanese Americans as well, except that the internal oppression did not emanate from the home country or its operatives but from the fallout of their mass incarceration by the US government during World War II. After having been falsely accused of being synonymous with the enemy, Nisei parents exerted a self-policing force over themselves and their children, which worked in tandem with Middle America to keep Japanese Americans in line. By tacit agreement—not unlike Jews' reticence to discuss the Holocaust or African Americans' reserve regarding slavery—Niseis did not talk about having been wrongfully incarcerated. Consistent with the dynamic of blaming the victim, sublimating the crime was a tactical if unconscious coping mechanism. When they did talk about the incarceration, it was only to each other—and only in code. "Where were you *before the war*? What *camp* were you in? Where did you go *after the war*?" Their world had been dichotomized into *before the war* and *after the war*, with a mysterious *camp* in between. Silence took on an ambiguity that permeated the Japanese American community after the war. The propaganda that insisted it was their patriotic duty to be

incarcerated, the euphemisms designed to mitigate its unconstitutionality, the humiliation of being betrayed by their own government, and
the psychological chaos these ironies created all conspired to blame the
victims. At the same time, our parents fostered cultural values: *gaman*
(to persevere), *enryo* (to think more of others than oneself) and to be
*otonashii* (respectful and polite). While endurance, consideration for
others, and respect are virtues, being silenced is a crime. Even as the
West is urged to "speak your mind," the Rest are admonished to "hold
your tongue" and "know your place."

Besides this conspiracy of silence, another internal suppressive force
within the Japanese American community was the coping mechanism
of striving to be 200 percent American. After the war, having grown
up as US-born Americans, my parents—and their generation—were
still trying to come to grips with how their American dream could go
so awry. With no public acknowledgement of their betrayal or societal
scrutiny of the government's un-American actions, and too socialized
to be righteously pissed off, many Niseis channeled their frustrations
the only way they knew how—by being 200 percent American, i.e., "as
good as white people."

As most people of color discover soon enough—whether with resent-
ment or resignation—to be "as good" as white people means that you
have to be better. In a kind of fuzzy magical realism, according to my
mother, the reasoning was that if we could prove to the government that
we were as good as Caucasians, they would realize (retroactively) what
a mistake it was to have imprisoned us. The overall effect was the creation of a widespread internal repression that fortified society's effort to
keep us in our place. In short, many Niseis believed—and taught their
children—that we should never rock the boat, always toe the line, work
hard, and never complain. Upstanding citizens, their underlying reasoning was phobic. This was our public secret.

### Racist Love

After the theme of being considered "alien," being the "model minority" has been an insistent and unshakable refrain in Asian America.

Despite mighty and continual efforts to expunge it, it just won't go away.

The propaganda started in the mid Sixties—six months after the Watts uprising—with the article "Success Story, Japanese-American Style" by sociologist William Petersen in the *New York Times Magazine*. He proclaimed, "By any criterion of good citizenship that we choose, the Japanese Americans are better than any other group in our society including native-born whites."[46]

By the end of the year, after another summer of civil unrest, another Asian ethnic group was the subject of another "success story" published in a major magazine. "Success Story of One Minority Group in the US" in *US News & World Report* called Chinese Americans "a model of self-respect and achievement." Openly naming African Americans as the negative other, it stated, "At a time when it is being proposed that hundreds of billions be spent to uplift Negroes and other minorities, the nation's 300,000 Chinese-Americans are moving ahead on their own, with no help from anyone else."[47]

A year later, *Newsweek* published "Success Story: Outwhiting the Whites." Returning to lauding Japanese Americans, the article began by quoting a hapless Nisei, triumphant at having proved himself to be 200 percent American, as saying, "I outwhited the whites," and ended with his restating the formula: "If a black family moved in next door, I wouldn't like it … If they want to get ahead, they have to work—just like the Nisei did."[48]

In the rising white fear of the growing black power, it was no accident that Asian Americans were cast as the good minority. In what political commentators Vijay Prashad called a "weapon in the war against black America"[49] and Scot Nakagawa called a "lever of white supremacy,"[50] the assertion of Asians as the model minority signified that the United States was not racist, as African Americans professed, but was the land of opportunity, as Asian Americans proved. Law professor Charles Lawrence pointed out that "African Americans are 'monitored' by the Asian American minority against the backdrop of both groups' subordination to the 'invisible majority' of whites and their racial privilege."[51]

But in the undertow of US racial relations, the Good Minority/Bad Minority game is not only played with Asians on one side and

African Americans on the other. Within the animal farm of shifting global relations, some Asians are sometimes better than others. When the Chinese first came to the United States, they were "good" because they filled a demand for low-cost labor but soon became "bad" when they were blamed for taking away jobs from white workers. Chinese became "good" again during World War II, when China was an ally of the United States and Japan was the enemy. Before the decade was up, however, during the occupation of Japan and Mao Zedong's rise to power, the Japanese became Good Asians, since they were now patrolled and controlled by the US military, while the Chinese were the Bad Asians, i.e., Communists.

In an analysis of race, class, and crime in San Francisco's Chinatown, criminologists Paul Takagi and Tony Platt noted that after the Chinese Revolution of 1949, when Chinese Americans became Bad Asians, "hegemonically, Japanese cuisine, architecture, art, film and culture came to be embraced in the United States, which facilitated the acceptance of Japan as a political ally." They contended that, in contrast to World War II just a few years earlier, it was this strategic, politically motivated love affair with all things Japanese—rather than any inherent cultural trait, like self-sufficiency or pulling yourself up by the bootstraps—that resulted in the lifting of social and legal barriers, which opened doors to housing, professional schools, and occupations for Japanese Americans, and accounted for the upward mobility of the Japanese in the United States.[52]

In 1972, six years after the rash of Asian American "success stories" in mainstream periodicals, Frank Chin and Jeffrey Paul Chan theorized the difference between the old-fashioned bigotry of "racist hate" and its more sophisticated counterpart of "racist love." Basically, racist love is the exhibition of flattering sentiments based on the logic that its obsequiousness outweighs its racist underpinnings. Ovations such as the mainstream media's testimonial that Japanese Americans were "better than any other group in our society including native-born whites" and that Chinese Americans were able to move ahead "with no help from anyone else" are blatant examples. Chin and Chan posited that stereotypes for racial groups come in two models—the acceptable and the unacceptable:

The hostile black stud has his acceptable counterpart in the form of Stepin Fetchit. For the savage, kill-crazy Geronimo, there is Tonto … For the mad dog General Santa Ana there's the Cisco Kid … For Fu Manchu and the Yellow Peril, there is Charlie Chan and his Number One Son.[53]

The acceptable model is acceptable because it is tractable. The unacceptable model is unacceptable because it cannot be controlled by whites. Chin and Chan warned of the impact of this thinking on Asian Americans. "If the system works, the stereotypes assigned to the various races are accepted by the races themselves as reality, as fact, and racist love reigns … One measure of the success of white racism is the silence of that race and the amount of white energy necessary to maintain or increase that silence."[54]

The cogency of the idea of "racist love" was foreshadowed in the mid Sixties when African American author Julius Lester wrote that the days of singing freedom songs and combating bullets and billy clubs with love were over. Whereas African Americans used to sing *We Shall Overcome*, he noted, "Now they sing, 'Too much love, Too much love, Nothing kills a nigger like, Too much love.'"[55]

But racist love is hard to spurn. Claire Jean Kim cites conservative educator Lance Izumi as criticizing liberal Asian Americans for adopting a "panminority ideology" that promotes black and Latino interests at the expense of their own. Likewise, she quotes conservative columnist Arthur Hu as saying, "The whole idea that we need to discriminate against an Asian because some white guy made a black person a slave is hard to understand."[56]

All people of color who grow up in the United States encounter a time when the rules of racial classification become all too clear. Social psychologist Claude Steele wrote that his first encounter was when he learned he was not allowed to swim in the local municipal swimming pool except on Wednesday afternoons, after which they presumably cleaned the pool. Like Bob Nakamura, who was likewise not allowed in his local public pool, it was a bitter awakening to the racial order that would dominate what should otherwise have been an ordinary childhood. Steele noted, "The implications of this order for my life seemed

massive—a life of swimming only on Wednesday afternoons? Why? …
I didn't know what being black meant, but I was getting the idea that it
was a big deal."[57]

We weren't white. We weren't black. We weren't the model minority.
It was time to determine who we were.

# ACT II: ONCE IN A MOVEMENT

*puckyoo sunn-obbaa-bit,*
*muderrpuckkerrrr!!*

Al Robles

## THREE

## Yellow Power

Fig. 3.1: *Los Angeles Free Press,* October 31–November 6, 1969

The *Los Angeles Free Press* (1964–78) was the first and most successful alternative newspaper of the Long Sixties. Having reached a circulation of 100,000 with a readership estimated to be double that number, it gained the reputation for being "*the* newspaper of the New Left" by the late 1960s.[1] So when the front page of the October 31–November 6, 1969 issue of that newspaper declared "Yellow Power Arrives!" it was like having made the society page of the New Left.

### *Speak a New Language So That the World Will Be a New World!*

Growing up Asian in a black-and-white world was a solitary experience. In our private efforts to be accepted, to be seen for ourselves, to be treated as Americans, we thought we were alone. After all, the experiences of being the only one from your Cub Scout troop to be refused entry into the public swimming pool, of realizing you too were an Eskimo, of being thrown onto the sidewalk by the seat of your pants, were mortifying. They were not things you talked about or even wanted to think about. And so we didn't.

Nor could we even if we had wanted to. We were literally at a loss for words. Ludwig Wittgenstein remarked, "The limits of my language are the limits of my mind. All I know is what I have words for."[2] Without words, experiences and feelings can hardly be thought, much less contemplated or articulated.

If we weren't "white," "black," "Oriental," or the "model minority"— all words that defined who we were not—then what words might define who we were? The thirteenth-century Sufi poet Rumi declared, "Speak a new language so that the world will be a new world!" Since speaking is a cultural practice and language is a mode of thinking, part of the cultural revolution was linguistic.

Words became moral imperatives, reflective of the social upheaval of the times. In 1966 Lenny Bruce was arrested for saying nine "dirty" words, most of which were included in George Carlin's 1972 monologue "Seven Words You Can Never Say on Television," in a case that made its way to the Supreme Court. "Pigs" became a common term for police. "Asshole" replaced tamer words like "phony" and "jerk," prompting linguist Geoffrey Nunberg to note, "Put simply, you have the right to treat assholes as assholes because the assholes have it coming."[3] The term "honky," a common pejorative since at least the 1940s, also took on a more nuanced meaning, insisting on the circuitousness of its definition. In Tom Wolfe's prickly 1969 *Esquire* article "The New Yellow Peril," he quotes San Francisco Chinatown youth organizer George Woo as saying, "I didn't call him honky because he was white. We have some white brothers who have done some of the things we should have done ourselves. I called him honky because he was a honky."[4]

Language reflected the changes that were occurring in social thinking. One of the most profound was the emergence of new terms for who we were. Tariq Modood, a leading proponent of multiculturalism, pointed out that, during the Civil Rights movement, the demand for equality was based on the assumption that we were all the same underneath our different-colored skins and that difference was a problem. The rise of Black Liberation replaced the goals of equal rights and opportunity with those of self-determination and empowerment. Difference was now valued over sameness, and the broader climate of progressive opinion recognized a multitude of groups, such as ethnic minorities, women, and LGBTQ, emphasizing identity and subjectivity. The new message was, as Modood asserted, "Respect us for what we are, don't try and change us into your conception."[5] However, as poet June Jordan cautioned, "There is difference and there is power. And who holds the power shall decide the meaning of difference."[6]

Naming thus became a critical part of the process of self-definition, as the evolution from "colored" to "Negro" to "black" to "Afro-American" to "African American" attests.[7] Kwame Turé, then known as Stokely Carmichael, who popularized the concept of Black power when he was chair of the Student Nonviolent Coordinating Committee, first theorized the concept of self-definition with political scientist Charles Hamilton in their electrifying 1967 bestseller, *Black Power: The Politics of Liberation in America*. In it they stated, "We shall have to struggle for the right to create our own terms through which to define ourselves and our relationship to the society, and to have those terms recognized."[8] Likewise, Gloria Anzaldua said that once they acquired the name Chicano and a language she calls Chicano Spanish, "the fragmented pieces began to fall together—who we were, what we were, how we evolved. We began to get glimpses of what we might eventually become."[9]

### Speak, Asian America!

Richard Aoki told his biographer Diane Fujino, "Up to that point, we had been called Orientals. Oriental was a rug that everyone steps on, so we ain't no Orientals. We were Asian American."[10] Best known for being one of the few non–African American Black Panthers, the point in time that Aoki referred to was that of the formation of the Asian American Political Alliance (AAPA) at the University of California, Berkeley, for which he had been a spokesperson. Coined by AAPA's founder Yuji Ichioka, the self-identifier "Asian American" marked a seismic shift in consciousness. More than just a descriptor, the term subverted the Orientalist tradition of lumping all Asians together—this time as an oppositional political identity imbued with self-definition and empowerment, signaling a new way of thinking. With the power of repetition, AAPA was the first organization to articulate the ideology of this New Man and Woman:

> We Asian Americans believe that we must develop
> an American Society that is just, humane, equal …

> We Asian Americans realize that America was
> always and still is a White Racist Society …

> We Asian Americans refuse to cooperate with the
> White Racism in this society …

> We Asian Americans support all oppressed peoples …

> We Asian Americans oppose the imperialistic
> policies being pursued by the American
> government.[11]

AAPA newsletters quickly circulated to other college campuses, and other formations of the same name appeared throughout the country although they were not considered chapters of the original organization. AAPA expressed an understanding of its catalytic imperative in an October 1969 newsletter. "AAPA is only a transition for developing our own social identity … . In fact, [the important link is not] AAPA itself … but the ideas generated into action from it."[12]

Even as Asian American students coalesced at the University of California, Berkeley, Asian American students began organizing at its sister campus in Los Angeles. Along with developing UCLA's Asian American Studies Center, the inaugural center of this new academic discipline, many of the same undergraduates launched *Gidra: The Monthly of the Asian American Experience*, the inaugural newspaper of the Asian American movement. Published between April 1969 and April 1974, during the primal years of Asian America, it not only provided alternative news, it served as a national forum for vetting alternative ideas. Untethered to any one organization or ideology and being eclectically inclusive—for which it was both criticized and praised—*Gidra* gained a national readership and inspired the birth of many other movement newspapers.

In 1972, at a time when alternative presses were rarely taken seriously by the mainstream, *Gidra* caught the attention of the *Library Journal*, the oldest and largest trade publication for librarians, which wrote that *Gidra* "effectively voices this new consciousness among Amerasians, simultaneously uncovering a century of wrongs committed by the white majority and enunciating a determination to make the future at once different and better than the past."[13] As momentous as its contents were, *Gidra* functioned just as importantly as a Petri dish for growing oppositional consciousnesses. With over 200 volunteer "staff" over its five-year tenure and a nationwide audience, *Gidra* contributed to the formation of political identities that gave rise to a generational cohort of activists and cultural workers.

Poet Audre Lorde maintained that, in order to know who we are, we needed first to "train ourselves to respect our feelings and to transpose them into a language so they could be shared," adding that, "where that language does not exist, it is our poetry which helps to fashion it."[14] Through their songs, troubadours Chris Iijima, Nobuko (then Joanne) Miyamoto and Charlie Chin were the first to transpose our untold feelings into words, fashion politics into poems, and render the politics and passion of the escalating Asian American movement into song:

> I looked in the mirror,
> And I saw me.
> And I didn't want to be
> Any other way.

> Then I looked around,
> And I saw you.
> And it was the first time I knew
> Who we really are.[15]

In 1972, Chris, Nobuko, and Charlie were approached by folk singer Barbara Dane, who they got to know from singing at anti-war rallies, to record an album. The result was *A Grain of Sand: Music for the Struggle by Asians in America*.[16] Their songs, now portable, were played at parties and rallies and sung by young and old across the country. *A Grain of Sand* thus became the soundtrack of the Asian American movement. Reflecting on those heady days, Charlie commented, "We were a vehicle, a delivery system to introduce people to the idea of Asian American consciousness." Chris agreed. "I think that what we were doing was to say, 'Look, our singing is part of what you guys are doing. Whatever you're doing, we're a part of that.' Our purpose was to tell people we're not alone."

### Yellow? Amerasia? Asian Nation?

As "Negroes" became "black" and Mexican Americans became "Chicano," what could signify our transformation? "Yellow"? "Amerasia"? "Asian Nation"?

Before "Asian American" became standardized, we tried on different names, each reflecting reasons that were part of the process of coming to terms with who and what we were. Some of the earliest attempts to organize Asian Americans did so under the banner of "yellow," no doubt in reaction to the color-coded black-and-white backdrop that had defined our existence.

As expressed in the 1969 *LA Free Press* headline, "yellow" reigned as the battle-cry of the times, an in-your-face inversion of the "Yellow Peril" and "yellow-bellied Jap" of yesteryear.[17] In the summer of 1968, "Are You Yellow?" was the name of the first Asian American conference —the first of many take-offs of the 1967 Swedish film *I Am Curious (Yellow)* that was popular at the time. In the first issue of *Gidra*, in April

1969, "Yellow Power!" was one of the first widely published manifestos of the new Asian American consciousness. Written by Larry Kubota, it declared:

> Yellow power is a call for all Asian Americans to end the silence that has condemned us to suffer in this racist society and to unite with our black, brown and red brothers of the Third World for survival, self-determination and the creation of a more humanistic society.[18]

Later that same year, *Gidra* published "The Emergence of Yellow Power" by Amy Uyematsu, which, reprinted on the first page of the *Los Angeles Free Press*, bore the headline: "Yellow Power Arrives!"[19] Despite its origins as an undergraduate term paper for one of the first Asian American classes, it has become the most anthologized article on the Asian American movement. As historian Scott Kurashige commented, the article "crystallized simultaneously the anger and the aspiration of [Uyematsu's] generation."[20] The article identified four main concepts that articulated the nascent movement's intellectual and philosophical underpinnings.

The first was the concept of identity. The supremacy of whiteness required all people of color to ruggedly declare their decolonized identity, as symbolized in the slogan "Black is beautiful." In the words of Black Panther and AAPA spokesperson Richard Aoki, "In the past I didn't think the identity issue was that important, but I realize that unless you have your identity, you can't go to the political level."[21] The second notion was that Asian Americans must come into their power both personally and politically. In a vicious cycle, the normalization of inequality had led to acquiescence on the part of Asian Americans, thereby perpetuating white supremacy. Third was the significance and challenge of creating a united front, the most obvious hurdle being the multiplicity of Asian ethnicities, each with its own language, culture, and history, the diversity of which was compounded both by historical antagonisms between ethnic groups and by social and economic stratifications. The article's fourth and last point was that, as Kubota had also written, the yellow power movement must join the Third World revolution "for the creation of a more humanistic society."

The term "Third World" came into its own during the Cold War, when representatives from Africa, Asia, and the Middle East came together at the Asian-African or Bandung Conference (1955) in opposition to the First World power of Western industrial nations and the Second World of the eastern bloc. While the Third World is often thought of as consisting of undeveloped or underdeveloped nations, Frantz Fanon and (more recently) historian Vijay Prashad have emphasized that it is not so much a place as a project.[22] For ethnic minority movements in the United States, the Third World became a unifying concept. W. E. B. Du Bois sent a message to the Bandung Conference stating, "We colored folk of America have long lived with you yellow, brown and black folk of the world under the intolerable arrogance and assumptions of the white race."[23] The term "Third World" was thereby adopted by progressive "colored folk of America" as a more accurate and appropriate designation than "minority." The idea of the Third World was empowering. In this cosmology, rather than being disenfranchised minorities, we were part of the vast majority.

In 1969 "yellow" was heralded in a variety of other iterations. A three-day conference called "Are You Yellow, Curious?" was co-sponsored by the Council on Oriental Organizations and the Los Angeles County Human Relations Commission. The Los Angeles–based self-help group Yellow Brotherhood was founded. The "Yellow Identity" conference at the University of California, Berkeley, attracted over 300 students nationwide, jump-starting the campus's Third World Liberation strike. "Yellow Seed" was a grassroots drop-in center for Asian American youth in Stockton, California. In the next few years, another group called "Yellow Seeds" was started in Boston; "Yellow Pearl" was both a song written by Chris Iijima and Nobuko Miyamoto as well as an innovative box of poems and drawings, produced by an ingenious crew that worked out of Basement Workshop in New York City.

In addition to "yellow," we tried on the compound label of "Amerasian." In a 1970 *Gidra* article titled "Amerasian Power," the Organization for Southland Asian American Organizations (more commonly called "the Umbrella") announced that it was changing its name to "Amerasia," noting, "Amerasia is not only an organization, it is also a state of mind."[24] Later that year, another *Gidra* article, "Amerasian

Culture," described Amerasians as having "a common history of oppression here in this country and therefore a common bond" in opposition to the term "Oriental."[25] That same year, an Amerasian chapter of the Japanese American Citizens' League (JACL) was formed.[26] In 1971, an "Amerasian Generation" conference was held at UCLA,[27] the Amerasia Bookstore in Los Angeles opened, Amerasia Creative Arts was established as a subsidiary of Basement Workshop in New York, and the *Amerasia Journal* was founded by a handful of students at Yale University. (Its publication continues today at UCLA, making it the longest-running Asian American academic journal.)

The term "Asian nation" made a brief appearance, more as a political concept related to the broader question of national oppression and liberation than as a term of self-reference.[28] As stated in a lengthy article in *Gidra*, "The concept of building an Asian nation here in North Amerika [sic] is an attempt at finding unity."[29] The article, which at the time of its publication was opaquely credited as "written and revised by two people from the collective,"[30] was penned by Shinya Ono while he was in the Cook County Jail in 1970, for his participation in the Weatherman's Days of Rage anti-war demonstration in Chicago, with editorial assistance, Ono wrote, from "a sister."[31] Although the article stated early on that, in referring to an Asian nation it did not adhere to the Stalinist definition of an historically constituted people with a common language, territory, economic life, and history, the use of the term was criticized on those grounds, debated, and eventually dropped.[32]

The term "Asian American" was also debated. Artist-activists Fay Chiang and Tomie Arai recalled countless debates on the question of whether "Asian American" should have a space or a dash. "Somewhere along the way," film scholar Peter Feng indicated, "the hyphen was voted out." Feng noted that the term was inherently problematic, beginning with the misassumption that "America" referred to the United States (and not other North or South American countries), while "Asian" typically meant East Asians.[33] Regarding the hyphenated identity, Feng noted that "although the difference between 'Asian American' and 'Asian-American' might seem trivial, for many the hyphen represents a persistent discourse which suggests that Asians will never be fully accepted as Americans."[34] Feng argued that, by yoking two identities together, the hyphen "strains to hold the terms together and apart." He complicated the discussion by pointing out that, as a bridge between two disparate identities, it preserved the notion of duality in binary opposition, thereby denying the creation of a stable third term.[35] Feng quoted a character in one of Maxine Hong Kingston's novels who states: "'Chinese hyphen American' sounds exactly the same as 'Chinese no hyphen American.' No revolution takes place in the mouth or in the ear."[36]

### To "P" or Not to "P"

As Peter Feng indicated, a significant caveat in defining the new Asian American is that we were not all Asian. Chinese, Japanese, and Filipinos made up the largest numbers of so-called Asians at the time, but Filipinos did not racially identify themselves as Asian. And while much of the new political identity was formed in opposition to being Orientalized, neither were Filipinos considered Oriental. Reflecting on this ethnic ambiguity was a 1971 *Gidra* article titled "I Am Curious (Yellow?)," in which Violet Rabaya wrote, "Being raised in a white society and having acquired white 'habits' is difficult enough to cope with when attempting to find pride in one's ancestry, but even more difficult is the alienation I find among my own people." Calling Filipinos "disoriented," she concluded, "To be an outcast in a white society and an outcast among other Orientals leaves the Filipino in that never-never land of social obscurity."[37] While Filipinos were included as part of the burgeoning Asian American movement, many felt marginalized within it—a condition reflected in the title of Fred Cordova's 1983 pictorial essay book, *Filipinos: Forgotten Asian Americans.*[38]

The most significant factor that distinguished Filipinos from their Chinese and Japanese counterparts was that the Philippines had been a subjugated colony—first of Spain, then of the United States—for 400 years. As colonized subjects of the United States, Filipinos were roller-coastered through a dizzying series of peculiar and fluctuating federal categories over the years. When the Philippines was annexed, its residents became "US nationals," which incongruously meant they owed sole allegiance to the United States but did not have the rights of citizenship.

Because they were not aliens, and hence not subject to national immigration quotas, Filipinos were heavily recruited as the third source of cheap Asian labor. In 1934, the Tydings-McDuffie Act, also called the Philippine Independence Act, combined two issues—provisions for eventual Filipino independence and the immediate reclassification of Filipinos from "US nationals" to "aliens," which rendered them subject to a restrictive immigration quota of a mere fifty persons per year.

In 1941, the Philippine Army was incorporated into the United States Armed Forces in the Far East to fight the Japanese invasion. In 1942, the United States granted citizenship to Filipinos who served in the US military—but four years later, when the United States gave the Philippines back its independence, Filipino veterans were stripped of the benefits they had been promised. While Chinese and Japanese felt the internal colonization of people of color in this country, Filipinos had been materially colonized in their own country, shaping a frame of mind they brought with them to the United States. As sociologist Antonio J. A. Pido wrote, "Migration to the United States merely transferred their colonial subordinate position from their native land to that of the colonizer."[39]

In 1970, Search to Involve Pilipino Americans (SIPA), which is still a vital organization in Los Angeles, organized a weekend "identity retreat." It was at this conference that US-born Florante Ibanez, recruited by SIPA co-founder "Uncle" Royal Morales, learned for the first time of the role the United States had played in the Philippines and of the subsequent history of Filipinos in the United States. Since this was not being taught in school, Ibanez said that the community had to shoulder its own self-education through seminars, workshops, and study groups.

It was during this time that, as part of the linguistic turn of the era, the spelling and pronunciation of Filipino became "Pilipino," partly because there is no "F" sound in any of the Philippine languages, but primarily to signal an anticolonial, progressive political stance. Florante recalled that it was Uncle Roy in particular who brought up the question of whether "to 'P' or not to 'P,'" as a discussion point in the dialogue around Filipino American identity and politics. Florante noted that, while the term "Pilipino" had been widely used throughout the 1970s, "Filipino," "Flip," and "Fil Am" were also used as labels of self-reference.

Fig. 3.2: Royal Morales in front of SIPA office, Los Angeles, c.1970

The Filipino Identity movement continued with a series of Young Filipino People's Far West Conventions. In 1971, Fred and Dorothy Cordova, who had founded Filipino Youth Activities (FYA) in 1957 in Seattle, initiated the gathering at the request, Dorothy said, of FYA youth who were interested in meeting other Filipino youth. However, with the attendance of Philip Vera Cruz and Larry Itliong from the United Farm Workers and the Kalayaan Collective, an anti-Marcos group from San Francisco, the conference took on an increasingly political role, and was held every year in various locations until 1982.[40]

Due to increased understanding of intra-Asian ethnic diversity from conferences such as the Filipino Peoples' Far West Convention, "Asian Americans" morphed into "Asian Pacific Islanders" in the late 1970s, in order to better reflect the inclusion of Filipinos, Samoans, Tongans, Guamanians, and other Pacific Islanders. While there are now Asian American and Asian Pacific Island associations and alliances for countless professions, occupations, and interest groups, there was a time when the people served by such groups were disregarded. The Asian American movement changed all that.

## Taking a Stand: Becoming a Movement

As Chris and Nobuko sang:

> By yourself, you are just by yourself.
> Together, we can all take a stand.[41]

Having broken through the double consciousness of seeing ourselves through the Orientalizing gaze of white America, we stopped trying to become who we were not. We stopped trying to assimilate into a society that, although considered the norm, we knew to be severely flawed. We realized, finally, that we could be both Asian and American, that we could eat both Chinese food and meat and potatoes. As C. L. R. James observed, "Those people who are in western civilization, who have grown up in it, but made to feel and themselves feeling that they are outside, have a unique insight into their society."[42] We took a stand.

Warren Furutani had been a weekend surfer and a cheerleader who was voted "Best Personality" in high school before he became one of the students of color in the innovative College Readiness Program of San Mateo College in 1968. One of the hallmarks of the program was for students from each of the participating racial groups to learn how to speak in public. Because there were few Asians in the program, Warren's turn came around often. When the program's funding was cut, Warren was one of the speakers at a rally on Friday, December 13, 1968, in support of the doomed program. When the football team started beating up demonstrators, a full-blown riot ensued, and Warren was arrested. "Here I'd been this kid from Gardena that always towed the line, did things the right way. I didn't want to be different. I wanted to be like everybody else. But when I started developing my voice, it gave me power. Jeez, it gave me power."

A charismatic orator then, as he is now, Warren was one of the first people called upon whenever a speaker was needed to address the rapidly growing Asian American movement, and he spoke widely across the nation. He commented:

Sometimes people think that the Asian American movement started with a leader or a group who traveled around the country and sowed the seeds of revolution, as it were. The reality was that it seemed like all of us came to the same threshold in history and stepped over simultaneously.

Warren, who later became a California State Assembly member (2008–12), is not the only one to tell this origin story. Nelson Nagai, one of the early members of Yellow Seed in Stockton, California, wrote that Steve Louie told him about another organization in Philadelphia called Yellow Seeds, that Warren Furutani had told him they were similar to Yellow Brotherhood in Los Angeles, and that Neil Gotanda introduced him to Richard Aoki of the Black Panther Party, Alex Hing of the Red Guard Party, and a host of people from the Japanese Community Youth Council, Asian American Hardcore, Asian American Draft Resistance, the newspaper *Rodan*, and the jazz fusion band *Hiroshima*. "I soon realized that Yellow Seed was part of a spontaneous action of Asian American youth in New York, Boston, San Francisco, San Jose, Los Angeles, and Hawai'i that were bringing attention to Asian community problems and creating programs to protect the Asian community."[43]

If, as Malcolm Gladwell described, a tipping point is an indiscernible boiling point that triggers mass contagious behavior, spreads mysteriously like a virus, has disproportionate effects, and happens in a hurry,[44] the spontaneous arisings that Warren and Nelson described marked the beginning of a nationwide Asian American movement.

Having stepped over the threshold, time also changed. We lived in a state of acceleration: fast-forward had become the norm. As the following chapters describe, in just a few years, Asian America came into its own. Whereas before 1968 there had been distinct Chinese, Japanese, Filipino, Korean, and other less populous communities, each with its own organizations, newspapers, and events, by 1970 there were at least forty progressive pan–Asian American grassroots organizations, four newspapers, and ten student and community conferences.

By the early 1970s, an explosion of Asian American activism erupted on a broad national scale. Distinct Asian American contingents were a visible presence in anti-war rallies. A pilgrimage to Manzanar in

Fig. 3.3. Warren Furutani with representatives of the Republic of
New Afrika and El Comite speaking at rally in Harlem, 1971

December 1969 was the first public national commemoration of the
World War II concentration camps, launching annual pilgrimages to
many other former detention sites. Asian Americans participated in
domestic Third World campaigns such as the movement to free Huey
P. Newton (1967–1970); the Occupation of Alcatraz (1969–1971); the
Black Panther trial in New Haven (May 1970); the National Chicano
Moratorium in Los Angeles (August 29, 1970); and the Occupation
of Wounded Knee (February–May 1973). Pat Sumi and Alex Hing
represented the Asian American movement in the 1970 US People's
Anti-Imperialist Delegation to North Korea, North Vietnam, and the
People's Republic of China. Asian Americans were active in the Tiao-yu
Tai Movement in 1970, protesting the renewal of the US- Japan Security
Pact in 1970, the reversion of Okinawa to Japan in 1971, and the dec-
laration of martial law in the Philippines in 1972.

Mike Murase commented:

The speed at which people got their consciousness raised was pretty
phenomenal. There was a feeling of urgency to decide what side you're
on. When you think in terms of a person transforming themselves in
a matter of six months, a year, two years—becoming a revolutionary
when you were an engineering student—it's a process that could take
a lifetime to figure out, but it was happening at warp speed.

It felt like we had to catch up, seize every moment, be everywhere at once. Or at the least attend more than one meeting a night. Back then—without cell phones, the internet or even faxes—the only way to be in more than one place at a time was to be there.

## FOUR

## Spontaneous Arisings

> *Whether it was LA, the Bay Area, Seattle,*
> *New York or the Midwest, people we ran*
> *into all over the country had the same*
> *epiphany at the same time.*
>
> Warren Furutani

In those days there was a there there. And it was everywhere. Asians of different stripes from various parts of the country were undergoing the same awakening at the same time. Three distinct alignments rose up in an independent co-existence of multiple beginnings. The first to blaze the way were what historian Eric Hobsbawm called "social bandits"—street people who were hemmed in by social and economic forces that they did not completely understand and over which they had no control. The second was a version of what W. E. B. Du Bois called the "Talented Tenth," college students who were symbolically 10 percent of their race, who took up the mantle of working for the betterment of their race as a whole. The third category consisted of middle-aged and established adults who were not only as outspoken and radical as their youthful counterparts, but in many cases served as the initial impetus for the politicization of young people. Together, these three groupings created a spontaneous and unprecedented partnership. Taking a giant step forward, they crossed the same threshold and, in less than two years, created a new world.

## Social Bandits

Many activists and academics trace the birth of the Asian America movement to the Bay Area, with the founding of the Asian American Political Alliance (AAPA) at the University of California, Berkeley and the Third World Liberation strikes at San Francisco State College and UC Berkeley in 1968. But if the Asian American movement was born in 1968, it had been conceived a decade earlier not on any campus, but in the streets. Before there were campus radicals there were street rebels characterized by the same Asian American pride, rage against the system, and nerve to confront it. They were hoodlums, delinquents—what we called *yogores* in Japanese. Although most of them were, no-doubt, actual thugs, some fit Hobsbawm's description of "social bandits"—prepolitical insurgents who flouted authority and championed the masses against oppression à la Robin Hood and Pancho Villa.

In Los Angeles in the 1950s and early 1960s, there were the Wombats, Black Quinns, Black Juans, Koshakus, Devastators, Decoils, and Buddha Bandits—and that was just on the Eastside. Their archrivals on the Westside included the Seinans and Baby Seinans, Constituents, Algonquins, Co-Gents, Ministers, and Dominators, with the Free-Lancers of San Fernando Valley somewhere in the mix. In San Francisco's Chinatown there were the Raiders, the Continentals, and the 880s, consisting mostly of ABCs—American-born Chinese. After the 1965 immigration influx, there were the Wah Chings, the Suey Sings, Hop Sings, and Chung Yee's or Joe Boys, who were primarily FOBs—immigrants "fresh off the boat."

Considered "gangs," they were chump change in comparison to today's gangs. Although they were delinquents in the eyes of the law, they exemplified what historian William Van Deburg called social banditry: "the act of being bad for a good reason."[1] Collectively, on their turf, might—not white—was right.

## JA gangs of LA

In the 1950s and 1960s, Japanese Americans formed gangs in Los Angeles because they faced racism. When the World War II camps closed in 1947, over 120,000 Japanese Americans were released back into

Fig. 4.1: Russell Valparaiso nominated for Optimist
of the Year, *Gidra* 2:12 (December 1970)

an America that was as hostile as before. As one former gang member declared, "Japanese American youths formed gangs because they felt they had to prove they weren't the 'buck-toothed, slant-eyed' traitors that the US government had portrayed them to be."[2] Russell Valparaiso, George Nakano, and Jim Matsuoka agreed.

Eleven-year-old Russell Valparaiso moved to Northern California from a pineapple plantation in Wahiawa, Hawai'i, and did itinerant work with his parents and siblings before moving to Los Angeles when he was sixteen—old enough to join the Tiny Black Juans, the fourth generation of Black Juans:

> When you're a minority, some people go backwards, they close their eyes to everything. Not me. I wasn't the kind of guy that was a bully, but I wasn't going to be pushed around. Personally not going to take shit from nobody. So I didn't care about getting a licking or getting in a fight. We dreamed of being good gangsters.

Russell eventually became a member of Asian American Hardcore, a group that worked with ex-cons, and Katipunan ng mga Demokratikong Pilipinos (KDP or Union of Democratic Filipinos), an anti-Marcos organization.

George Nakano, a former member of the Constituents who went on to become a member of the California Assembly (1998–2004), said there was an explicit political awareness among street gangs:

> We would talk about how Japanese, Asians, were portrayed. We were rebelling against society and reacting in the only way we knew how. Looking back, we tended to be nationalistic. Given the nature of things at that time, it was the only thing you could fall back on in order to maintain your self-dignity and pride.[3]

Jim Matsuoka's tactical ability to choreograph rumbles during his days as a Black Juan earned him the nickname "the General." Ray Tasaki, a former Baby Black Juan, the third generation of Black Juans, recalled:

> Jim would be the one to get everybody together. "Okay, we're going to take these three cars—you come around this side …" He was the one who actually saw all of the parts and put it together, figured out what should take precedent and who should flank, and all that.

Jim himself admits that he became the arms master of J-Flats. "Maybe there's passive Asians, but we certainly weren't. I mean, hell, we'd give tit for tat. December 7, we'd wear the rising sun all day." Jim, who later co-founded the Pioneer Project (a support group for elderly Japanese Americans) and was an original member of the National Coalition for Redress and Reparations, said:

> [gang members] knew that somehow society was pulling shit on them but they didn't know how it was being done. There was no Malcolm X. There wasn't even a Martin Luther King at the time. Segregation in 1953 was an accepted way of life. We knew something was wrong in this society, but we didn't know how to articulate our position.[4]

## Yellow Brotherhood

Some *yogores* (thugs) who did articulate their position and matriculated into "good gangsters" were former members of the Ministers,[5] a dominant Crenshaw gang that later founded a self-help group called Yellow Brotherhood (YB). The original Ministers disbanded in 1962, after a shoot-out with the Buddha Bandits sent some to prison and others into the service. When Victor Shibata returned from the Air Force, he found that his community had changed substantially. A new adversary had moved into the neighborhood—a drug epidemic that killed dozens of Japanese American youth in a single year. He also found that the original street code of honor—the brotherhood of never abandoning your friends—was gone. Asian American youth were no longer merely fighting and committing minor crimes. Hard drugs were creating addicts, young people were overdosing, and students were dropping out of school in alarming numbers. Not only was nothing being done about these problems—they were largely ignored by an overwhelmed community that had just begun to regain its footing after the mass incarceration of World War II.

In November 1968, Victor and other members of the original Ministers met to talk about what could be done. After meeting with young people, alarmed parents, old gang friends, and concerned community members, they formed the Yellow Brotherhood in February 1969. YB developed a variety of programs—both conventional and unconventional—around education, extracurricular activities, sports, and work projects. Older members, although only in their early twenties, sponsored younger members and were responsible for making sure their people stayed off drugs and in school. YB became one of the earliest organizations to implement and promote what was commonly called "Serve the People" programs.

## Yow Yee, Joe Boys and Leways

In San Francisco's Chinatown, Yow Yee, meaning "have righteousness," organized to improve their condition as immigrant youth. The organization grew in number—but also in disillusionment, because of lack of any real improvement. By the late 1960s they were being enticed by the tongs (originally organizations formed to assist the immigrant

Fig. 4.2: Yellow Brotherhood member Ronnie Nakashima speaking at Optimist Club dinner. Thanks to community advocacy, Nakashima was released in 2013 after thirty-eight years in prison.

community that became associated with organized crime) to carry out illegal activities. Some Yow Yee members opposed the tong connection and wanted to stay true to their original ideals, claiming, "We were Yow Yee. We wanted to do what's right, to have the guts to do what's right."[6] This faction renamed their group "Chung Yee," but they were better known by the name the police and media gave them: "Joe Boys," after Joe Fong, one of their leaders. As Bill Lee, a former member of the Joe Boys who wrote a memoir of his gang life, recalled:

> Average folks didn't trust the officials or government. You had these bandits in China who were very well known and were looked upon as heroes—Robin Hood-types. Certain bandits would rob from the rich and give to the poor and the Joe Boys adopted that model.[7]

Around the same time, American-born Chinese teens (often referred to as ABCs) started a self-help group called Leways, which stood for "legitimate ways." Its president, Denny Lai, stated, "Most of us cats are misfits, outcasts with a rap sheet. What we're trying to do is to keep the hoods off the streets, give them something to do instead of raising hell."[8] Sociologist Stanford Lyman, who taught a class called "The Oriental American" at UC Berkeley as early as 1957, wrote that the police "refused to believe in the efficaciousness of methods that eschewed official surveillance, sporadic shakedowns and the not always occasional beating of a youth 'resisting arrest.'"[9]

According to criminologists Paul Takagi and Tony Platt, "Perhaps more than any other development at this time, the activities of Le Way [*sic*] brought the police into Chinatown, to sweep the streets clear of youth for tourists."[10] Publications as divergent as the revolutionary I Wor Kuen newspaper *Getting Together*,[11] a report by the California Organized Crime and Criminal Intelligence Branch,[12] and the *San Francisco Magazine*[13] all reported unwarranted police harassment of Leways—with the knowledge and blessing of the Six Companies, the power elite of Chinatown.

## The Red Guard

Alex Hing was, as he put it, "kind of a rebel from the get-go." Feeling that Chinatown was the home village that you could never leave, hemmed in by a Confucian society enforced by the Six Companies and a strict father, Alex had been in and out of correctional facilities for stealing cars and petty theft throughout his youth. When Alex was locked up, he read a lot of world history and was struck, he said, by two things: that American society was inherently racist and that the resolution of societal problems was not achieved through war. When he was released, Alex joined the Peace and Freedom Party to put Eldridge Cleaver on the ballot. He read *Red Star Over China* and *The Autobiography of Malcolm X*. He followed the recently formed Black Panther Party for Self-Defense. In 1968, he went on the Poor People's Campaign in Washington, DC, and when he returned, he said, "OK, now I can go back to Chinatown because now I'm going back with a purpose—to organize the lumpen crowd I grew up with to be revolutionary."

When he got to Chinatown, he discovered that the people he was going to politicize had already formed Leways. By that time Leways was under siege—by both the police and the Chinatown elites—and some members felt they had to make a fundamental change. "So when I got there they were armed. They were studying. They were talking politics and trying to transform themselves." Alex joined this group of eight to ten people within Leways who wanted to build a revolutionary organization like the Black Panthers. They broke away and formed the Red Guard. Their platform stated, "We the Red Guard want an end to the exploitation of the people in our community by the avaricious business-men and politicians who are one and the same."[14]

Stanford Lyman noted, "After all, Leways had tried to be good, to play the game according to the white man's rules, and all it had gotten for its pains was a heap of abuse and a few cracked skulls." Lyman asserted that the Panthers had provided language that depicted the situation that young people in Chinatown were up against. "Police were 'pigs,' white men were 'honkies' … and the goal to be attained was not integration or material success, but power."[15] To Lyman, the Red Guards represented the modern-day social bandit. Articulating what Ling Chi Wang would later call "dual domination," Lyman noted, "They stand against two power structures in their opposition to oppression and poverty, that of old Chinatown and that of the larger metropolis." Lyman made his point by describing the Red Guard in Hobsbawmian terms:

> They cry out for vengeance against the vague but powerful complex of Chinese and white elites that oppress them. They dream of a world in which they will have sufficient power to curb their exploiters' excesses; meanwhile, they operate as best they can to right local wrongs and to ingratiate themselves with the mass of their Chinatown compatriots.[16]

### The Talented Tenth

The baby boom, the Asian War Brides Act, and the loosening of exclu-sionary immigration laws in 1965 resulted in more Asian Americans attending college in the late 1960s and 1970s than ever before. As then UC Berkeley undergraduate Belvin Louie commented, "We were like the Talented Tenth, the first in many families to go to college," using Du Bois's term for the 10 percent of African Americans who would be "leaders of thought and missionaries of culture" for their race. The Asian American Talented Tenth were not simply all Asian Americans to go to college. Rather, Belvin and his politicized cohorts were among the few who, although initially striving for academic achievement and eventual economic gain, like everyone else, were moved to become "leaders of thought and missionaries of culture"—the front-runners of the early Asian American movement.

## The Asian American Political Alliance

As indicated in the previous chapter, the first group to unify under the banner of "Asian American" was the Asian American Political Alliance (AAPA) founded in 1968 at UC Berkeley. This is not to say there were no Asian American political activists before AAPA. As early as 1904, the San Francisco Japanese Socialist Party was formed,[17] and in 1914 the Chinese Socialist Club was established, also in San Francisco.[18] Japanese sugar plantation workers in Hawai'i were the first to strike for better pay and conditions in 1905, and Filipino farmworkers and cannery workers organized throughout the West Coast in the 1930s.

There were also individual Chinese, Japanese, and Filipino American activists who participated in the civil rights, Free Speech and anti-war movements. As AAPA founder Yuji Ichioka commented:

> There were so many Asians out there in the political demonstrations, but we had no effectiveness … We figured if we rallied behind our own banner, behind an Asian American banner, we would have an effect on the larger public. We could extend the influence beyond ourselves, to other Asian Americans.[19]

To identify potential AAPA recruits, Yuji said he and his wife Emma Gee, who were members of the recently formed Peace and Freedom Party, "went down the list and picked out identifiable Asian names."[20] Richard Aoki was already a member of the Black Panther Party when Emma approached him on campus to come to a first meeting. He recalled, "I was astounded at that AAPA meeting to see so many political Asians. Don't forget, up to this point there was no such thing as an [Asian American movement], and only a few known Asian American radicals"—referring to Yuri Kochiyama in New York, Shoshana Arai in Chicago, and Grace Lee Boggs in Detroit, who had all been active in the Black movement.[21]

V. Wong wrote that AAPA consciously and carefully chose the words "political" and "alliance" as a critical part of the group's name in order to distinguish itself from previous ethnic organizations that were more social in mission.[22] In addition to veteran activists who had been involved in previous political struggles, Floyd Huen commented that AAPA also appealed to "alienated students who had eschewed groups like the Chinese Student Club," adding that he was representative of mainstream Chinese American students who were then undergoing changes in their identity and consciousness.[23]

## The San Francisco State College Strike

If AAPA at UC Berkeley was the seminal organization that first articulated the new Asian American consciousness, the San Francisco State Third World Liberation Front (TWLF) strike for ethnic studies was the event that gave it legs. While ethnically specific organizations were commonplace, alliances between different races and ethnicities were rare. In 1968–69, when an army of blacks, Latinos of various ethnicities, Asians of various ethnicities, and Native Americans of many tribes crossed ethnic lines to form the boldly named "Third World Liberation Front," first at San Francisco State College and then at UC Berkeley, it no doubt felt like a bona fide revolutionary uprising.

The San Francisco State TWLF Strike of 1968–69 is widely known as being the longest campus strike in US history, lasting for almost five months. Protesting the dire lack of diversity in the academy, the heavily Asian American–infused TWLF—of over 200 students, faculty and supporters organized by the AAPA at SF State, Intercollegiate Chinese for Social Action, and Philippine American Collegiate Endeavor—was also the first major event that put the concept of Asian Americans and the ideology of the Third World on the line. The ethnic studies classes that resulted were built, as historian Gary Okihiro argued, "with the stones hurled through closed windows at San Francisco State in 1968. The hands that threw them were the same hands that lay railroad tracks, planted vineyards, and sewed garments."[24]

Ethnic studies professor Daryl Maeda indicated that the strike was a singularly significant moment in Asian American history, as it exemplified a clash between competing paradigms of identity: assimilation —embodied by S. I. Hayakawa—and leftist tactics—embodied by the new Asian American.[25]

Dressed in his signature tam-o'-shanter and acting with authoritarian bravado, Hayakawa became a colorful nationwide symbol of repression of people of color by a person of color, and hence the perfect foil for the emerging Asian American movement. When he was offered the presidency of San Francisco State, Governor Ronald Reagan quipped, "If he'll take the job, we'll forgive him for Pearl Harbor." Even as Hayakawa was racialized, he distanced himself from Japanese American associations, proclaiming that ethnic-based organizations retarded assimilation into mainstream society. During the strike, Hayakawa made no apology for his disdain for black militants and was especially hostile toward Asian American activists. That his contempt was discernibly personal was apparent in a 1970 newspaper article in which he sarcastically moaned:

> Pity, therefore, the little Oriental girl of the Asian American Political Alliance at UCLA or San Francisco State, looking in the mirror at her long and black but hopelessly straight hair, realizing sadly that it just can't be arranged Afro style. Right on![26]

## Behind the front

The Third World Liberation Front at UC Berkeley that lasted from January to March 1969, like San Francisco State, demanded more relevant education in the form of ethnic studies and support for Third World students. Belvin Louie recalled the many debates and discussions that preoccupied him before he decided to join the strike. Belvin was a US-born Chinese from the agricultural area of Salinas, California. His father had come to the United States at the age of fifteen, when the Japanese invaded Taishan, and was drafted into the US Army just three years later. Belvin's mother was one of the first to enter the United States under the 1946 Chinese War Brides Act, which circumvented the restrictive quota system based on nationality by allowing Chinese wives of US citizens to immigrate. Belvin started out as a pre-med major ("like a lot of

Chinese students at the time"), and several friends counseled him not to get involved in the strike because it would jeopardize his future. "I said, 'Well if it's a future that you want to make, you have to be part of it.'"

Belvin became part of the leadership of the TWLF:

> We met every night. And after the TWLF steering committee meeting each [ethnic/racial] group would meet. You're on the picket line all day long, and then it's like meeting, meeting, meeting. On the line and out in the open we always showed a united front. But internally, oh my God, it was intense discussion and disagreements. Every night we'd meet, debate and yell at each other. The tension and the stakes were very high, because you knew that every time you were out on the line it could break out into a riot and people could get hurt and busted.

The TWLF strike at Berkeley was shorter but more violent than the one at San Francisco State. Governor Ronald Reagan had declared "a state of extreme emergency," and the California Highway Patrol, Alameda County Sheriffs, plainclothes police and the National Guard were deployed to the campus. Mace and tear gas were liberally used. By the end of the strike, there were dozens of injuries and over 150 students arrested.

As a field marshal, Belvin had to be on the line day in and day out, as well as think on his feet:

> You know you're going to make decisions that are going to impact people and the principle thing for me was the safety of our people. We would be in the front line taking the frontal assault—face to face with the police, the National Guard, and the Blue Meanies.[27] Then the "support" would be in the back—some anarchists and what we called agent provocateurs essentially tossing stuff, provoking the situation— and then we'd get beat up for it! While all of this stuff is happening on the picket line, negotiations are going on, and this is dragging on and on, right? And it's like, "Goddamn, I gotta wake up tomorrow and get back on the picket line. Am I gonna survive this one?"

Posttraumatic stress disorder (PTSD) was first defined in 1980. Although primarily applied to soldiers who suffered in combat, it can be triggered by many types of traumatic events. Wilbur Sato, a Nisei who survived America's concentration camps during World War II, said that many camp survivors experienced symptoms of PTSD, thirty years before there was a name for it. Belvin also referred to posttraumatic stress. "A lot of us avoided Sproul Plaza for over a year because there were all these 'John Doe warrants' out. Even when the strike was over, we knew these warrants were floating around. They didn't know your name, but they knew who you were from all the pictures they took." Belvin ended up dropping out of school while remaining active in community issues like the campaign to maintain the International Hotel in what used to be Manilatown in San Francisco. He returned to the university many years later and completed his degree.

## Cultivating Asian American Studies

Until *Roots: An Asian American Reader*, the anthology published by the then-fledgling UCLA Asian American Studies Center in the fall of 1971, course readings consisted of a jumble of badly mimeographed reprints stapled together into makeshift readers and reproduced for makeshift classes across the country. Artist-activist Fay Chiang remembers coming to California from New York City during the summer of 1971 looking for curriculum material:

> I was looking for Visual Communications. I was looking for Yellow Brotherhood. I was looking for *Gidra*. I had started an Asian American studies course at Hunter College and our friends were pushing for a department at City College, but we had no curriculum. So I was just collecting all the mimeograph sheets and ditto sheets I could get my hands on.

With the publication of *Amerasia Journal* in March 1971, Asian American studies became a bona fide academic discipline. Don Nakanishi and Lowell Chun-Hoon were then undergraduates at Yale. Don recalled, "Somehow Lowell and I had the outrageously ambitious idea that we could make a contribution to the development of this new field called Asian American Studies, and decided to start a journal." Lowell and Don decided they would each raise $500 during the summer between their junior and senior years. When they returned, Lowell brought in his share but Don did not. "So," Don said, "Lowell had first pick of positions and wanted to be the editor. And even though I didn't raise any money, I became the publisher." Don had a vision of *Amerasia Journal* being long-lasting, but he also had the foresight to realize it would probably not be at Yale, because "it did not have an alumni base, it did not have a community base, and with one guy who couldn't get $500, it clearly was not going to go very far." After many discussions with Alan Nishio, acting director of the UCLA Asian American Studies Center, *Amerasia Journal* moved to UCLA and has grown from a student-initiated project to the discipline's premiere academic journal.

After UCLA's "Are You Yellow?" conference in 1968 and the success of UC Berkeley's Yellow Symposium in January 1969, students in different parts of the country organized their own regional conferences. The first nationwide conference on Asian American Studies was held at Berkeley in September 1969. Sponsored jointly by UC Berkeley, UC Davis, and UCLA, it attracted representatives from sixteen campuses, fourteen of which planned to offer Asian American studies courses the following academic year.[28] On the East Coast there were four major Asian American studies conferences—two at Yale and two at Pace College—between 1970 and 1972. At the University of Hawai'i in 1971, a four-day ethnic studies conference featured talks by Juan González on the Young Lords Party, Ysidro Macias on the Chicano Movement, and Carmen Chow on I Wor Kuen, as well as Kalani Ohelo on the Hawai'i Movement.[29] In 1973 there were conferences in San Diego and San Jose; California State University, Long Beach, held an entire Asian American Week. In April 1974, the First Midwestern Asian American Conference was in Chicago, with a second at the University of Wisconsin, Madison, later that year.

### Over Thirties

The Asian American movement is thought of primarily as a youth movement; matters such as identity, campus reform and the draft were key concerns. And anyway, "you can't trust anyone over thirty," warned a popular slogan of the youth-crazed Sixties. But the broader concerns of racism and imperialism that gave rise to the social movements of the era were not limited to the young, and first responders were not confined to those under thirty.

## The Asian Coalition for Equality

In Seattle, before there were Asian American student activists there were Asian American middle-aged activists and the Asian Coalition for Equality (ACE). According to veteran activist Bob Santos, "The Asian Coalition for Equality was one of the earliest Asian American advocacy groups in Seattle, if not the nation, and was particularly ground-breaking because it was the first political advocacy group which crossed Asian ethnic lines." Bob added that ACE was likewise significant in having "mature leaders."[30] ACE founder Phil Hayasaka noted that since its active core members consisted of clergymen and professionals, he knew they could not easily be written off.

Although ACE was officially born in June 1969, Phil—who was then the first director of Seattle's Human Rights Commission—thought of the idea two years earlier. Phil is a Nisei who was born and raised in Seattle and was incarcerated at Minidoka in Idaho during World War II, after which he returned to Seattle where he made a living as an insurance salesman. He initially joined the Jackson Street Community Council—a community service organization established after the war to forge links between Seattle's often divided communities of color[31]—as a potential business network. He became a board member, was elected as president of the board, and then was asked to be its executive director.

From this vantage point, Phil realized that civil rights was perceived to be a predominantly black-and-white issue in which Asians had no part. The prevailing attitude was that Asians had no problems, and therefore warranted no attention. In order to overcome that stereotype, Hayasaka felt it was necessary to bring the major Asian ethnic groups—Chinese, Japanese, and Filipinos—together in a united effort:

> There was a lot of mistrust between Japanese and Chinese and Filipinos at that time, mainly because we didn't know each other. We

had common problems, so I thought we should get together and do this as a team. No one group should have to do it alone.

As was common nationwide, Chinese, Japanese, and Filipino communities themselves maintained that they had no problems, much less saw a need to work together. Historically up against a hostile external society, each group was used to fending for itself, which reinforced traditional family values, resulting in the predominant attitude that each group needed to take care of its own. It took Phil two years of heart-to-heart discussions with individuals in each group to break through their shared reticence. When I asked him how he had been able to convince them, he simply said, "Persistence, I guess."

In an op-ed announcing the organization, Phil emphasized that, while the initial reason for coming together had been concern over racial injustices in Seattle, ACE was "not interested in just mere intellectual discussion" but would be "action-oriented" in its dedication to "win human rights for all persons."[32] In addition, according to Phil's wife Lois, who had been active from its inception, ACE members called themselves "Asian Americans" independently from the students of AAPA at UC Berkeley. Lois recalled, "There was a great deal of discussion about identification," which at that time was "Oriental." "So we discussed what to call ourselves at great length, and finally came together on 'Asian American.' We knew of no one else at that time who had that identification."

One of the most far-reaching activities in ACE's history was its participation in a protest against the discrimination of black and minority trainees on publicly financed construction projects. When the demonstration erupted into violence that resulted in property damage and several arrests, it was ACE members who most adamantly made the charge of police brutality. Startled that Asians would take such a strong stand on civil rights issues, the title of a feature article in the Sunday edition of the *Seattle Times* asked, "Should Orientals Join Blacks in Racial Protest?" The opener read, "Suddenly, the Seattle Oriental is becoming identified with civil rights and the protest movement," asking, "Yellow power: A new concept in the black and white of civil rights—or an exercise in futility?"[33] ACE members were quoted extensively throughout the article. "Orientals should be participants in, rather than specta-tors of, the struggle for equality," said ACE spokesperson, Reverend Mineo Katagiri. Reverend Lincoln Eng insisted, "Racism is not directed solely at the blacks, and to combat it we have to assert ourselves." Dr. Joseph Okimoto added, "The Japanese still experience discrimination in housing, pay and job promotions, but most of them have accommo-dated psychologically for racism."

In March 1970, ACE again rocked multiple boats by simultaneously protesting the Elk's Club for its whites-only membership policy and the Nisei Veterans organization for patronizing a facility that would not allow them to become members. As guests arrived in their finest attire, they were met by ACE members and supporters carrying signs declar-ing: "I wouldn't let my kid marry an Elk," "Elk-k-k," and "Elks, moose and skunks." Phil and Lois recalled that, although there were under-standably some bad feelings, one Nisei who had come for the dinner instead picked up a sign and joined the demonstration.

### Asian Americans for Action

Around the same time, a similar group of activists over thirty came together in New York City. In the 1960s, amid the throngs of African Americans who went to hear the likes of H. Rap Brown, James Farmer, Stokely Carmichael, and Eldridge Cleaver were two seemingly unlikely enthusiasts. Kazu Iijima and Minn Masuda had been members of the Young Communist League in the 1930s, and each had accumulated more than thirty years of political activism. Although they undoubtedly seemed anachronistic, in reality they were as radical, or more so, than the young African Americans with whom they stood. Kazu said that while she and Minn had already subscribed to revolutionary ideas, their Communist Party analyses were from a white perspective:

To listen and read about racism, the nature of oppression, mis-edu-cation, imperialism, beauty standards, etc. from a black perspective was heady and challenging to us, and we talked about it a lot. We were deeply impressed by the Black Power movement's "black is beautiful" slogan, and confronting racism not only politically but cul-turally. Minn and I kept saying, "We wish our children could be in a movement like that." That's when we decided, "Well, look, nobody's doing it. So you and I are going to do it."

They talked it over with their children, and Kazu's son Chris (who would soon team up with Nobuko Miyamoto and Charlie Chin) urged them to make it—whatever it would be—not just Japanese American but pan-Asian, because he felt the Japanese American community was too small and conservative to effect a "movement." At that time, Kazu said, because there were no links between the ethnic Asian communities, "We decided to contact every Asian we saw at the demos. And of course, many of them just couldn't make us out. These two little old ladies talking about a movement and starting an organization. So on April 6, the day of the meeting, we thought, 'I wonder if anyone's going to come?'" To their delight, about twelve to fifteen people attended.

Like ACE, these women wanted action. As Kazu wrote, "We called ourselves Asian Americans for Action [Triple A] because we knew we were going to be active. We met once a week from eight until past midnight, but we also had two or three meetings during the week to plan actions and to study." In July 1969, their first newsletter rolled off the mimeograph machine, announcing their statement of purpose:

> We recognize that this country is racist and that there are contradictions within the society which are responsible for the problems of Asian Americans. We feel that it is our responsibility to effect changes. We have united to establish a political voice for the Asian community and a means for group actions. We invite Asians to join us.[34]

Yuri Kochiyama, who was already active in the black movement, wrote in her memoir: "I was drawn into the Asian American Movement by Kazu Iijima who was the most informative and compelling Asian American woman on the East Coast."[35] Yuri also recalled that the younger members disliked the fact that older women were the force behind the group.[36] Kazu felt that it was also a matter of difference in tactics: "The young people were for confrontation, but whenever they got arrested we older ones were the ones who were putting out all the money for bail. So we said, 'I don't think we're financially ready for this kind of action, nor is the community ready to accept it.'"[37]

No doubt the generational disagreements were also a reflection of their different orientations to white society. The Nisei wanted to change the broader society from which they had been excluded. Sansei, on the other hand, were bristling against having been whitewashed into thinking they had been part of white American society. Kazu indicated that Niseis tended not to use rhetorical language because they wanted to reach the greatest number of people possible, but that for young people taking their first political stance "the tendency was to be very rhetorical, very militant." She said that it was "part of the catharsis." Her son Chris observed that, realistically, the reason there were both old and young activists in Triple A was because it was the only political Asian American organization around at that time: "And the reason I think it didn't work was because of political immaturity on the part of a lot of young people."

Despite these inner struggles, Triple A continued to grow. Its December 1969 newsletter reflected the major themes of the Asian American movement at large:

> Among the many actions taken were: organized demos against the War, two major demos (covered by the *New York Times* and *Washington Post*) against the US-Japan Security Treaty, established communication with the Asian movement in California and with the Black and Latino movements, demonstrated against Edgar Hoover's racist slurs against Chinese Americans, organized films and forums on Cuba, China, Taiwan, and Ceylon, co-sponsored a hugely successful conference on US Imperialism in the Pacific Rim, met with representative of the Peace Movement in Japan, demonstrated for community control of the schools and the young people in Chinatown were helping out in education, recreation, medical and draft counseling. All that in only eight months![38]

The newsletter concluded with the statement: "Just as important, we have worked, played and struggled together as political Asians, so long alienated from one another, and have grown together personally and politically, young and old, Chinese, Japanese, Ceylonese and East Indian, Nisei and Sansei, Juk kuk and Juk sing."[39]

In 1970 Triple A underwent structural changes. Kazu wrote:

> The young people, who were increasingly involved in Chinatown, felt the need for a Chinatown-based organization which would be more disciplined and ideologically oriented in Marx-Lenin-Maoism. So they all, except for a few, left to form the I Wor Kuen, which eventually became a pre-Party formation, the first of its kind on the East Coast. We older AAA members understood this need and had no quarrel with this new formation.

They considered dissolving. "But at what we thought might be our last meeting a young woman [Pat Sumi] who had just returned from a visit to North Korea, came and, inspired by her trip, urged us to continue. So after some discussion, we voted to do so but at our own pace."[40] With a core group of about fourteen, their "pace," however, hardly broke stride.

When the International Ladies' Garment Workers' Union mounted an anti-"Made in Japan" campaign, Triple A, recalling similar anti-Japanese propaganda during World War II that had landed Japanese Americans behind barbed wire, mounted a countercampaign to pressure the union to "redirect their energy and funds toward resolving basic problems right here at home." At the 1971 Hiroshima-Nagasaki Day demonstration, Triple A distributed 2,000 cellophane packets of ashes that linked the nuclear bombings to the Vietnam War. In 1972 Triple A sent representatives to the historic Emergency Summit Conference of Asian, Black, Brown, Puerto Rican and Red People against the Vietnam War. As Kazu wrote, "The fact that we were an older group was advantageous as we had no peer pressure to contend with and were free to be ourselves."

## A multitude of over-thirties

ACE and Triple A were not the only "mature" activists that helped make Asian America. The 1967–71 campaign to repeal Title II of the 1950 Internal Security Act, the so-called "concentration camp act," was spearheaded by Northern California Niseis Raymond Okamura, Mary Ann

Takagi, and Edison Uno, who were soon joined by many other "mature" activists, such as Hiroshi Kanno in Chicago, ACE member Don Kazama in Seattle, Min Yasui in Denver, and my uncle Pat Okura in Omaha. Through their leadership, backed by mass action by AAPA, ACE, Triple A, and many other Asian American organizations and individuals, the Emergency Detention Act was repealed in September 1971.

Larry Itliong was fifty-two years old and Philip Vera Cruz was sixty-one when, in 1965, they founded the Agricultural Workers Organizing Committee, later to become the United Farm Workers. Sue Kunitomi Embrey, who was a reporter and editor for the *Manzanar Free Press* while she was incarcerated there during World War II, became the backbone of the Manzanar Committee after she attended the first Manzanar Pilgrimage in 1969. Koji Ariyoshi, who had befriended Mao Zedong and Chou Enlai while he was in the Military Intelligence Service (MIS) during World War II, was a labor activist who championed the establishment of the University of Hawai'i's Ethnic Studies program, teaching one of its first classes. Labor organizer Goso Yoneda, who changed his name to Karl in honor of Karl Marx, was a proud, card-carrying Communist who had also served in the MIS and remained an activist all his life. Grace Lee Boggs cut her revolutionary teeth in the Black Liberation movement in the 1940s and 1950s.

From their various standpoints, these over-thirty rebels, along with social bandits from the streets and the Talented Tenth from campuses, challenged the social order by standing up to a system they saw as unjust, and together became the pioneers that blazed a trail for the emergence of Asian America.

## FIVE

# Gooks

> *The Oriental doesn't put the same high price on life as the Westerner. Life is plentiful, life is cheap in the Orient, and as the philosophy of the Orient expresses it, life is not important.*
>
> General William Westmoreland

I t is no accident that Asian America was born at the **peak of the Vietnam War.** In addition to fighting against an unjust war, one of the most subjective reasons Asian Americans came together at this time was because of our collective identification with the Vietnamese. *Gidra* staff writer Bruce Iwasaki articulated in 1973:

The US involvement in Vietnamese affairs began around the time we were born; stayed hidden from the national consciousness during our years of innocence; escalated as we matured; and has reached climactic proportions while our generation gains the will and seeks the means to end that involvement. Much as we forget, ignore, or grow numb to it, the war has been a constant shadow in our lives.[1]

As Kazu Iijima of Triple A said, "The Vietnam War **made Asian identity much more clear. It clarified** in many minds what racism was all about."

By 1968, US troops in Vietnam reached a staggering 550,000, with over 16,500 killed and 110,000 wounded in that year alone. The war was costing the United States some $25 billion a year; further casualties were reported every day as the nation watched the war on television like a serial drama; and increasing numbers of people around the world were questioning the mayhem. As many as 40,000 men were drafted each month, adding human fuel to the firestorm. By 1969, one out of every two Americans personally knew someone who had been killed or wounded in Vietnam, and over half thought the war was a mistake. By the end of the war, over 58,000 American soldiers and an estimated 1.5–3.6 million military and civilian North and South Vietnamese, Laotians and Cambodians—all someone's sons and daughters, mothers and fathers—were dead.

By 1968, the anti-war movement was also at its peak, and individual Asian Americans were part of this worldwide protest. Adna Louie combined creativity with sheer pluck in her anti-war activities. Four years before her younger brother Belvin became a field marshal for the UC Berkeley Third World Liberation Front strike, when Barry Goldwater attempted his unsuccessful bid for president in 1964, Adna went around crossing out Barry and writing in "Bury" on posters and bumper stickers throughout their hometown of Salinas, California. Working after school and on weekends in her parents' restaurant, she inserted anti-war literature in the take-out orders even as her mother was the head of their benevolent association's anti-communist league. During the Vietnam Summer of 1967, she and Belvin, with two friends, wrote, mimeographed and distributed their own anti-war paper, of which the only known surviving issue showed up in Belvin's FBI files. In October 1967 she was among the thousands who participated in the Stop the Draft Week at the Oakland induction center, and was one of many—including Joan Baez—to be arrested.

Harvey Dong also joined the Stop the Draft Week protest—just after resigning from the ROTC. "I was following the path of my dad and uncles. I thought if the military worked for them, it should work for me too." Harvey grew up in Sacramento, a product, he said, of the GI Bill and the War Brides Act. While they lived outside Chinatown, in a fairly integrated tract home development, the only social institutions his parents related to were the family associations and the Chinese Baptist Church. Raised by his grandmother and immigrant mother, he did not speak English until he entered elementary school. There, Harvey said, "I remember being confronted with racism wherever I went. So that put my guard up—fearful of violence, and then also ready to protect myself and friends and brothers."

As a freshman at UC Berkeley in 1966, Harvey's dorm was split over the war. "Myself and two others were in the ROTC program. Then there were conservative students who were for the war and those who were anti-war." Harvey said this mix of opinions "stirred up a lot of questioning, so I went and investigated [the war] on my own." In the meantime, ROTC officers told the cadets not to read or even talk about the war because of the certainty of communist infiltration. "After going through sessions like that, we decided to quit. It was a big decision." And it was also a huge leap for Harvey as he then became more and more involved in the anti-war movement.

> We would assemble at Sproul Plaza at, like, four in the morning, and from there go by caravan to the Oakland Induction Center on Clay Street where we would try to stop the inductees from being shipped out. It was supposed to be nonviolent, but the police were really hitting people. A lot of students were getting beaten. One time we really felt we had to run for our lives. We ran from the Oakland Induction Center all the way back to Berkeley. Yeah, it was pretty heavy.

In 1969 Asian Americans became a visible presence in the anti-war movement—both collectively and as leaders. In that one year, Asian Americans for Peace in Los Angeles was formed; Shinya Ono, a member of the Weather Underground, was arrested during the disastrous Days of Rage in Chicago; Warren Furutani spoke at the first national Moratorium Against the War at Long Beach State College; Professor Isao Fujimoto spoke at the Moratorium at UC Davis; the first Asian American contingent, 300 strong, marched in the second national Moratorium in San Francisco; and Pat Sumi helped organize a third anti-war Moratorium in Oceanside as part of the Movement for a Democratic Military.

As Asian Americans gained the will and sought ways to end the war, more Asian American contingents appeared in marches and rallies across the nation, and Asian-specific anti-war organizations, such as the

Bay Area Coalition Against the War and the Asian Coalition in New York, were formed. The broader goal was to stop the war, so why wasn't just participating in the broader US anti-war movement sufficient? Why were Asian American contingents necessary?

### Stop Genocide!

Although the imperialist nature of the war was addressed by the mainstream anti-war movement, its racist underpinnings were not. On April 24, 1971, the largest bicoastal demonstration against the war brought an estimated 200,000–500,000 protesters to Washington, DC, and 150,000 to San Francisco. In New York, a flier generated to organize an Asian American contingent to Washington, DC, rhetorically asked, "Why an Asian Contingent?" The answer: "Because … America is perpetrating a systematic cultural and physical genocide of Southeast Asian people."[2] Simultaneously, on the other side of the country, at the San Francisco rally, speaker Patsy Chan asserted, "The vicious imperialism which seeks to commit total genocide against the proud people of Indochina is the same imperialism which oppresses those of us here in the US by creating dehumanizing conditions in our Asian communities."[3]

The racist nature of the war was clearly pronounced when Kwame Turé (a.k.a. Stokely Carmichael) defined the draft as "white people sending black people to make war on yellow people to defend the land they stole from red people."[4] And although the phrase "No Vietnamese Ever Called Me Nigger!" was erroneously attributed to Muhammad Ali when he defied the draft in 1967,[5] it nonetheless got the point across. Asian Americans riffed on the theme, with placards that read: "No Vietnamese Ever Called Me Chink" and, after Vice President Spiro Agnew referred to a Nisei journalist as a "fat Jap"[6]: "No Vietnamese Ever Called Me a Fat Jap."

"No Vietnamese Ever Called Me Nigger!" was also the title of a documentary film on the disproportionate number of black soldiers sent to Vietnam.[7] Writing about the film, professor Sylvia Shin Huey Chong noted that the black anti-war movement used "the abuses of the Vietnam War to stage a larger critique of white racism and gesture

Fig. 5.1. Placard "Stop Genocide" behind Mike Murase in first
Asian American anti-war rally in Los Angeles, January 27, 1970

Photo by Robert A. Nakamura

toward a Third World internationalism that aligns American blacks with
the Vietnamese as brothers in a common struggle."[8]

Chris Iijima asserted, "Asian American organizing around opposition
to the Vietnam War crystallized around identification of the racial implications of the war—particularly when traditional anti-war organizations
were unwilling to address those issues."[9] Because of the increasing differences between the mainstream anti-war movement and activists of
color, an historic meeting of Third World people against the war con-
vened at a Holiday Inn in Gary, Indiana, on June 3–4, 1972. Called
"The Emergency Summit Conference of Asian, Black, Brown, Puerto
Rican and Red People against the Vietnam War," it comprised over
300 delegates, including representatives from more than fifty grassroots
organizations, meeting for the first time on a national scale. Its main
political principles were victory to the Vietnamese and other Indochinese
people and complete support for the seven-point peace proposal of the
Provisional Revolutionary Government of South Vietnam—two points
that Asian American contingents regularly stressed. At least twelve
Asian Americans attended from throughout the United States. They
formed an Asian Caucus that selected its representatives to the People's

Solidarity Committee: Yuri (then known as Mary) Kochiyama and Dr. Anthony Kahng of Triple A from New York, Russell Valparaiso (the social bandit discussed in Chapter 4) from Los Angeles, and Roy Nee from San Francisco.[10] A conference report summed up the major differences between Third World and mainstream perspectives in the fight against the Vietnam War:

> All of us who met at Gary have been daily faced with the problem of not only the aggression of the US against the Indo-Chinese people but also how to deal with the concrete problems that we face as oppressed nationalities in North America.[11]

### *"Makibaka!"*

Another reason Asian American contingents were formed was because the Vietnam War was seen as the latest episode in a prolonged history of racism against Asians. Placards at anti-war rallies that declared "Makibaka!" (Tagalog for struggle) "Remember Manzanar!" and "Remember Hiroshima-Nagasaki!" connected the Vietnam War with injustices of the past.

The Philippine-American War (1899–1902) was an exceptionally brutal conflict between the United States—which had acquired the Philippines as part of the spoils of the Spanish-American War—and the people of the Philippines, who saw the war as a continuation of their struggle for independence. After 300 years of Spanish rule, Filipinos were not about to submit to further colonization without a fight. The ensuing war was so vicious it prompted Mark Twain to unflinchingly, albeit patronizingly, refer to US troops as "our uniformed assassins," in the killing of "six hundred helpless and weaponless savages."[12]

In 1971, on the heels of the My Lai massacre and stories of other atrocities in Vietnam, Pat Sumi wrote an article titled "US War Crimes in the Philippines." In it was a quote from a 1901 editorial about the extermination of "men, women, and children, prisoners and captives, active insurgents and suspected people from lads of ten and up" that sounded eerily like a report from the Vietnam War. The article also referred to a *Los Angeles Times* article that appeared just a month before in which an ex-Marine recounted massacres and search-and-destroy missions that he had both witnessed and participated in. "They said My Lai was the first time American soldiers in a war had killed so many unarmed civilians, I knew that wasn't so. We did it in the Philippines over seventy years ago."[13]

World War II was another flash point in the history of racism against Asians that contained lessons for the present. "Remember Manzanar!" evoked the wholesale rounding up and imprisonment of Japanese settlers who were denied naturalization, along with their US-born offspring, without due process of law. While the United States was also at war with Italy and Germany, only immigrants from Japan were incarcerated for being "enemy aliens." When Isao Fujimoto spoke at the first National Moratorium on October 15, 1969, at UC Davis where he was a professor, recalling his own experience during World War II, he drew moral implications from personal acts of kindness.

> When I was being taken away to a concentration camp in this country during the last war, a few friends who dared come see us off brought with them coffee and doughnuts. These were acts of generosity and appreciated as such. But people of good will should be reminded that this is all you'll be able to do if you wait till a time of crisis to speak up and act.[14]

Asian American anti-war activists used commemorations of Hiroshima and Nagasaki to remind the US public that the atomic past was the genocidal present. In *Gidra*, Charles W. Cheng wrote, "Let us not forget that what occurred in Hiroshima is now occurring in Vietnam, Laos and Cambodia—a policy of race extermination." He alleged that the nation was insensitive to the atomic destruction because "We are *gooks* in the eyes of White Americans."[15]

Before physicist Michio Kaku became a best-selling author and renowned popularizer of science, in 1973 he was the keynote speaker at a Hiroshima Day Commemoration where he and other scientists took a public oath not to participate in war research. He pointed out that the equivalent of a Hiroshima bomb had been dropped on Vietnam and Cambodia every week for seven years. "The casualties of Hiroshima and Nagasaki number in the hundreds of thousands. The casualties of Vietnam and Cambodia number in the staggering millions."[16]

At a Hiroshima/Nagasaki Day event in August 1971, Triple A distributed 2,000 cellophane packets of ashes, along with a picture of Cambodian Buddhist priest Ta You, who had died on July 8, 1970 from napalm-related injuries. Designed by artists Arlan Huang, Karl Matsushita, and Jim Tsang, stapled to each packet was a card with the following poem by Vietnamese patriot Ngo Vinh Long:

> On this land
> Where each blade of grass is human hair
> Each foot of soil is human flesh
> Where it rains blood
> Hails bones
> Life must flower.

On the other side was printed: "Hiroshima–Nagasaki, August 6, 1945–August 9, 1945. Must it continue?"[17]

### "Kill that gook, you gook!"

If, as Charles Cheng wrote, "We are *gooks* in the eyes of White Americans," Asian American soldiers in Vietnam were that much more compromised. Racism against Asian American soldiers in the US military—as well as Vietnamese, and Americans of Asian descent back home, particularly women—was another reason Asian American contingents against the war were formed.

One of the first reports of the US military's racist behavior in Vietnam was the article, "The Nature of GI Racism,"[18] written by my brother-in-law Norman Nakamura in the June–July 1970 issue of *Gidra*. Recently returned from a tour in Vietnam, he wrote that generalized disrespect and mistreatment of Vietnamese was the norm because "the land is not populated by people but by 'Gooks.'" Soldiers were taught that no Vietnamese could be trusted and that even South Vietnamese soldiers

Fig. 5.2. Cover, *Gidra* 4: 5 (May 1972). Art by Alan Takemoto

were not dependable. Because racist behavior was not only sanctioned but taught by the US military, GIs generally felt morally exonerated of responsibility or guilt, were officially immune from reprimand or punishment, and felt culturally and physically superior to the Vietnamese.

First written for *Gidra* and later reprinted in the Asian American anthology *Roots*, Nakamura's article was the source and inspiration for an editorial written by Pulitzer Prize-winning journalist Frank Orr, who concluded:

Mr. Nakamura comes to the same conclusion many others have—that we should be out of Vietnam—but for a specific reason: "It seems ridiculous and hypocritical to be antagonizing the very people you are supposed to be aiding ... Rather than bringing civilization to Vietnam, the American GI has brought racism to the Vietnamese people."[19]

January—the coldest month in Detroit, with an average low of 17°F—was made even colder in 1971 by the chilling testimonies of Vietnam veterans who gathered there for the Winter Soldier Investigation, sponsored by the Vietnam Veterans Against the War. Scott Shimabukuro, identified as "L/Cpl. (E-3), 'C' Battery, 1st Bn, 13th Marine Reg., 3rd Marine Division," declared that, while the focus of the investigation was how US soldiers mistreated the Vietnamese, "it goes deeper than that. It goes into American society, which is all you people out there." Throughout his testimony, the ex-Marine emphasized that the racism that was rampant in the military started at home in the United States. As Nakamura had done, Shimabukuro also pointed out the deliberate dehumanization of the Vietnamese by the military. "Once [Americans] get into the military, they go through this brainwashing about the Asian people being subhuman—all Asian people." Shimabukuro said, "All during boot camp, I was used as an example of a gook. You go to class, and they say you'll be fighting the VC or the NVA, but then the person giving the class will see me and say, 'He looks just like that, right there.'"[20]

Mike Nakayama, "1st Battalion, 5th Marines, 1st Marine Division," was another of the 109 veterans and sixteen civilians who were fed up enough to speak of the unspeakable at the Winter Soldier Investigation. Nakayama was then, and continues to be, one of the most outspoken Asian American veterans against the Vietnam War. In addition to the Winter Soldier Investigation in Detroit, and countless talks at campuses and communities across the country, Nakayama also testified at the Winter Soldier Investigation sponsored by the California Veterans Movement in Los Angeles later that year—along with fellow ex-Marine Nick Nagatani, with whom he founded Asian Movement for Military Outreach and the Asian American Vietnam Veterans Organization.

At the Winter Soldier Investigation in Detroit, Nakayama testified that he had also been used as an example of what the enemy looked like.

Notwithstanding this humiliation of being made to stand up and turn around like a circus bear, so his fellow recruits could see "what a gook looks like," Nakayama fought fearlessly in combat, and went on to be awarded a Bronze Star. A Bronze Star, however, did not keep Nakayama from almost being left for dead, because he still looked like a gook.[21] It happened the second time he was wounded—just three weeks after the first:

> When I was shot, I had shrapnel in my skull, my eardrums were blown out, my lung was pierced. We were overrun, and the helicopters finally came and got us out. We got to Da Nang hospital, and I knew from my training that you deal with head wounds and bleeding first. Two guys in my squad who didn't have head injuries were being treated. I was just laying there, and finally I said, "Hey man, when are you going to deal with me?" and they said, "Oh you can speak English, we thought you were a gook.[22]

Both Shimabukuro and Nakayama linked the racism they experienced in the military to the racism their families and communities experienced at home. Ironically, Shimabukuro's father, who had been a member of the segregated 442nd Regimental Combat Team during World War II—the most decorated unit of its size in US history—insisted that there was no more racism in America because, he maintained, "We won the right to be Americans. I fought for you to be an American," Nakayama noted:

> Our experiences are similar to those of our parents fighting for equality abroad while their families back home were incarcerated in concentration camps; similar to the experiences of our Asian sisters who have been accosted and propositioned while walking down the streets of their communities.
>
> Those who disassociate themselves from the contradictions of society and become hippies, those who are confused with the contradictions and abuse drugs, those who ignore the contradictions and find escape in books; we all feel the presence of alienation and racism whether it be in the military or in our communities.[23]

## Bringing the War Home

In his article "GI Racism," Norman Nakamura noted, "Frustration and racism have made racist bullies out of many GIs in Vietnam … but will it end in Vietnam or will it color a negative stereotype toward all Asians?" He speculated that for some GIs, this was "the first contact with Asian peoples, so it is highly unlikely that this experience would not affect them."[24]

In 1970, the *Los Angeles Times* reported that two Japanese college students studying in the United States were attacked and beaten by two Vietnam veterans in Georgia, who shouted, "We just got back from fighting you communists in Vietnam!"[25] At the Winter Soldier Investigation in Detroit, Nakayama and Shimabukuro both told the story of two friends of theirs who had been mistaken for Vietnamese and beaten up so badly that they were in the hospital for months. These were not isolated cases.

Asian women—in Vietnam and in the United States—were a specific target of the war's physical and psychological violence. Books like Mark Baker's *Nam: The Vietnam War in the Words of the Men and Women Who Fought There* (2001) and Wallace Terry's *Bloods: An Oral History of the Vietnam War by Black Veterans* (2006) are filled with ghastly first-person accounts of viciousness against Vietnamese women. One soldier admitted, "In the Nam you realized that you had the power to take a life. You had the power to rape a woman and nobody could say nothing to you."[26] Another conceded: "It's like institutionalized insanity. When you're in combat, you can do basically what you want as long as you don't get caught."[27]

Mike Nakayama shared a perspective from an Asian American point of view in the film *Looking Like the Enemy* (1996) that I produced and Robert A. Nakamura directed:

> So I see these guys lined up like they're waiting to see a movie in front of one of these pre-fab, small, cinder block kind of structures. I looked in, and there's a family sitting there eating dinner, around a table, sitting on the floor. And the father is telling the daughters to hurry up and eat and go finish their work because there's like ten guys standing at the doorway in line. They were prostitutes. And that was very weird to see because it was like looking in on my family.[28]

Off camera, Mike also related how a drill instructor had taken Mike's wallet, found a photo of his sister, and announced, "Hey, I fucked her when I was in Japan." Mike added, "You know, normally you wouldn't take that kind of talk from anybody on the street, but you're in a situation where you could die, so you got to just keep pushing on and not let it show that it affects you at all. To him it was a big joke, to me it was my sister."

An example of the lethal effects of racism against Asian women in the United States is the monstrous murder of Le My Hanh, a seventeen-year-old honors student living in Queens whose tightly trussed body was found stuffed in a closet after being beaten, raped, sodomized, and strangled by Louis Kahan, a Vietnam veteran. According to his defense attorney, Kahan had done what he was trained to do and was ultimately found not guilty by reason of insanity. In a book about the case titled *Aftershocks: A Tale of Two Victims* (1986), David Haward Bain wrote:

> Rape was an ever-present coercive force … The procedure in the units to which Kahan was attached was to isolate the woman from the rest of her family and village. She would be tied up, threatened and raped regardless of what she told her captors … The men took turns as each occasion arose, thus reinforcing the credo that "they were all in it together"; "they had all participated." There were no exceptions, and there were no objections.[29]

## Identity and Imperialism

Chris Iijima pointed out that there is an indelible link between identity and imperialism. As Asians in America, we were fighting for self-determination at the same time as people who looked just like us in Vietnam were fighting for their lives. Like Marine Mike Nakayama, the New York Asian Coalition stated, "As Asians, many of us have seen in the faces of our Vietnamese sisters and brothers, the faces of our children, our families, our people."[30]

Civil rights leader Bob Moses noted that black opposition to the Vietnam War "does not come from what we know of Vietnam, but

Fig. 5.3: Cover, *Kalayaan International*, July 1971, reflecting Asian America's identification with victims of war in Southeast Asia.

Fig. 5.4: Mike Nakayama in Nixon mask leading Thai Binh and Van Troi Youth Brigades at Nisei Week parade, Los Angeles, August 1972.

from what we know of America." Asian American opposition to the war, however, came not only from what we knew of America, but also from empathy for and identification with the Vietnamese. Rather than just appealing for peace and an end to the war, Asian Americans adopted the Vietnamese goals of self-government and an end to imperialistic interference, specifically calling for support of the seven-point peace proposal of the Provisional Revolutionary Government of South Vietnam as the only genuine settlement of the war. First presented in Paris on July 1, 1971, its three basic points were setting a date for complete withdrawal of US troops and weapons, for the United States to stop meddling in South Vietnam's internal affairs, and for the United States to end support for dictatorships.

From March 31 to April 7, 1971, the Anti-Imperialist Women's Conference was held at the University of British Columbia in Vancouver, Canada. There, six women from North Vietnam, South Vietnam, and Laos met with 200 women from North America, sharing their personal experiences in an effort to end the war. Pat Sumi, one of the conference organizers, asked Mike Nakayama to act as security for the Vietnamese women. In a 1971 article for *Gidra* he wrote, "Knowing that, as veterans, we had invaded and destroyed their land, and murdered and raped their families and friends; yet these women met and talked with us as brothers and sisters—stone revolutionary examples." In a recent interview, when recalling how some of the speakers who had been held in the infamous tiger cages spoke of their prolonged and agonizing tortures, Mike had to stop, overcome by his memories.

Moral support for the plight of the Vietnamese was transformed into direct action with a nationwide Medical Supply Drive in 1972. Initiated by the Asian Movement for Military Outreach in Los Angeles, and joined by Asian American anti-war organizations across the country such as the Bay Area Asian Coalition Against the War and the Los Angeles and New York-based Asian Coalitions, the national drive raised over $5,000 for medical supplies. While the campaign fell short of tapping into the more affluent segment of Asian American communities that could have also been educated by the effort,[31] it furthered the Asian American anti-war effort, which, in itself, functioned as a dynamic vehicle in helping to build the consciousness of Asian America. The New York Asian

Coalition, for example, wrote that since it was "possible for a small nation to defeat the most powerful nation on earth," Asian Americans, a small group in the United States, might also be "capable of winning a victory for the control of our own lives."

In the summer of 1972, Nguyen Thai Binh, a South Vietnamese anti-war activist and former student at the University of Washington, was brutally killed during his last desperate appeal to stop the war. Deported, he knew he would be killed or jailed for his anti-war activities when he landed in Saigon. So Thai Binh wrote an open letter to explain his action—an attempted hijack of Pan Am Flight 841 with two lemons wrapped in foil. He wrote:

> My name is Thai Binh, which means Peace. My parents name it to me to express the deepest aspiration of the Vietnamese people … I know my voice for peace cannot be heard, cannot defeat the roared sound of B-52, of the US bombings unless I take this dramatic action … my only bomb is my human heart … if I fail, a million Vietnamese will replace me to fight until the war ends.[32]

In the Long Sixties, there was an epidemic of skyjackings that Brendan I. Koerner chronicled in his book, *The Skies Belong to Us: Love and Terror in the Golden Age of Hijacking* (2013). About Thai Binh's attempt, he writes that the flight's captain, Eugene Vaughn, "knew that one of his passengers, a retired San Francisco police officer, had come on board with a .357 Magnum. He told the ex-cop to be prepared, for he would soon have an opportunity to end Binh's life."[33] Under the pretext of making a refueling stop in Saigon, Vaughn pinned Thai Binh down as the cop shot him five times at close range. The captain then picked up Thai Binh's body and threw him out onto the tarmac. As he would later recall, "I got a good football hold on him and he went just like a football."[34]

Two years later I named my first child Thai Binh.

At the annual Nisei Week Parade in Los Angeles that year, 150 youth marched in youth brigades named after Thai Binh and Van Troi (another Vietnamese martyr). Their joint statement read, "We are a group of young Asian brothers and sisters who have united to show our opposition to the genocidal war being waged by the US government against the Southeast Asian people, and to show our love and support to the just struggle of our Vietnamese cousins."

As can be gathered by the Thai Binh Brigade and through my own example, Asian Americans were deeply inspired by this Vietnamese martyr, as were non-Asian Americans. Every year for nine years after his assassination, Thai Binh's friends and teachers at the University of Washington gathered to remember him. In 1992 a memorial ceremony was held in Seattle to mark the twenty-year anniversary of his death.[35] In 2010 in Vietnam, he was given the title of Hero of the People's Army Forces for his anti-war activities while a student in the United States. In 2013 his remains were reburied in the martyr's cemetery of his home-town of Long An Province, where a ceremony was held in his honor.[36]

As Asian Americans, we were moved and motivated by the relent-less determination of the Vietnamese people. But, as the ever-discerning Bruce Iwasaki cautioned in 1973, "Vietnam's victory should inspire us—but we shouldn't get a high off of it." Bruce, who is now a Los Angeles County Superior Court Judge, counseled:

> Vietnam's victory should inspire us—but we shouldn't get a high off of it. Doing so really diminishes their achievement. Why? … When we romanticize Vietnam we impose an unreality in order to bask in some borrowed glory … If there is anything we should learn from their self-reliant drive for self-determination is that our revolution must be fought and won, first, in our own behalf.[37]

## SIX

## To Serve the People

> *The notion of serving the people was like the power behind the opening shot in a pool game that catapulted the balls in different directions, energizing people to do things beyond the self-serving.*
>
> Robert A. Nakamura

The Panthers popularized the term "Serve the People," although it originated with Mao Zedong, who was in turn inspired by the revolutionary writer Lu Xun in 1942:

Fierce-browed, I coolly defy a thousand pointing fingers
Head-bowed, like a willing ox I serve the children.

Heavy, but too esoteric for Bob Nakamura. When Bob first heard the idea of serving the people, it was simply liberating, vindicatory and instantaneous. "We're not part of the larger white society; integration and assimilation are myths. So what can you do? Make money? At the end of the day you're still not part of anything. Serving the people made me feel useful, relevant when I used to feel irrelevant."

The idea of serving the people signaled a new definition of community, which at its core is simply the subjective feeling of belonging—a combined sense of solidarity and shared identity. Although the term "community" has been considered vague and variable as a social-scientific tool, for social movements of the 1960s and 1970s, the model of community—as epitomized by Martin Luther King's "beloved community"—served a greater purpose as an organizing tool. More than a geographical space, it was a multiple site in which theory met practice, acting as a touchstone by which a variety of progressive agendas were shaped and measured. In the area of ethnic studies, for example, Gary Okihiro argued that "all ethnic studies history may, from one point of view, be judged good or poor by the extent to which it contributes to our understanding of community."[1] In the arts, theorist of the Black Arts Movement Larry Neal declared that it was "radically opposed to any concept of the artist that alienates him from his community."[2] Asian American studies scholar Elaine H. Kim noted, "Without the reconciliation of the self to the community, we cannot invent ourselves. This 'community' begins with but extends beyond the boundaries of our families, far beyond Chinatown to wherever resistance to domination is taking place."[3]

Although the theoretical conception of community was a founding principle of Asian American studies, when tangible problems emanating from the Little Tokyos, Chinatowns and Manilatowns across the country were uncovered, community needs overtook campus concerns, and the locus of activism shifted from the seasonal status of students to the perennial actuality of real life. With newfound energy galvanized by the commitment to rectify communal concerns and wired by a "What have we got to lose?" spirit to try new ideas and solutions, a profusion of grassroots programs sprouted across the country. Among them, the Kearny Street block in San Francisco, the Japanese American Community Service's Asian Involvement office in Los Angeles, Basement Workshop in New York, and the International District in Seattle became major epicenters of Asian American community building.

### The Kearny Street Block, San Francisco

Kearny Street was described by poet and musician Norman Jayo as "an intersection in the heart … an intersection where humanity comes together and finds itself."[4] This juncture began when Asian American students marched from the campuses in San Francisco and Berkeley to what was left of Manilatown on Kearny Street, which is now part of Chinatown, to join the fight to save the International Hotel (I-Hotel) from corporate expansion. Pumped and primed from their high-octane battle with the university, student activists were quick to rally around the besieged manongs and elderly Chinese tenants of the hotel, who reminded them of their grandparents.

In 1969 the recently developed Asian American Studies Program at Berkeley had made inroads into San Francisco's Chinatown, whose overcrowding and poverty provided a breeding ground for the highest tuberculosis and suicide rates in the nation.[5] Among the demands of the Third World Strike were work–study positions in the community, which brought Harvey Dong, the ROTC cadet turned student activist, to Self-Help for the Elderly in San Francisco's Chinatown. "There I got introduced to real issues and problems that the elderly face—housing, mental illness, poverty, crime, drug abuse—the elderly had all of those." Because he was conversant in several dialects, Harvey was given assignments like, "Mr Tong is at the park waving a knife around. Can you go there and get him to take his medication? Or so and so's in jail, can you bring him home and make sure he gets settled?"

Harvey also worked with Chinatown youth. "These were like gang kids who got summer jobs. Afterwards they would hang out in the street and I would hang out with them and get to know about their lives." The contrast between the mean streets of Chinatown and the ivory tower of academia motivated Harvey and others to advocate for an Asian Studies Field Office at the I-Hotel to facilitate campus to community involvement. When residents of the single-occupancy rooms at the I-Hotel and other residential facilities with no place to gather began to hang out there, it morphed into the Asian Community Center (ACC).

One of ACC's popular activities was the film program that had begun at Self Help for the Elderly. According to Harvey, "At first we just showed movies we got from the library, and some of those movies were pretty boring—like how to mow your lawn—but people came because they had nothing else to do." When they found films about China, even if they were overtly anti-Communist, the old men, long separated from the country of their youth, would applaud. "The politics of the film were secondary to their feelings of nationalism for China. When we showed *The East Is Red*,[6] we had to show it fifteen times because there was a line of people outside waiting to get in." The Kearny Street block had begun.

Because the I-Hotel was under threat of eviction, it had many empty storefronts, which soon came to be occupied, at various times, by a multitude of service programs and revolutionary organizations. In addition to ACC were other community groups like Leways (the Chinatown youth group), Asian Draft Help and Legal Services (which became Asian Legal Services when the draft was eliminated in 1972), Everybody's Book Store (the first Asian American bookstore in the United States) and the Manilatown Information Center.

There were several political formations: the Red Guard Party that split off from Leways and was later absorbed by I Wor Kuen (IWK), a Marxist-Leninist formation that originated in New York; Kalayaan International, an anti-Marcos collective that became Katipunan ng mga Demokratikong Pilipinos (KDP); Wei Min She (WMS), an anti-imperialist organization that formed out of ACC; and the Chinese Progressive Association, the mass organization of IWK. As will be described in chapters 7 and 8, all had newspapers that spread their word and each played leading roles in the struggle to save the I-Hotel from eviction and demolition.

One of the most ambitious endeavors on the Kearny Street block was the Chinatown Cooperative Garment Factory, which started as a UC Berkeley Asian American Studies class project, and continued to the point where its workers ran and controlled its operation for four years. At the co-op the workers were paid an hourly wage, while at that time an estimated 3,500 women were employed in Chinatown sweatshops, earning $1 to $2 for a dress that retailed at $25. In addition, during their breaks at the co-op, they had English lessons, exercise classes, and classes on current events.[7]

The most durable organization that emerged from the I-Hotel complex was the Kearny Street Workshop (KSW), an artists' co-op that offered classes in a variety of arts and literature free of charge. After the residents and occupants of the I-Hotel were evicted in 1977, KSW moved to a new location and, when necessary, moved again and again, surviving

Fig. 6.1: Advertisement for Chinatown Cooperative
Garment Factory, *Rodan* 2:4 (November 1971)

as the oldest Asian American arts organization in the country. In addition to classes, KSW sponsored exhibitions such as one about Angel Island (the immigration station through which Chinese and Japanese were interrogated and detained) and initiated events such as the Asian American Jazz Festival, which KSW produced for seventeen years. Over the years, KSW has adapted to new challenges and appealed to new audiences while maintaining its original motivation to make artists out of community members and community members out of artists.

Steve Yip, a founding member of Wei Min She, described the Kearny Street block as "a meeting place and training ground for immigrant and native-born rebels of different ages, nationalities and socio-economic backgrounds, from Iranian students opposing the US puppet, the fascist Shah of Iran; to Asian sisters protesting the sexist Miss Chinatown pageants."[8] Estella Habal, a member of KDP and one of the key organizers of the I-Hotel anti-eviction struggle, wrote:

> The elderly bachelors had found enduring respect and recognition from the children they had been prevented from fathering. The students had found their history, their cultural roots, and their living forbears along with the possibilities of political activism rooted in concrete community concerns. At that moment, an assertion of community consciousness could be rooted in an actual place.[9]

## Japanese American Community Services, Los Angeles

The gravitational center of Serve the People programs in Southern California was the Asian Involvement program of the Japanese American Community Services, known as JACS-AI. When the grassroots endeavor opened in January 1970, Rocky Chin wrote in the New York–based *Bridge Magazine* that JACS-AI marked a significant change within the movement, in which "community needs replaced campus concerns and theoretical concepts were tested by concrete practice."[10] When JACS-AI grew—offering legal and draft services, youth and parent counseling, health and medical referrals, and job development—it moved to the Sun Building on Weller Street, where the Japanese American Citizens League (JACL) and Pioneer Center were already located. There it became a hub for other Serve the People programs and organizations, such as Joint Communications (communicating with Asian prisoners), Asian Sisters (providing drug education and counseling), the Japanese Welfare Rights Organization, Creative Workshop (working with young people), the Amerasia Bookstore, Involved Together Asians (a service group located on the Westside), and the Asian Women's Center.

The history of JACS-AI is tesimony to the fact that Serve the People programs were not the invention of Sixties activists but were a continuation of earlier efforts. In 1912, the Japanese immigrant community established the Rafu Jindokai (Japanese Humane Society of Los Angeles) to help young women fleeing from picture-bride marriages or prostitution. Two years later they opened the Shonien (Japanese Children's Home) to care for children of single mothers or financially struggling parents.[11] The Shonien operated for twenty-five years, until World War II sent its founder Rokuichi Kusumoto to a camp in Missoula, Montana, and the children to Manzanar, north of Los Angeles.[12] After the war, the board sold the Shonien building (which served as a postwar hostel for Japanese Americans who had lost their homes during World War II), the proceeds of which eventually seeded JACS in Southern California.

After three years of false starts JACS was finally incorporated but could not quite get a program up and running. In the meantime, local student activists attracted over 200 participants to a conference on Asian American identity, organized over 100 protesters to demonstrate against S. I. Hayakawa, and coordinated a successful countywide campaign to reverse the racially motivated firing of Los Angeles coroner Dr. Thomas Noguchi. The success of these efforts was not lost on the JACS board. In August 1969, two Sansei student activists—Alan Nishio and Miya (Linda at the time) Iwataki—were asked to join the board. Cautiously, the board then approved a one-year pilot program called Asian Involvement (AI), which opened in January 1970. JACS-AI continued for four years.

One of the significant characteristics of JACS-AI, as well as other Serve the People programs in Los Angeles, was its ability to bring together unlikely partnerships, including students, professionals, and street people, as well as the generations of Issei, Nisei and Sansei.

Young and old came together to form the Pioneer Center for elderly Issei. Los Angeles' Little Tokyo—like San Francisco's Chinatown/Manilatown and Seattle's International District—was populated by aging bachelors, victims of the history of restrictive immigration and anti-miscegenation laws, who lived in run-down residential hotels with no place to gather and little to do. Mr. Nishimura, one of these elderly bachelors, fashioned an unused room in the Sun Building into a makeshift drop-in center for seniors.[13] When it was discovered and closed down, he asked two former gang rivals—Jim Matsuoka and Mo Nishida—for help moving out. Instead, Jim and Mo recruited young people to clean, paint, and transform another room into what would become the Pioneer Center, where elders could gather, play cards, as well as attend outings organized by Sanseis who continued on as a support group.

Another unusual partnership was the coalition of street people, students, and professionals who came together around Asian American Hard Core, a self-help group spearheaded by Mo Nishida and Richard Toguchi, to help ex-offenders adjust to life outside of prison and prevent recidivism.[14] Students provided transportation and other support services. Established professionals were instrumental in positioning Hard Core as a viable alternative to incarceration. Coroner Thomas Noguchi provided Hard Core with its first residential facility. Jeffrey Matsui, of the Pacific Southwest JACL, social worker Jim Miyano of the Los Angeles County Probation Department, and John Saito of the Human

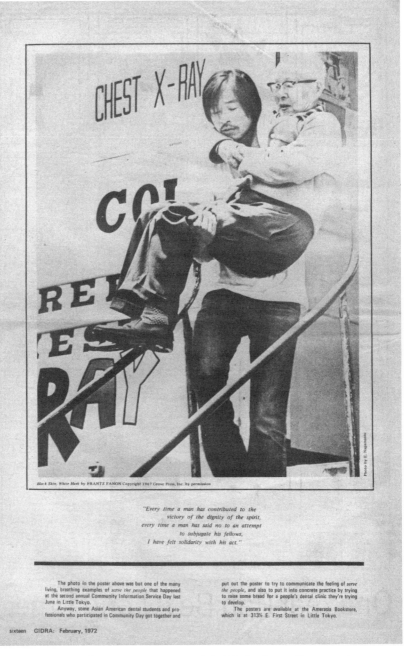

Fig. 6.2: Nick Nagatani assisting Mr. Nishioka at Community Information Service Day in Los Angeles, February 1972

Relations Commission worked in the background, helping to broker the system and legitimize this grassroots organization. Mo Nishida recalls that Shinya Ono was paroled to Hard Core after serving time for his part in the Weathermen Days of Rage in Chicago. A member of the Tiny Black Juans was paroled to Asian American Hard Core instead of being sent to Folsom.

Hard Core also had many female members. One, who had been on probation between the ages of eighteen and thirty-six for "getting into one beef after another," was summoned for an evaluation to determine whether she was a "menace to society." Since she had a habit of not showing up for her court appearances, Hard Core orchestrated an all-out community intervention. A carload of people fetched her from her home to make sure she got to the court for her hearing. By the time her case came before the judge, the courtroom was packed with supporters, from "suits" to "dopers" to "George who was in the back cleaning his silencer." She recalled:

> Mo and others rallied people and brought them by the van load. It really impressed the judge. My public defender, who never gave me the time of day before, saw all these potential clients and passed out his business cards saying to call him if they ever needed help.[15]

When former Baby Black Juan Ray Tasaki got out of prison in the summer of 1969, having been in and out of the joint for most of the 1960s, he met Mo Nishida and Warren Furutani, a popular speaker in the Asian American movement:

> Mo'd be rappin' to us. Warren'd be rappin' to us. Mo and Warren, any chance you give 'em, any subject, they'd just blah, blah, blah, but I would listen. It was becoming clear that I didn't have nothing at stake in this society. The only thing I could do was something for my people.

Ray became one of JACS-AI's two paid staff members. There he helped start Joint Communications, a program to connect prisoners with the outside through letter-writing and visits. Another unlikely pairing, when Ray the ex-con met Jerry Enomoto, the director of the California Department of Corrections. Ray recalled, "I put the question directly to him. 'Can you get us a list to reach Asians in prison?' And to my surprise, within a few days, I had this printout with 248 names."

Ray commented, "Campus people were coming to the community and street people were now able to find a direction to give back to the community and find direction to their life." He recalled that Evelyn Yoshimura, who attended Long Beach State College and Sandy Maeshiro from UC Santa Barbara, "took time with us *yogores* and explained things." Yet the relationship between street and students was not always serious, and it was not only work that brought them together. Ray recalled,

> We would drop acid together and, hey, one of the strangest things was at someone's apartment in the bathtub. You bend a clothes hanger and hang it over and go "bing" on the side of the tub with your head in it. The echo—and if you're under acid—you go, "Whoa!"

### Basement Workshop, New York Chinatown

When Fay Chiang first went to Basement Workshop in the spring of 1971, she was not impressed. It was literally a dark, dingy basement in one of New York Chinatown's many tenements, most of which had been built before 1901 when "Old-Law Tenements" were outlawed.[16] It had faulty plumbing that would create small tide pools on the concrete floor, which the volunteer staff, Fay said, would "ease towards the drain with a broom." Rocky Chin, who was showing Fay around, pointed to an orange crate with four or five books on it, and a four-drawer file cabinet, saying that was the Asian American Resource Center—"the only collection of its kind on the East Coast." "I looked around and said to Rocky, 'Wow, okay, maybe I'll see you in the fall.'"

That fall Fay did return, and this time found a small horde of about thirty Asian American artists and writers squashed in for a meeting for "Yellow Pearl," the innovative boxed production of lyrics, poems, and graphics produced under the auspices of Basement Workshop in 1972. They were sitting on boxes of *Bridge Magazine*, a glossy-covered monthly

that Basement had just begun to produce. A door they had found on
the street served as a table. They were sipping Cold Duck, which they
kept chilled in the toilet tank. Chris Iijima, Nobuko (then Joanne)
Miyamoto, and Charlie Chin, whose songs were to be reproduced,
were there, as well as cartoonist Larry Hama, graphic designer Alan
Okada, project coordinators Arlan Huang and Takashi Yanagida, and
many others. While Fay had crossed paths with many of them through
anti-war and Asian American studies activities, she had never seen so
many Asian American artists, writers, and musicians in one place before.
They were debating—very passionately and heatedly—"What is Asian
America? What does it mean? Who are we?" Fay said to herself, "Oh
my gosh, these are my people! I was nineteen and felt for the first time I
had come home." Like the I-Hotel in San Francisco and the JACS office
in LA, Basement Workshop was the safe house on the east coast, where
Asian American cultural fugitives found shelter and gained sustenance.

Basement Workshop, which would become the first multidisciplinary
Asian American cultural institution on the East Coast, was the brainchild of Danny Ning Tsun Yung, a newly graduated urban planner out of
Columbia University. Born in Shanghai and raised in Hong Kong, Yung
returned to Hong Kong in 1979 and is now a world-renowned artist.
When he first came to New York in the late 1960s, Chinatown was in
turmoil. The 1965 Immigration Act had rescinded restrictive national
quotas and, according to the New York City Planning Department,
by 1970 it was estimated that 6,000 to 10,000 new immigrants were
absorbed into the already densely populated Chinatown each year.

With the momentous increase in population and the realization that
government aid to neighborhoods was tied to official census figures,
college students like Legan Wong—who became one of Basement
Workshop's office coordinators from 1971 to 1973—joined the Chinatown Census Committee to educate its residents about the importance
of the upcoming 1970 census.

I participated in doing a survey of every single building in Chinatown
and the surrounding Lower East Side. This is when I realized that
behind these old tenement buildings was a hidden building. If you
kept going towards the back where there's no light and where all the

garbage cans are, across a little alleyway there was a whole other set of apartments.[18] There were literally hundreds of Chinese living there who were not being counted. In our broken Chinese, we would try to talk to them about the census, but there was a lot of fear. Many were undocumented, having come under false papers, which is the history of our first generation of Chinese Americans.

Compounding and complicating the population explosion in Chinatown was the targeting of Chinese Americans in the dragnet of FBI red-baiting. In 1969, J. Edgar Hoover had testified before the House Appropriations Committee that there were over 300,000 Chinese in the United States who might "assist Red China in supplying needed material or promoting Red Chinese propaganda."[19] By 1971–72, Hoover was posting leaflets—in Chinese and English—on the walls of every major Chinatown in the country urging its residents to report suspected communist activity. In this politically and socially charged context, Danny Yung established the Chinatown Study Group, which surveyed 565 residents in Chinatown[20] and wrote the first report on its rapidly changing demographics. Believing that "research without subsequent implementation is meaningless,"[21] he founded Basement Workshop to put the research to use.

Danny's sister Eleanor was part of the Chinatown Study Group. She recalled the day Danny called her to come to 54 Elizabeth Street in Chinatown.

Walking down a flight of metal stairs, I found myself looking into a basement room about 16′×16′, with a small window in one corner. Danny was beaming, standing in the middle of the empty room, and exclaimed happily, "Well, what do you think?" Then he went on to say that he had just rented this basement, and this will be the place from which we can operate our activities and programs for Chinatown. On that day, Basement Workshop came into existence. It took us another six months or so before we became legal. There were five of us on the legal paper,[22] and about a dozen of us who chipped in to pay the rent. In the spring of 1970, Basement Workshop Inc became official.[23]

As the Asian American movement took hold in New York, veteran activist Rocky Chin brought a progressive, pan-Asian direction to the otherwise Chinese-specific Basement Workshop. Rocky had been part of a stellar Asian American student grouping at Yale that included Don Nakanishi and Lowell Chun-Hoon who started *Amerasia Journal*, long-time teacher and activist Glenn Omatsu, and Bill Lann Lee who went on to serve as Assistant Attorney General for Civil Rights. In addition to being involved in the anti-war effort, supporting the Black Panthers at the 1970 New Haven trial, and helping organize one of the first East Coast student conferences, Rocky wrote his master's thesis on the post-1965 changes affecting New York's Chinatown. Published as "New York Chinatown Today: Community in Crisis" in the inaugural issue of *Amerasia Journal*, it relied heavily on data from Danny Yung's 1969 Chinatown Study Report, as well as a 1970 Chinatown Health Report, while interpreting their findings through the lens of the new Asian American consciousness.

When the idea of the cultural production "Yellow Pearl" surfaced—inspired by requests to reproduce the song lyrics created by Chris Iijima, Nobuko Miyamoto, and Charlie Chin—Rocky helped write a proposal to fund the project. In the proposal, "Yellow Pearl" was presented as an attempt "to build a new identity and culture which is Asian American."[24] As Rocky recalls, "We ran it up to the New York State Council for the Arts in time for the deadline and we got the grant, $3,000."

Following the successful publication of "Yellow Pearl," Basement started to receive outside funding. With financial support, Basement grew into a multidisciplinary community enterprise, the likes of which had never been seen. In four different locations, Basement managed to publish *Bridge Magazine* every month; ran the highly successful Amerasia Creative Arts program of classes in silk screening, photography, dance, music, and creative writing; developed the Asian American Resource Center from an orange crate and file cabinet to an extensive oral history program in Chinatown; and implemented a Community Planning Workshop program that offered weekly English and citizenship classes, as well as children's arts and crafts. In addition to administering and running the programs, Basement supervised Neighborhood Youth Corps and college Urban Corps interns each summer.

Fay Chiang became the director of Basement Workshop in 1975 and stayed until it closed in 1986. "When we started," she recalls, "we were the first Asian American cultural organization in Chinatown, in New York City, on the East Coast. By 1986 it closed, since a lot of the projects split off to become non-profits in their own right." Basement's Asian American Dance Theatre became the Asian American Arts Centre. Their writers' program morphed into the Asian American Writer's Workshop. The Asian American Resource Center was donated to the Chinatown History Project, which became the Museum of the Chinese in America. People from Basement started Asian Cinevision and the Asian American Arts Alliance. At the time of writing, all these organizations still exist.

### The International District, Seattle

The International District of Seattle—or ID, as it is affectionately known locally—is unique in Asian America for being the only place in the continental United States where Chinese, Japanese and Filipinos comprise one multiethnic community.[25] Originating as a Chinatown in the late 1890s with Nihonmachi as its neighbor, by the early 1900s the area had become a haven for Filipino immigrants and in the 1920s was also infused with African American and Native American inhabitants and businesses. The ID was the setting for such Asian American literary classics as Monica Sone's *Nisei Daughter* (1953) and John Okada's *No-No Boy* (1957); it is where Carlos Bulosan (*America Is in the Heart,* 1946) worked as a labor leader. One of the oldest neighborhoods in Seattle, a substantial portion of the ID is now on the National Register of Historic Places.

Its identity as the International District emerged after World War II, at a time when people of color—already thrust together in overlapping neighborhoods—often vied with each other for jobs and housing. In 1952 the mayor proclaimed it the "International Center" ostensibly to recognize the contributions of the area's Chinese, Japanese, Filipino, and African Americans, while promoting it as a tourist destination. Local businesspeople established the International Improvement Association and sponsored such events as an International Festival, an International Art Exhibit and an International Queen contest, with four queens representing the Chinese, Japanese, Filipino, and African American communities.

As previously described, the Asian Coalition for Equality, founded by Phil Hayasaka, was the first pan–Asian American activist organization in Seattle. It was the forerunner of the International District Improvement Association (Inter*Im), a multiethnic group formed to improve the declining conditions of the ID. According to Bob Santos, who served as executive director of Inter*Im during its years of fighting for the preservation of the ID (1972–86), "Phil actually was the one who got a lot of us involved."

Affectionately called "Uncle Bob," an honorary Filipino appellation of respect, Bob began a lifetime of activism after being cajoled into joining his first picket and realizing that discrimination did not have to be a fact of life. When Bob became the head of CARITAS, a social service action agency, he managed the St. Peter Claver Center, which he opened up to a variety of activist groups including the Black Panthers, United Farm Workers, United Indians of All Tribes, and El Centro de la Raza. From that time forward, whenever the Asian American or the International District needed widespread support, they would inevitably call on Uncle Bob, who would call out the troops. At Inter*Im, whenever a hostile issue would arise, Bob and his staff would retreat to what they ceremoniously called "the war room," which Bob confessed was a card table:

> But we wanted a military-sounding place where we would strategize about attacking the enemy. I considered each issue to be part of the strategy of what I used to call "payback." I never screamed racism. I never talked about being discriminated against. It was always about getting even.

The battle surrounding the building of the Kingdome, a multipurpose stadium that encroached on the already depressed ID in 1972, became a cause célèbre that, as journalist Mayumi Tsutakawa reported, spurred the Asian American community's coming of age.[26] When the

Photo by Eugene Tagawa

Fig. 6.3: Sherrie Chinn, Susan Alfonzo, Reme Bacho, Norris Bacho, Bob Santos and Al Sugiyama in march on HUD, Seattle, November 12, 1972

county held the dedication for the groundbreaking, then student activist Al Sugiyama recalled, "That's when Frankie [Irigon] posted a note on the Asian Student Coalition [at the University of Washington] door and said, 'Let's go protest against the Kingdome.' I called him and asked, 'How many people do you have?' He said, 'Two—me and you.'" Two became twenty-five, and with shouts of "Stop the Stadium" and dirt clods thrown in the general direction of the podium, Al said their goal was not to stop it, but "to disrupt the party, to show the press and elected officials that we wanted our voices heard."[27] And that's what they did.

As the Seattle Civil Rights and Labor History Project noted, the media coverage that was generated brought attention to concerns that had up to that time been ignored and challenged stereotypes about passive Asians.[28] Since nothing could be done about the building of the stadium, community activists parlayed the resulting energy and attention into securing public and fiscal support for building low-income housing for the elderly and providing bilingual social services—both long-identified needs. They succeeded on both counts.

After studying neighborhoods in cities along the Pacific Coast such as Chinatown/Manilatown in San Francisco and Little Tokyo in Los

Angeles, Bob testified before the Seattle City Council. "Urban centers all across the nation are losing downtown neighborhoods to progress at the expense of the pioneers who built these cities. And we in the International District refuse to follow this trend."[29] Within the decade, in addition to several low-cost housing units subsidized by the Department of Housing and Urban Development, a variety of service groups and agencies were established to address the health and welfare of the ID and ensure its preservation.[30] The ID is still going strong. As testament to its endurance, of the many Sixties activists I spoke to about the Asian American movement—specifically regarding how and why it ended—those in Seattle alone said it had never stopped.

### Power to the People

In the August 1970 issue of *Gidra*, Mo Nishida wrote an article stressing that the way to achieve "Power to the People" was to "Serve the People." Taken at face value, Mo maintained that Serve the People was little more than helping others, a missionary attitude that fostered dependency. He asserted that its real meaning was to create institutional change. It

Photo by Robert A. Nakamura

Fig. 6.4: Mo Nishida (left) at Little Tokyo
Information Day, June 1971

is this communalization—activity that promotes a sense of collective belonging—that is the basis of community as an organizing tool.

A second critical factor of Serve the People programs was the engagement and dedication of a mix of many people. There was so much to be done that a large number of people were needed who were able to do different things. Harvey Dong recalled that "people from all walks of life were drawn into activism." These programs laid the groundwork for the many present-day Asian American service-oriented institutions and associations.

Not that everything always ran smoothly. Not everyone saw eye-to-eye or amicably agreed to disagree. Although Serve the People programs addressed urgent needs in the five designated areas of food, medical care, education, shelter, and employment, the age-old problem of meeting people's immediate living requirements in the context of the larger need for deep societal change was a critical issue then, as it is now. Nevertheless, those who were able to learn to struggle with each other despite differences and disagreements, to find common ground upon which to work, to keep their eyes on the prize while putting one foot in front of the other, might be able to say, as did Bob Nakamura:

> All of a sudden, with that one idea of "let's get together and serve the people," the thought that you could actually effect change gave me a sense of value, of empowerment really. It was an epiphany.

## SEVEN

## Arts of Activism

*Ah, Pilipinos*
*if you only knew how brown you are*
*you would slide down*
*from the highest*
*mountain top*
*you would whip out your lava tongue*
*& burn up all that white shit*
*that's keeping your people down.*

Al Robles, "Rappin' with Ten
Thousand Carabaos in the Dark"

In his essay, "Poetry Within Earshot: Notes on an Asian American Generation 1968–1978," poet, editor, and artist Russell C. Leong wrote, "Because I wanted to relearn—and relive—the stirrings of an Asian American generation, I sought out its poetry. For poetry, like a hammer, can nail down the times."[1] And, of course, it was not just poetry that reflected "the stirrings of an Asian American generation."

We learned, as Rumi said, to "speak a new language so that the world will be a new world," and, as Audre Lorde said, to "give name to the nameless so that it can be thought," and our new lingua franca did not consist only of words but included pictures and music as well. With this new language of words, pictures, and music we unleashed a torrent of posters, poetry, photographs, newspapers, visual art, songs, theater, dance, and film that gave shape to the explosive energy and impassioned power of the moment. Together these cultural productions not only reflected a new consciousness, they created a new culture—of resistance and renaissance—that became the heart of Asian America. They were not just the *means* of representation, they were *makers* of meaning.

### Posters: Art for the People

The most iconic art form of the Sixties was the silk-screen poster. Poster art was a practice of politically engaged cultural production that not only promoted issues and events but also democratized the aesthetics and distribution of what was considered "art." Poster art curator Lincoln Cushing indicated, "Synonymous with rebellion and visual wit, these fragile documents were densely packed cultural viruses capable of transmitting such abstract concepts as 'solidarity,' 'sisterhood,' or 'peace' all over the world."[2] Activist-artist Josh MacPhee locates its origins with the Cuban internationalist group, the Organization in Solidarity with the Peoples of Africa Asia and Latin America, that included folded-up posters in their publication, *Tri-Continental*, which at its height was distributed to eighty countries in multiple languages.[3] Regarding the production of Asian American posters, Leland Wong of Kearny Street Workshop (KSW) in San Francisco said, "It was natural for us to get into the screen-printing business at that time because it was the most economic way to print anything. You know, it didn't take a lot of money to set up, and the product was very strong, the colors were very vibrant."[4] KSW was one of the most prolific sources of poster art during the Asian American movement. Conceived in 1972 by artists Jim Dong, Lora Foo, and Mike Chin at the International Hotel in San Francisco, KSW conducted numerous classes and workshops in arts, crafts, music, and dance. Even given its long and impressive resume, the quality and quantity of its poster art is unparalleled. As art historian Julianne P. Gavino wrote:

How the posters subsequently conveyed KSW's mission is as much a part of the story as the aesthetic of the posters themselves. By their very placement in the selected communities, the posters communicated a significant subtextual message: Asian American ethnic communities are to be valued and made visible in society.[5]

*Bridge Magazine* commemorated its tenth anniversary in 1982 with a retrospective of poster art. In greatly reduced size, some in black-and-white and others in their original color, *Bridge* showcased eighty-eight posters that had been created in various parts of Asian America between 1968 and 1982 (see Fig. 7.1).[6]

In the introduction to the commemorative issue, art director C. N. Lee remarked, "Through the posters we can see how we identify, celebrate, listen, 'get down,' give, struggle and remember. The posters act as a prelude to what is to happen and as a historical reminder of what did."[7] Indeed, these posters reflect the major themes and topics in the evolution of Asian America. The underlying motif of ethnic dignity and determination is apparent in all of the posters, made especially potent against the dearth of positive images that preceded them. Community was another broad-based theme that included local political issues (such as Asian Americans for Equal Employment's fight for Asian construction workers for Confucius Plaza in New York, and anti-eviction struggles in San Francisco and Los Angeles), "Serve the People" and cultural programs (such as Qris Yamashita's posters of a women's health fair and community events) and arts programming (such as Nancy Hom and Zand Gee's posters of dance, poetry, music and film, most of which were printed at KSW). The movement goal of historical recovery was embodied in Leland Wong's poster for a KSW exhibit on Angel Island, Paul Kagawa and Rich Tokeshi's Japan Arts and Media poster for an annual Day of Remembrance, and Miles Hamada's poster remembering the victims of the atomic bomb. The theme of Third World solidarity was represented by posters in support of Kampuchea by the Kampuchea Support Committee and support for the democratic struggle in the Philippines by Dahong Palay.

Women artists were particularly powerful and prolific. Art director Chuck Lee noted, "Styles become recognizable; the palm trees motif in some of Qris Yamashita's work, the delicate line work in the facial features of Tomie Arai's pieces, the solid block of colors preferred by Nancy Hom."[8]

Peter Eng, Chung Goa/Asian American Film Festival 1978

Zand Gee/Kearny St. Workshop. 1980

Gail Aratani/JAM Workshop. 1980

Qris Yamashita/Little Tokyo Art Workshop. 1980

Nancy Hom. 1980

Qris Yamashita/LTAW. 1979

Tomia Arai. Mid '70s

Zand Gee/Kearny St. Workshop. 1981

Fig. 7.1: From a retrospective of poster art in *Bridge* 8: 1 (Summer 1982)

Jack Loo/JAM Workshop. 1978

Tomia Arai. 1977

Nestor Gener 1979

Kagawa, Rich Tokeshi/JAM Workshop. 1979

Leland Wong/Kearny St. Workshop. 1976

Tomia Arai/Basement Workshop. 1973

TO FIGHT DISCRIMINATION IN CONSTRUCTION INDUSTRY!

Various Artists/AAFEE. 1974

Qris Yamashita attended California State, Long Beach, a relatively diverse college. She had been raised as a Buddhist and had grown up in the all-encompassing Japanese American cosmos of Gardena, and it was the first time she had been in a non-Asian-centric environment. When she took an art history class, she discovered that she was unfamiliar with the many biblical references others took for granted; she was astonished to learn how the standard of art was so predominantly Judeo-Christian. As a graphic artist, she noted, "You need some point of reference to pull from in order to convey information. I think that's why my imagery is so Asian American."

Tomie Arai went to the High School of Music and Art in New York and then to the Philadelphia College of Art, where she majored in painting. After returning from an anti-war march in Washington, she "woke up one morning and said, 'What am I doing here?'" To escape, Tomie went across country with her white hippie boyfriend, staying at communes, living off the land. "Everyone was on their way to Canada for a peace conference. It was a sea of white people. When anything Asian came up, they'd look at me and I didn't know what to say." Along the way she met filmmaker Christine Choy, who asked her, "What are you doing

Fig. 7.2: Poster for Yellow Pearl by Tomie Arai, Amerasia Creative Arts, Basement Workshop, New York, 1972

here? You should be in New York with the Asian community!" In 1971 she returned to New York and found out about a project in Chinatown called "Yellow Pearl" being produced out of Basement Workshop. "They said, 'Can you draw?' I said, 'Sure.'"

When Nancy Hom was a student at Pratt Institute, her goal was to become a gallery artist—until Chris Iijima and Nobuko (then Joanne) Miyamoto came to perform. "They sang of things that resonated with me, songs of garment workers and railroad builders, people like my parents."[9] She remembers that day distinctly, because when they performed, "there was some kind of 'bing!' that went off in me." When she shared her enthusiasm with one of her art teachers, "He looked at me and said, 'Get the hell out of my office.'"

## Music: Songs for Ourselves

Bernice Johnson Reagon described how, during a march, "the sound of protestors singing preceded them as they walked, so that by the time they reached their destination their voices had already occupied the space in a way the police could not reclaim."[10]

Chris Iijima, Nobuko Miyamoto, and Charlie Chin exemplified the role that music played in social movements and cultural transformation. In 1968, Chris was a student activist during the Columbia University strike:

> I spent a summer with the black students. When they took over the building I didn't go because I wasn't black. I didn't feel I should be there and they didn't feel I should be there either. So I got involved in SDS [Students for a Democratic Society], but SDS was mostly white and I didn't feel at home there either. I was ready for something different and something related to being Asian.

Nobuko was a professional who can still be seen singing and dancing on late-night television with Natalie Wood in the 1961 film *Westside Story*. Charlie—whose given name is William David but, being the only Asian kid on the block on the Upper Eastside, was instead

Fig. 7.3: Poster for Asian American Dance Collective by
Nancy Hom, Kearny Street Workshop, San Francisco, 1979

called "Chop Chop" and "Charlie"—had once been called "the only
Chinese in rock" by early *Rolling Stone* writer and senior editor Ben
Fong-Torres.[11]

Chris and Nobuko started singing together when they were among the
early Asian American activists who descended upon the 1970 national
convention of the Japanese American Citizens League in Chicago to
pressure the middle-of-the-road organization to take a stance on the
Vietnam War. There they wrote their first song, "The People's Beat."
As Nobuko recalls, "Somehow we had the guts the next day to sing it
in front of this conference, and the response was an electric moment.
It was making a statement about, 'This is who we are and this is our
song.'" Later that year Chris and Nobuko were accidentally paired
with Charlie at the Asian American Reality Conference in New York
when time ran short. Charlie recalls, "So they start singing and playing
and I'm playing behind them going, what are they singing about? 'The
masses, the people …' I've been hearing about this stuff but I've never
heard Asians carrying on like this."[12] From that time on, Charlie made
the duo a trio.

Of their music, Nobuko said, "We wanted to reach people in a way that speech couldn't. We wanted to touch their heart. We wanted to move their spirit." Through the years Chris, Nobuko, and Charlie have erroneously been called "A Grain of Sand," after their album, or "Yellow Pearl," the title of one of their songs—which was how John Lennon introduced them to a nationwide audience on the *Mike Douglas Show* in 1973. However, although they played together for three years, they never gave their group a name, symbolically reflecting their political standpoint that it was not so much about them, or even their music, as it was about the message.

Some forty years later, Charlie reflected, "In terms of Chris, Joanne and Charlie as a group, it functioned for a purpose for a time. The trio only really represented a reflection of the time and the place."[13]

### Newspapers: Yellow Journalism Unplugged

Historian Elizabeth Eisenstein argued that societies have been informed and transformed by the capacity to reproduce and thereby distribute ideas through the technology of print even more fundamentally than by the ability to read and write.[13]

Foreign-language and bilingual newspapers have played a vital role in shaping the history and experience of ethnic Americans in this country. Before World War I, there were approximately 1,300 foreign-language newspapers in the United States. Now there are 1,300 Spanish-language newspapers alone. American Studies professor A. Gabriel Meléndez asserted that the function of the ethnic press was an "organized movement against cultural erasure."[14]

The earliest African American newspapers, like *Freedom's Journal* in 1827 and Frederick Douglass's *North Star* in 1838, fought for abolitionism and rights for free blacks in the North. In the 1960s, the *Black Panther* newspaper and the agitprop art of Emory Douglas gave concrete expression to the political values of the Black Power movement. What American Studies professor Todd Vogel said of the black press was true of the Asian American movement press as well: it gave voice and agency to those denied both by the mainstream society.[15]

Likewise, the dissident press—often referred to as "underground" or "alternative"—has been an integral part of social movements. In 1965 there were only a handful of dissident newspapers, but four years later—driven by dissatisfaction with mainstream media, and made possible by the new technology of offset printing—the count was 150 and rising.[16]

Communicating the new consciousness of Asian America were newspapers and magazines like *Gidra*, *Chinese Awareness*, *Rodan*, *Kalayaan International*, *Getting Together*, *New Dawn*, *Asian Family Affair*, *Yellow Seeds*, *International Examiner*, *Bridge Magazine*, *Hawai'i Pono Journal*, *Hawaiian Ethos*, *Hawai'i Free People's Press*, and *San Francisco Journal*.

Each publication had its own mission, constituency, style, and geographical reach. They sometimes disagreed, but more often overlapped and shared articles and information. While all reflected the issues and activism of the Asian American movement from the late 1960s to the late 1970s, most targeted specific audiences, and many did not last too much beyond vol. 1, no 1.[17] Some were organs of anti-imperialist organizations. *Kalayaan International* was the newspaper of the Kalayaan Collective in San Francisco and continued when the collective became KDP. *Getting Together* was the newspaper of IWK, which began in New York's Chinatown and became national when it merged with the Red Guard Party in San Francisco. *Wei Min Bao* was the newspaper of Wei Min She, and *New Dawn* was the "newsmonthly," as they called it, of the J-Town Collective; both were based in the San Francisco Bay Area. *Come-Unity* was the short-lived newspaper of the Storefront, a multiethnic political organization in Los Angeles.

Many newspapers were directed to the specific geographical areas in which they were based—especially those in Hawai'i, as the issues confronting the islands were often considerably different from those in the continental United States. The *International Examiner* addressed the activities and needs of the International District of Seattle. *Rodan* was geared to the Northern California Asian American community. Some publications focused on the needs of particular ethnic communities in specific areas, such as the bilingual *Yellow Seeds*, geared toward Philadelphia's Chinatown, and *Chinese Awareness*, which focused on Los Angeles' Chinatown.

As previously mentioned, *Gidra: The Monthly of the Asian American*

*Experience* was the first newspaper to give material expression to Asian America. Spitting forth biting and provocative political commentary and social criticism in the form of essays, poetry, graphic art, and photographs, *Gidra* was as irreverent as it was earnest and as thought-provoking as it was reflexive. The brainchild of Mike Murase and a handful of other UCLA undergrads, it soon moved off campus and quickly went nationwide, as copies were passed from person to person and subscriptions came in from all parts of the country.

*Bridge Magazine* was the first Asian American periodical in magazine format. It began in 1971 as a publication of Basement Workshop. Unlike most other movement publications, *Bridge* was created through the skills of professional journalists like Frank Ching, a former editor with the *New York Times* and later chief of the *Wall Street Journal's* Beijing bureau; Margaret Loke, who was an editor for the *New York Times Magazine*; and Peter Chow, who, with Danny Yung and others, later founded Asian CineVision. Like *Gidra* and other publications of the times, the issues of *Bridge* are now mini time capsules—preserving historic caches of artifacts and information that chronicle Asian America in the making.

### Literature: Nailing Down the Times

In his introduction to the literature section of the anthology *Counterpoint: Perspectives on Asian America* (1976), Bruce Iwasaki wrote:

> Third World writing provides a critique of America from people who are uniquely prepared to provide one, discouraged from doing so, and able to illuminate how these two conditions are related. Thus I impose upon the writer an active duty to know his or her time.[18]

*Liwanag: Literary and Graphic Expressions by Filipinos in America* was a collection of short stories, poems, essays, photographs, and artwork produced in San Francisco in 1975. A collaborative production of words and images, the anthology's structure and presentation prioritized the work and minimized the maker, thereby embodying the philosophy of allowing the work to speak for itself. Its contents—poetry, prose, photo-graphs, and graphics—were presented without introduction or analysis. Even the artist's or author's last name only appeared in the upper corners of the pages next to the page number. *Liwanag* was dedicated to poet Serafin Malay Syquia, who had died a few years earlier, at the age of thirty. As Bruce Iwasaki exhorted writers to know their time, Syquia knew his, stating in his essay:

> The nature of the times requires, no, demands realism, both in politics and poetry. A people starving cannot be fed on pictures of gourmet dishes. A people with nowhere to live cannot live inside 21-inch tele-vision sets. To feed people obscure thoughts perpetuates the obscurity of such thoughts.[19]

*Aiiieeeee! An Anthology of Asian American Writers* (1975) was edited by Frank Chin, Jeffery Paul Chan, Lawson Fusao Inada, and Shawn Wong—the literary bad boys of the Asian American movement. Esteemed writers all, they interpreted what they knew of their own time into plays (like *The Chickencoop Chinaman*), short stories (like *The Chinese in Haifa, Each Year Grain*), poems (like *Before the War, Legends from Camp*), and novels (like *Homebase*). They were also rogue archeologists digging for and resuscitating literary works from a buried past, and as such were part of a group called the Combined Asian Resources Project, which, as Elaine Kim wrote, "spearheaded an effort to find, revive, and reprint little-known works of Asian American literature that express unstereo-typed aspects of the Asian American experience."[20] *Aiiieeeee!* was one of the results of their archeological digs—an anthology of the work of fourteen Chinese, Japanese, and Filipino American writers, some nearly forgotten, some previously published in mainstream presses but long out of print.

Poet Russell Leong believed that, for our generation, "poetry was the most broadly based of crafts."[21] Certainly, in movement publications like *Gidra*, even people you would never suspect of reading, much less writing poetry—highbrows and lowbrows alike—became bards, if only for a moment, probably because, as Audre Lorde said, "Poetry is the way we help give name to the nameless so it can be thought."[22]

Alongside Bruce Iwasaki's dictum that a writer's duty is to know his or her time, Russell Leong added it was poetry that could nail it down. Quoting N. V. M. González, who described the Filipino writer as one who mines the "inherited deposits of experience," Russell listed key shared experiences of Chinese, Japanese, and Filipinos that served as motifs in their writing: coming to the United States, family and culture, women's roles, the Vietnam War, civil rights, Black Power, and ethnic studies.[23] Uninhibited by grammatical conventions of sentence structure or syntax, poems can strike at the heart of the matter, wriggling into spaces too tight for prose.

Lawson Inada is a Sansei who was born and grew up in Fresno, California. His grandparents were sharecroppers, his father was a dentist, and Lawson became the first Asian American to publish a collection of poems with a major New York publishing house—*Before the War* (William Morrow, 1971). In another genealogy, during World War II, Lawson was first sent to a so-called "assembly center" set up at the Fresno County Fairgrounds, then to the concentration camp in Jerome, Arkansas, and finally to the officially designated Granada War Relocation Center in Colorado, which everyone called Amache. A longtime resident of Oregon, Lawson was the state's fifth poet laureate (from 2006 to 2010) and arguably Asian America's first poet laureate—not only because he was the first Asian American to have a book of poetry published by the mainstream press, but more importantly because he provided snapshots of our Asian American life. On growing up alien:

> So we went to school with
> Spanish-Merkans and Colored Folks
> and maybe an occasional Injun
> when the moon was full,
> and we was a-tryin our darndest ta talk proper-like
> & keep our shirt-tails tucked in
> but I mean, you know, man, it just didn't take.[24]

On "Looking Back at Camp":

> I work on campus.
> I try to concentrate.
>
> Still, things sneak
> up to remind me:
>
> "This is not Amache!"[25]

On "Being Asian American":

> Of course, not everyone
> can be an Asian American.
> *Distinctions are earned,*
> *and deserve dedication.*[26]

And on the Asian American movement:

> The Revolution
> not yet over
> Asian America
> just begun.[27]

### *Political Cartoons: Subversive Weapons*

One of the deadliest weapons in the arsenal of the arts of activism is the political cartoon. With the capacity to spar swiftly and deftly with serious issues, it can strike at the heart of social issues with exaggerated caricature, stinging reversals, and droll but profound impropriety. In the political cartoon, irony is a source of knowledge and a means of understanding.

Larry Hama, now best known as the original writer of the Marvel Comics *GI Joe* series, hooked up with Basement Workshop in New York where he produced illustrations for "Yellow Pearl" and *Bridge Magazine*.

Born in Manhattan and raised in Queens, he sold his first work in comics when he was sixteen years old. When he went to DC Comics in the mid 1970s as an editor, Asian characters were still colored bright yellow. Larry went to the head of the production department to ask why. When he was told that was the way it had always been done, Larry said, "Well, maybe we should stop." That's all it took, he said. From then on, Asian coloring was less strident.

Speaking of "yellow," in another take-off of the popular 1967 Swedish film *I Am Curious (Yellow)*, which served as fodder for other articles and conferences during the early movement, Larry poked fun at racism, identity, and male-female relationships (see Fig. 7.4a & b). Before being "politically correct" circumscribed social commentary, Larry knew his times and nailed it as only an artist can.

Alan Takemoto's brilliant *Gidra* cover, "Kill that Gook, You Gook!" in Chapter 5 (See Fig 5.2) was worth a thousand words of anti-war treatises and dealt a double blow to the war's inherent racism as well as the dilemma of looking like the enemy, all in a single, nonrhetorical line drawing. Alan's prolific graphic genius, like that of graphic artists David Monkawa, Glen Iwasaki, and Dean Toji, articulated *Gidra*'s signature style. As high school students, they had all been handpicked to be part of the Tutor/Art program for disadvantaged youth founded by graphic artist Bill Tara, and taught by such ground-breaking African American artists as Bill Pajaud and Charles White.

Before the term "graphic novel" was popularized in the late 1970s, Alan illustrated a sixteen-page booklet written by Bruce Iwasaki, Greg Fukuda, and Nick Nagatani, in speech bubbles and text boxes that broke down the complexities of US imperialism, Japanese militarism and the PRG seven-point peace plan into simple terms. Produced for distribution at the anti-war "take-over" of Nisei Week in August 1972, it was reproduced in its entirety on four full-size pages in *Gidra* the following month.

Placed within the front-matter of *Gidra*—between the staff listing and the Volume/Number designation, occupying a mere four inches by two inches—Alan's simple yet evocative drawing (see Fig. 7.5) might easily have been missed. Typical of *Gidra*'s—and specifically Alan's—shrewd and witty commentary, it illustrated the dilemmas and decisions

# I AM YELLOW...CURIOUS??

Fig. 7.4a&b: "I Am Yellow…Curious??" by
Larry Hama, *Bridge* 2: 4 (April 1973)

WE BEGIN TO FORGET, AND START APPLYING WHITE VALUES TO OURSELVES...

...THE TROUBLE WITH ASIAN MEN IS THAT THEY'RE ALL HUNG LIKE HAMSTERS!

...YEAH AND THEY ALL TREAT YA LIKE SHIT!

...AND THEY'RE SO *CHEAP!*

ASIAN WOMEN ARE REALLY OUT OF IT, MAN THEY AIN'T GOT NO TITS TO SPEAK OF!

... EVEN IF THEY GOT SOME, *YOU* SURE AS HELL AIN'T GETTIN' NONE!

...AND THEY'RE ALL GOLD-DIGGERS ALL THEY WANT IS YOUR BUCKS!

AND WHAT ABOUT THESE GUYS? THEY KNOW DAMN WELL THE GOLDEN MOUNTAIN HASN'T COME FOR THEM, NO MATTER WHAT COSMOPOLITAN SAYS!

SPECIAL TODAY! BANANAS EN FLAMBE

RACING FORM

AND WHAT ABOUT YOU? DO YOU THINK FUCKING IS DIRTY AND EVIL EVEN WHILE YOU ENJOY IT!? ARE YOU STRUGGLING WITH A WHOLE SHITLOAD OF SEXUAL GUILT? ARE YOU SUPPRESSED REPRESSED AND UNDER-LOVED? FILL OUT THIS HANDY QUESTIONNAIRE AND MAIL IT RIGHT AWAY! IT WON'T HELP YOU ANY BUT IT DOES A DANDY JOB OF FILLING UP HALF A PAGE!

- - - - - - - - - - - - - - - - - - - - - - - CUT HERE - - - - - - - - - - - - - - - - - - - - - - - - -

# THE I AM YELLOW...CURIOUS QUESTIONNAIRE?

FILL OUT AND MAIL TO: BRIDGE MAGAZINE c/o BASEMENT WORKSHOP 22 CATHERINE ST. CHINATOWN N.Y.

**CHECK ONE**

1. I AM: ☐ASIAN ☐BLACK ☐LATINO ☐OTHER
2. I AM: ☐MALE ☐FEMALE ☐BOTH ☐NEITHER
3. I LUST AFTER: ☐WHITE MEN ☐WHITE WOMEN ☐BLACKS OF BOTH SEXES
4. I FIND ASIAN SEXUAL PARTNERS TO BE: ☐INFERIOR ☐MEDIOCRE ☐GREAT ☐NON-EXISTANT
5. I HAVE HAD EROTIC DREAMS ABOUT: ☐CHINA LEE ☐KEY LUKE ☐RAQUEL WELCH ☐MARLON BRANDO ☐MINNIE MOUSE
6. WHILE MAKING LOVE, I THINK ABOUT: ☐INFINITY ☐TOMORROW ☐GETTING OFF ☐SOMEBODY ELSE
7. I WOULD LIKE TO GO TO BED WITH: ☐MISS CHINATOWN '73 ☐TOSHIRO MIFUNE ☐CATHERINE DENEUVE ☐MICK JAGGER ☐ALL FOUR
8. I THINK PEOPLE SHOULD BE MARRIED BEFORE THEY GO 'ALL THE WAY.' ☐YES ☐NO
9. I GO TO COCKTAIL PARTIES AND CAN'T UNDERSTAND WHAT PEOPLE ARE TALKING ABOUT. ☐YES ☐NO
10. I AM OFFENDED AND EMBARRASSED BY THIS QUESTIONAIRE. ☐YES ☐NO

**ESSAY QUESTION** **EXTRA POINTS!!**
ON ANOTHER SHEET OF PAPER IN 100 WORDS OR LESS, EXPOUND ON ONE OF THESE TOPICS
1. THE AUTHOR IS FULL OF SHIT, I KNOW THE TRUTH!
2. THE MATING HABITS OF THE GIANT PANDA
3. GOOD THINGS COME IN LITTLE PACKAGES
4. EATING OUT IN CHINATOWN

ALL REPLIES WILL BE KEPT STRICTLY CONFIDENTIAL UNLESS OTHERWISE STIPULATED
THIS HAS BEEN A PUBLIC SERVICE CARTOON BROUGHT TO YOU BY THE UNITED ASIAN COMIC BOOK WORKERS OF THE WORLD,

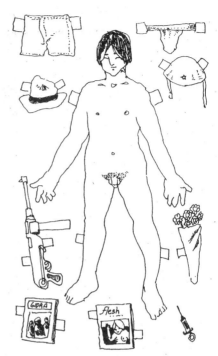

Fig. 7.5: "Make This Picture Decent!" by Alan Takemoto, *Gidra* 5: 11 (November 1973)

MAKE THIS PICTURE DECENT !
*sponsored by Gidra Freaks for Creative Decency.*

Fig. 7.6: Cartoon by David Monkawa, *Gidra* 5: 5 (May 1973)

facing the newly born Asian American. Problematizing the theme of identity, it reminded viewers that agency and choice were involved. By depicting the figure as a paper doll and providing a variety of possible accoutrements, the cartoon placed the decision-making responsibility squarely on viewers, reminding them that they had options and alternatives. Of his work at *Gidra*, Alan commented, "I wasn't interested in the commie stuff, I was there to fight racism."

In May 1973, Bruce Iwasaki brought attention to the continued war in Southeast Asia in his article, "A Separate Peace: War." Although the Peace Agreement signed in January 1973 indicated that all military activities in Cambodia and Laos would end, Bruce pointed out that a full-scale war in Cambodia was continuing, adding "The American news blackout in Cambodia has been total." Accompanying Iwasaki's article was David Monkawa's illustration of the news blackout (see Fig. 7.6). David's penetrating depiction of Nixon conjures up cartoonist Doug Marlette's assessment that "Nixon was to cartooning what Marilyn Monroe was to sex. Nixon looks like his policies. His nose told you he was going to invade Cambodia."[28]

David joined the staff of *Gidra*, where, he said, "every illustration, every cartoon, picture or article I did … was like a way to get back at the system." His searing *Gidra* cover, "Little Tokyo 1984?" (see Fig. 8.2) was as astute an analysis of capitalism-gone-wild as the best political discourse. He combined the dystopias of three distinct eras: Orwell's 1949 novel *Nineteen Eighty-Four*, the dark fantasy of the 1982 film *Blade Runner* that would appear almost ten years later, and (most ominously) the real-life nightmare of September 11, 2001, twenty-eight years later. When I asked him how he had come to draw with such prognostic detail, he answered, "I have no idea. I was loaded."

Glen Iwasaki was another of *Gidra's* graphic guerrillas and another product of Bill Tara's Tutor/Art program. In a destabilizing inversion of the ubiquitous American image of disposable chopsticks complete with instructions (see Fig 7.10) Glen confronted the question: What is foreign and to whom? Preferring the velocity of drawings to the bulk of rhetoric, in the last issue of *Gidra*, in an article titled "What *Gidra* Means to Me," Glen wrote, "I like pictures w/ words. *Gidra* has words. I have pictures."[29]

Fig. 7.7: Illustration by Glen Iwasaki, *Gidra* 5: 12 (December 1973)

When the humor embedded in political cartoons is self-deprecating, it is all the more powerful. Mike Murase, who spearheaded *Gidra*, created the "Stereotypes" cartoons that appeared consecutively in *Gidra*'s first four issues.

Disarmingly naive and guileless, the simple figures look forward directly and unabashedly at the viewer. Contextual embellishments are sparse and quickly read. By utilizing pre-existing symbolism, Mike relied on public familiarity with Orientalized depictions in order to drive home the point that the societal values that made them so omnipresent were bigoted and xenophobic. Instead of raging against ethnic stereotypes, each cartoon exaggerated them, reversed their meaning, and messed with the viewers' sense of propriety. By reaching in and pulling out embedded kernels of truths, Mike undermined the stereotypes, simply but definitively throwing them back as subversive representations of the racializations they resisted.

Fig. 7.8a–d: "Sterotypes" by Mike Murase, *Gidra* 1: 1–4 (April–July 1969)

### Pictures: See What I'm Saying

Photography did for pictures what the printing press had done for the word: democratized art for mass consumption. Walter Benjamin argued that the ability to mass-produce art realized its revolutionary potential.

### Photography

Bob Nakamura was a professional photographer when he stumbled across the second issue of *Gidra* in May 1969. Feeling that fears and desires he had buried for decades were now outpictured in this alternative rag, Bob immediately found his way to the *Gidra* office to volunteer his services. There he met Alan Ohashi, Eddie Wong, and Duane Kubo, who would all soon join him as the filmmaking core of Visual Communications. But at the time, being a good ten years older than these *Gidra*-istas, his reception hardly matched his enthusiasm. Duane recalls, "In walks this guy with a sport coat. He had a real job. We wondered, 'Is he part of the Asian undercover?'" And Eddie said, "We were just a bunch of goofy kids, expect for Bob. He was obviously the most professional person among us. And he was an adult!"

Undeterred, Bob taught a photography class for the first Asian American Experimental College in the summer of 1969, and rented a space down the block from the *Gidra* office that he turned into his darkroom and studio. Alan remembers, "When Bob invited me to his dark room on Jefferson, I was just blown away. This was what I wanted to do!"

In December 1969, Bob was one of the pilgrims who went on what would become the first Manzanar Pilgrimage—an event that now continues annually and inspired pilgrimages to other campsites. It was the first public commemoration of the forsaken World War II concentration camps in the country and the first time Bob had been back since he had been incarcerated there as a boy. His iconic photograph of the Manzanar monument first appeared in *Gidra* as a centerfold rimmed with faces of fellow pilgrims, each one a story (see Fig. 7.9). The photograph was later reproduced as a poster that wallpapered the dorm rooms, hallways, and offices of Asian America.

The photograph in Fig. 7.10 of Nobuko (Joanne) Miyamoto and Chris Iijima was taken by Bob Hsiang at a Martin Luther King Day commemoration in New York in 1971. It is one of the many he took, capturing the Asian American movement in New York. Bob had been radicalized by the civil rights and anti-war movements when he had been an undergraduate at the State University of New York. His portal to Asian America, as for many on the East Coast, was the storefront called "Chickens Come Home to Roost," named after one of Malcolm X's speeches and which served as a lighthouse for many fledgling Asian Americans in New York looking for solid ground. When they were kicked out of that space, Bob, with Nancy Hom (who would become his wife), Nobuko Miyamoto, Gordon Lee, John Kao, and Corky Lee formed the Asian Media Collective, a loose-knit group with a variety of media skills and interests. Bob recalls that the collective "came out of the thought that we could create and control our own media, that we didn't need other people to tell us how to think and how to present images and stories."

Corky Lee was born Lee Quoork—the fictitious last name made up by Corky's father to confound the restrictive US immigration quotas of the time. Corky was a conscientious objector during the Vietnam War and worked in Chinatown as a community organizer before becoming a photographer. At this time, having shot an estimated 800,000 pictures in the past forty plus years, Corky has earned his self-conferred title as the "Undisputed Unofficial Asian American Photographer Laureate." If he is within running distance of an Asian American event, Corky is there to document it. True to his title, Corky has declared many times, "Every time I take my camera out of my bag, it's like drawing a sword to combat indifference, injustice, and discrimination."

That is what he did on May 18, 1975, when he took a photograph of police brutality at a demonstration against police brutality (see Fig 7.11). On this day, Corky estimated that some 20,000 people marched from Chinatown to City Hall to protest the police beating of Peter Yew, who had complained of police mishandling in Chinatown. The storefronts of Chinatown even closed their doors in support of the protest. In a detailed chronicle of that day, Henri Chang wrote:

10:15am. From Chambers Street it was impossible to see either the beginning or the end of the line of marchers. In all directions all

Fig. 7.9: First Manzanar Pilgrimage, California, December 1969
by Robert A. Natamura, *Gidra* 2: 1 (January 1970)

MANZANAR RELOCATION CENTER
December 27, 1969
[photographs by Bob Nakamura]

Fig. 7.10: Nobuko (Joanne) Miyamoto and Chris Iijima
performing on Martin Luther King Jr. Day, New York, 1971

Fig. 7.11: Rally against police brutality, New York Chinatown, May 18, 1975

that one could see was Chinese, and suddenly it happened, the one thing that the marshals were instructed to contain. The outbreak of violence.[30]

Before the convenience of auto focus, figuring he was about five feet away from the action, Corky set his lens at 28mm. "I was like a wide receiver. I ran on the sidelines, coming back in to photograph. I knew I had something. I ran from City Hall though Chinatown to the [*New York*] *Post*. The photograph came out in the afternoon edition."

## Film

In February 1970, Bob Nakamura was asked to create a photo display for the campaign to repeal Title II of the Internal Security Act. Rather than just photos to hang, Bob designed a free-standing exhibit consisting of thirty-two 12″×12″ cubes covered with historical photographs of the camps from the National Archives, as well as photos he had taken on the first Manzanar Pilgrimage. This was one of the first times that the general public, as well as the Asian American community, had seen documentary photos of the camps, and the exhibit was displayed widely.[31] When he made more copies to meet the requests for exhibition, Bob called it a production of "Visual Communications" (VC)—a name that had been conceived by Kaz Higa, an artist and then chair of the Ethnic American Cultures Department at Los Angeles City College. When the Pacific Southwest Council of the Japanese American Citizens League asked them to become a committee, Kaz riffed off the CBS logo of an eye and, putting a rakish slant on it, designed VC's logo, which remains in use over forty years later.

In addition to Bob and Kaz, VC was first staffed by Ron Hirano, who with Kenyon Chan coordinated Asian American Studies Central; Norman Nakamura, Bob's brother, who had written "GI Racism" for *Gidra*; and Alan Ohashi, who had visited Bob's studio a year earlier. After Bob went back to school as a graduate student in the EthnoCommunications program of the film school at UCLA, *Gidra*-istas Eddie Wong and Duane Kubo soon joined the program as undergraduates. Eddie joined VC first, and recalled, "We talked about who we could bring into the group and decided to recruit Duane. And

Fig. 7.12: L-R: Alan Ohashi, Eddie Wong, Robert A. Nakamura
and Alan Kondo on Visual Communications shoot, c.1971

he agreed, knowing that it was going to take a long time, take a certain
amount of sacrifice, but in the end we would learn a lot and have fun
doing it." Duane said, "I think we understood that we were creating
for the first time a new American media and that made it very excit-
ing." Rounding out the core filmmaking team of VC, Alan Ohashi
specified, "eventually the refugee from Canada, Alan Kondo, came on
board."[32]

Bob's film *Manzanar* (1970), about his boyhood memories of camp;
Eddie's *Wong Sinsaang* (1971), a poetic profile of his father; Alan Kondo's
*I Told You So* (1974), on the poet Lawson Inada; Alan Ohashi's *Kites and
Other Tales* (1975), a children's film on the origin of kites featuring Alan
Takemoto's illustrations; and Duane's *Cruisin' J-Town* (1975), on the
groundbreaking jazz fusion band "Hiroshima"—these became the inau-
gural films of VC and some of the earliest films in the country to depict
Asian America. According to Bob,

> Growing up when the only media depictions of Asians were Charlie
> Chan and the Dirty Jap, I didn't want to change other people's image

of Asian Americans as much as I wanted to change our own views of ourselves. We all came together at the right time. A group like ours only happens once in a lifetime.

By day, Chonk Moonhunter is Curtis Choy. "Chonk" is a term he and poet George Leong created in 1970 to self-define that which is Chinese American. "Moonhunter," as his website indicates, is "a component of Iron Moonhunter, the legendary Chinaman-built railroad created from stolen Central Pacific Railroad parts that would take them home to China."[33] In addition to Curtis's landmark films, such as *The Fall of the I Hotel* (1983), which features actuality footage that he shot on the night of the eviction, Curtis organized the first Asian American Film Festival in 1977. Held over two days in San Francisco, its program warned: "Welcome to the most diverse showing of heart, mind and guts to burst out of Asian America's closet: staggering, puking, sprouting hair in strange places. We ain't messin' around no more" (see Fig. 7.13).

## Art as Social Theory

The arts of activism functioned as alternative epistemologies encoding and communicating what has become our intellectual and cultural heritage. Ron Eyerman and Andrew Jamison argued that music in the Sixties functioned as another kind of social theory.[34] They noted that, because processes of personal and political change were linked to a common project of liberation, some musicians became "movement intellectuals."

This was certainly true of singer-songwriter and law professor Chris Iijima, who theorized Asian Pacific American identity as political resistance to oppression; and of activist and musician Fred Ho, who wrote extensively on the Asian Pacific American left as well as on interactions between black and Asian American politics and culture. Creative writers like Frank Chin and Jeffrey Paul Chan, who developed the concept of racist love, and Russell Leong, who wrote about lived theory, also doubled as "movement intellectuals."

In the liner notes to *A Grain of Sand*, Chris Iijima and Nobuko Miyamoto wrote a lengthy statement on how they theorized their music

Fig. 7.13: Poster by Leland Wong for the first Asian American Film
Festival, produced by Chonk Moonhunter, 1977, San Francisco

in terms of content, form, and context. Regarding content, they argued
that revolutionary songs were not just slogans set to music, but rather
that music had the power to move people to act. Quoting the Cuban
Institute of Cinematographic Arts and Industries, they wrote, "We
now understand that it is possible to be genuinely entertaining while
making our ideological points clearly and poetically." About form, they
wrote: "Some people feel that as long as the content is 'correct' there is
no necessity to struggle further. We reject that mode of thinking as we
feel it our responsibility to communicate our politics not just to recite
them and the form that we choose will either aid or detract from that
communication." On context: "we see our work in the context of time:
that certain conditions dictate certain responses whether it be unions in
1900 or Asian identity in 1970." They concluded: "We owe our music
to the movement and the struggles of oppressed people. Without them
our music is irrelevant. Without them—without you—we have nothing
to sing about."

In *Aiiieeeee!*, editors Frank Chin, Jeffrey Paul Chan, Lawson Fusao Inada, and Shawn Wong wrote an introduction that stands as a conceptual polemic on the role of literature for people of color in the United States: "The subject matter of minority literature is social history, not necessarily by design but by definition." They admonished, "The white writer can get away with writing for himself, knowing full well he lives in a world run by people like himself. At some point the minority writer is asked for who he is writing, and in answering that question must decide who he is."[35] They also professed, "Our anthology is exclusively Asian American," describing Asian Americans as US-born Filipino, Chinese, and Japanese Americans "who got their China and Japan from the radio, off the silver screen, from television, out of comic books, from the pushers of white American culture that pictured the yellow man as something that when wounded, sad, or angry, or swearing, or wondering whined, shouted or screamed 'aiieeeee!'"[36]

In the elongated era of the long Sixties, Asian Americans generated a new language, new ideas, new theories, and new knowledges that had not previously existed. The arts of activism intersected the lives of those touched by them, creating meaning, defining purpose, and acting as a catalyst for change. The preponderance of creative expressions alongside critical analyses of US imperialism and manifestos of anti-racist programs attests to the cultural as well as political revolution that gave birth to Asian America. As Salman Rushdie reasoned, "Art is not entertainment. At its best it is revolution."[37]

## EIGHT

Other Wars

> *If you're not afraid, join us. If you are*
> *afraid, this isn't the place for you.*
> Slogan of the Jung Sai Garment
> Workers Strike, San Francisco, 1974

David Monkawa, the artist who drew the premonitory drawing of two airplanes crashing into two skyscrapers for the cover of *Gidra* (see Fig. 8.2), no longer wanted to "just do *Gidra*":

> Okay, here I'm doing art and culture and that's fine. There's a role, a place for art and culture. Then I figured, "I want to be a soldier on the front line." I felt like a war correspondent, you know what I mean? Like I was behind the camera. And that's okay, but I wanted to be on the front line because I wanted to get them more. I don't know how to explain it. I just wanted to get them more.

Like Bob Santos and his staff retreating to what he called the "war room" to strategize the next battle confronting the International District in Seattle, the combat analogy that originated on the front lines of the 1968 Third World Liberation Front strikes at San Francisco State and UC Berkeley prevailed throughout the 1970s as Asian American activists engaged in a multitude of struggles around the world and around the block. Among the many political campaigns that Asian Americans felt strongly about, two that hit closest to home were the fights to preserve our historical and spiritual geographical centers against the expansionism of urban renewal and rural removal and labor struggles for equitable wages, working conditions, and in some instances the right to work at all.

### Urban Renewal, Rural Removal

Throughout the nation, Chinatowns, Little Tokyos (also called *Nihonmachis*), and Manilatowns—in addition to rural farmlands in Hawai'i—were being eaten up by civic and corporate expansion. Each of these geographical communities exuded what architectural historian Delores Hayden called a "power of place" which, when demolished, also wiped out imprints of the rich cultural legacy of the United States.[1] As city redevelopment enterprises partnered with private development companies to sweep out residential hotels, mom-and-pop businesses, and small farms to make way for parking lots, five-star hotels, and condominium complexes, they erased generations of public history. Even as Asian America was evolving, its historic foundations were targeted for destruction, and activists rose up to save what was left. As each of the following examples illustrate, many of the original centers were lost but thanks to battalions of activists, they were not totally eradicated, and alternative provisions were created.

### The Fall and Rise of the I-Hotel

Among the many anti-eviction struggles across the country, the nine-year battle to save the International Hotel in what used to be San Francisco's thriving Manilatown, and its resurrection nearly three decades later, have become legendary in Asian American movement history. It was even immortalized in *I Hotel: A Novel* (2010) by Karen Tei Yamashita, one of the few Asian American movement moments that figures in recent literature.

Having fallen into disrepair but sitting on prime real estate, the International Hotel had been slated for demolition by its owners in 1968 to make way for a parking lot. A massive David and Goliath fight ensued to keep a roof over the heads of the mostly elderly Filipino and Chinese men who had made the hotel their home for decades and had nowhere else to go. In 1969 a mysterious fire killed three elderly tenants on the eve of a momentous lease-signing that subsequently fell through, and students joined tenants in their fight, helping to refurbish the hotel and oppose the impending eviction.

In June 1977, the I-Hotel earned a place on the National Register of Historic Places. Two months later, in the still-dark morning of August 4, 1977, its 150 elderly occupants were forcibly evicted by 400 riot police on horseback, who charged through a 3,000-person barricade of protesters linking arms to defend the hotel.

A 2010 public radio documentary evoked the intensity of the early-morning raid. Using actuality sound from Curtis Choy's 1977 documentary film *The Fall of the I Hotel*—of SWAT teams breaking through the human blockade and using sledgehammers to break down the doors—the radio documentary featured contemporary interviews with eye-witness participants. Anti-eviction organizer Emil De Guzman described the police as "Roman legions coming in the night," fellow organizer Estella Habal likened the raid to "being under siege," and David Prowler, who worked for the San Francisco Human Rights Commission, called the incident "the brutality of unregulated capitalism".

*On August 3 around ten o'clock at night, they heard that the police were mobilizing and heading toward the International Hotel.*

PROWLER: I went down there and there were thousands of people in front of the hotel, chanting … [the police and sheriffs had] so many walkie-talkies in that area they all jammed each other … And then this fleet of police cars and sheriff's cars with sirens and lights, coming up Kearny street … The red lights, bouncing off the buildings, the sirens, and then horses. It was like an invasion.

DE GUZMAN: … people had fortified themselves outside in the human barricade and the police were just running their horses into the crowd and beating people. It was a massacre. They were beating people indiscriminately.

HABAL: So by the time they finished, it must have been about five hours … four o'clock in the morning. It was a cold morning, we were just shocked … And they pushed us off into the street.

According to KDP member Helen C. Toribio, the ten-year span to save the hotel "paralleled the evolution of various left formations which, in the late 1960s emphasized 'serve the people' activism, but by the late 1970s had become focused on 'party-building' with each formation contending to be the vanguard of the U.S. revolution."[3] Three pre-party formations —I Wor Kuen (IWK), Wei Min She (WMS), and Katipunan ng mga Demokratikong Pilipinos (KDP)—played major roles in the I-Hotel struggle.

KDP organizer Estella Habal, who has written the most definitive book to date on the I-Hotel struggle, claimed that "radical leftists had been in the forefront of the mass movement to defend the I-Hotel. The dedication, energy, and self-sacrifice of all of the different leftist groups and factions gave the struggle much of its dynamic, bottom-up character."[4] However, Alex Hing, one of the founders of the Red Guard Party, wrote: "The I-Hotel would still be standing, but come the I-Hotel eviction night,

© Bob Hsoing Photography

Fig. 8.1: Police charge demonstrators on the night of the
I-Hotel eviction, San Francisco, August 4, 1977

one wing was fighting the other … and they, the system, saw that and
moved in."[5] Toribio indicated, "In the I-Hotel, the polemical relationships among the various left groups amplified the already bitter struggle
against eviction."[6] More specifically, Habal concluded, "Tendencies to
adopt positions of dogmatic militancy … to put the interests of their
own organization-building projects ahead of the mass movement tended
to isolate the revolutionaries farther from their 'mass base.'"

Even Calvin Trillin, in the *New Yorker,* knew that "the International
Hotel protest movement is divided into three organizations partly for
reasons that have nothing to do with the International Hotel."[7] These three
organizations were the International Hotel Tenants Association, which
was affiliated with KDP; the Support Committee of the International
Hotel, of which IWK played a leading role; and the Worker's Committee
to Defend the International Hotel, which included members of the
Asian Community Centre (ACC), Everybody's Bookstore, and WMS.[8]

According to ethnic studies professor Daryl Maeda, KDP analyzed the
battle for the I-Hotel as primarily a working-class struggle for housing
and chose to cooperate with liberals who opposed the eviction; WMS
also viewed the fight as class-based but refused to cooperate with what
it considered "reformists"; and IWK cast the eviction as an example of
racism or "national oppression."[9]

These divergent perspectives were not only ideological, they played
out on the ground. Warren Mar, a member of the Chinese Progressive
Association (CPA) and its parent organization IWK, said that—as at
large-scale anti-war rallies to which different coalitions brought their
own constituencies—on the night of the eviction, although it looked
like everyone was part of one demonstration, it was "really a bunch of
little demos … ACC would have their own contingent. CPA would
have their own contingent. KDP would have their own contingent."[10]
Another activist added that, on the night of the eviction, one contingent
purposefully let the police through the human barricade that had been
erected to defend the hotel. "Everybody knows that. They didn't think
we would succeed, so they tried to claim victory by saying, 'Look at the
capitalists. Look what they've done!'"

The sequel to the dramatic eviction was the near-miraculous rebuilding of the hotel nearly thirty years later through the persistence of Asian

American activists. The physical demolition of the hotel after the forced eviction pounded the final nail into the casket, only to give rise to a citizens' advisory committee that eventually facilitated not only the rebuilding of the hotel but a revitalization of Filipino community life. Like an empty gravesite, the hole in the ground was sacrosanct, guarded against any development that did not include affordable housing. Finally, thanks to St. Mary's Catholic Center, the Department of Housing and Urban Development, and city funding, the International Hotel Senior Housing and Manilatown Community Center opened in 2005.

KDP organizer Emil De Guzman located the resurrection of the hotel within the context of making Asian America. "The whole period with the Vietnam War where Asian people were being killed, the farmworker movement, the Civil Rights movement. It did a lot for us young people to get a sense of who we were, that we are part of a community, part of this history."[11] Bill Sorro, who with Guzman and poet Al Robles comprised the backbone of the effort to resist and rebuild, tempered the triumph of the resurrection within the larger scope of the struggle: "People ask, 'Do you feel vindicated now that they are filling that hole up?' No, we don't. We don't feel vindicated because justice don't work like that. Justice isn't something simple, so that if you fill the hole up with this much justice then you're equal … It is not OK."[12] Robles explained that the I-Hotel was "the life of the manongs, the life of the Filipinos. It was their heart, it was their poetry, it was their song."[13] This heart, this poetry, this song, is commemorated each year on the anniversary of the eviction at the International Hotel Manilatown Center.

### "Something's Rotten in Little Tokyo"

Such was the conclusion of Luis Abita, one of the many long-time residents of Little Tokyo who was destined to be evicted because of redevelopment: "Modernization is inevitable—but people should not be victimized by it, they should benefit from it. It shows that something's very rotten. Not in Denmark but in Little Tokyo."[14]

To its mostly poor and elderly residents, Little Tokyo was home, with all the practical and emotional nuances that "home" entails. Yet, according to the LA Master Plan, which included the creation of an "International Zone" encompassing neighboring Chinatown, Olvera

Street, and Little Tokyo, and the multinational Kajima International Corporation, which planned to build a luxury hotel and commercial complex in the area, Little Tokyo was a blighted area that stood in the way of profits and needed to be "redeveloped."

The history of Little Tokyo is similar to that of Chinatowns, Manilatowns, and Little Tokyos across the country. Formed in part by segregationist policies, these indigenous hubs served as centers for cultural and spiritual life not only for those who lived and worked within them, but for compatriots in the surrounding areas. Usually located in the oldest parts of the city, they became the metropolis's "inner city"—a euphemism for decrepit, neglected districts where minority and poor people live. Occupying valuable real estate, however, city governments—dependent on the substantial bed and sales taxes that big hotels and shopping centers generated—prioritized big business, at the expense of low-income residents, small establishments, and cultural and community groups. Government and corporate partnerships sought to capitalize on the areas by accentuating their quaint and colorful character and turning Chinatowns and Little Tokyos into sites designed to attract tourist trade.

When Little Tokyo was targeted for redevelopment, drawing a comparison to the mass eviction of Japanese Americans during World War II, a succession of grassroots organizations were formed to fight City Hall. The Little Tokyo Redevelopment Association tried to encourage local businesses to rebuild in Little Tokyo and succeeded in holding off the expansion for a number of years. The Little Tokyo Development Corporation attempted to raise enough funds to construct a shopping mall for local businesses forced to move. The Little Tokyo Community Advisory Committee formed to provide community input and to advise and work with the Community Redevelopment Agency, the municipal body responsible for arranging affordable housing and new commercial spaces for displaced residents and small businesses. The Little Tokyo Anti-Eviction Task Force, and subsequently the Little Tokyo People's Rights Organization, were formed to pressure the Community Redevelopment Agency to deliver on its promises.[15] The many community groups, such as Japanese American Community Service-Asian Involvement, that were housed in or connected to the Sun Building

Fig. 8.2: Cover *Gidra* 5: 8 (August 1973).
Art by David Monkawa.

targeted for eviction, as well as other Asian American movement organizations such as *Gidra* (which published a special supplement on redevelopment) and Visual Communications (which produced the video "Something's Wrong with Little Tokyo") went into overtime to stop the destruction and dispersal of Little Tokyo.

The cover of *Gidra*'s August 1973 special bilingual edition on redevelopment was created by David Monkawa, the artist who wanted to be on the front line. Visualizing the future of an overdeveloped Little Tokyo controlled by big business, it invoked the literary dystopia of George

Orwell's *1984* (see Fig. 8.2). Eerily prophetic, David's illustration featured futuristic monorails with spaceshiplike vehicles and oversized billboards hawking Japanese corporate interests that prefigured the visual universe of Ridley Scott's *Blade Runner*, which would be made eleven years later. Even more premonitory are his searing images of not one but two planes crashing headfirst into two towers, complete with bodies falling from a skyscraper—a harbinger of the real-life dystopia of September 11, 2001. Monkawa's audacious illustration served, as Mike Murase remarked, as "a call to action."

An army of activists went into action. Mark Masaoka, who was both a Little Tokyo hotel resident and an active member of the Little Tokyo Peoples' Rights Organization, recalled the redevelopment struggle:

> What galvanized the community's response was that local owner-developers were to be given the first opportunity to develop the hotel parcel on Weller Street. At the time, all the owners of that block were local. But a week before the deadline for bids, Kajima International, intent on building a luxury hotel complex, bought a small parking lot from a local owner and submitted what became the winning bid.

Mark recollected guerrilla tactics like amplifying the theme song of the movie *Bridge over the River Kwai* during the groundbreaking ceremony of the resulting high-rise hotel, as well as age-old strategies like packing city council meetings, refusing to leave, and getting arrested. "Our demands were: no evictions until housing for seniors was built, [as well as] affordable places for small businesses to relocate, and a community center for cultural and community organizations."

Mike Murase added that, although the new center was envisioned as a gateway for Japanese arts and culture, because the community insisted on local tenancy and relevance to the local Nikkei community, they struggled over the name of the new center, which was finally named the Japanese American Community and Cultural Center. "A small but important concession," he said. Although not all of the CRA's promises were kept, due to community pressure, evictions from certain hotels were halted until senior housing was completed, residents were given relocation assistance, community groups offered low-rent alternative space, small businesses provided with rental subsidies, and the Japanese American Community and Cultural Center had been built. All testified to the fact that it had been worth fighting City Hall.

### Fighting Rural Removal in Hawai'i

The long arm of corporate expansion not only invaded the urban enclaves of Chinatown and Little Tokyo, it also reached across the Pacific into the rural valleys of Hawai'i. What had been a fight against urban renewal in the inner cities took the form, in Hawai'i, of a battle against urbanization by small farmers. Land was the base of power in Hawai'i—*mana* to the *kanaka maoli* (Native Hawaiians) whose sustenance and spirit were rooted in the land, and profits and control to the missionaries and capitalists who overran the islands after Captain Cook's fateful arrival. Before Hawai'i had been colonized, land was determined by use, not ownership. After colonization, as Tracy Takano wrote in 1982 almost three decades before the Occupy Movement, "Less than 1 percent went to 99 percent of the population."[16] During the late 1960s the state owned 38.7 percent of Hawai'i, the federal government owned 9.8 percent, and a mere seventy-two large private landowners owned 47 percent (almost half the state), leaving less than 5 percent for everyone else.[17]

The first mass eviction took place in 1970 in Kalama Valley, where small farmers were uprooted for a modern housing development. Because it was the first, and because the adversary was the mighty Bishop Estate—the largest single landowner in Hawai'i—the rural Hawaiian, Japanese, Filipino and Portuguese farmers in the area had little choice but to comply. Only a stubborn few, like Portuguese pig farmer George Santos, refused. A support group called Kōkua Kalama was formed, initially consisting of student activists who had fought for the Ethnic Studies Program at the University of Hawai'i.

Mary Choy, a second-generation Korean American who, like most Asian American activists, had been politicized by the anti-war movement and the struggle for ethnic studies, recalls that the final eviction was on Mother's Day—May 21, 1971. "The State of Hawai'i's special force was there in full battle dress and assault weapons. The young people climbed to the rooftop of George's house, to be brought down one-by-one. George was the first to be dragged out of his house."[18]

An underlying issue in the Kalama Valley fight was the *malahini* ("outsider") factor. As Soli Niheu, one of the Native Hawaiian organizers of Kōkua Kalama, wrote, Hawaiians "were hesitant to support us because whenever the topic of Kalama Valley came up on the TV screen, too many *haole* were seen, especially the hippie type."[19] Kōkua Kalama then decided that only *kanaka maoli* and locals would speak on behalf of the organization. Niheu commented that this was "an important move on our part, and I must say that some of the whites understood the reasons and rationale—people like John Kelly and John Witeck, who were quite active."[20] John Witeck, who was originally from Virginia, commented:

> The Kalama Valley activists wanted to have a tactical separation, to show that this is not outside agitators or hippie culture … For myself, as a *haole* with civil rights movement experience, it was sort of a repeat of that understanding in the mid-'60s that whites may have a different role to play than black activists, that we needed to work with our own communities.[21]

Kalama Valley was sacrificed, but the struggle provided the necessary experience and indignation to spur more people to fight the onslaught of other evictions. Community struggles in Hawai'i were based in the land. Some twenty different land struggles were waged, including Ota Camp, in which evicted Filipinos succeeded in obtaining another location and the funding to relocate; People Against Chinatown Eviction, which was formed to prevent urban evictions in Honolulu's Chinatown; and Waiāhole-Waikāne, where protest strategies included blocking the Kamehameha Highway and establishing a system of lookouts with air horns in trees to warn of approaching law enforcement and possible evictions.[22]

Seisuke "Sei" Serikaku, who had farmed in Waiāhole for fifty years, recalled the involvement of the Revolutionary Communist Party (RCP) during the early days of the land struggle: "They were the ones who taught us how to protest, do civil disobedience and organize against the big boys. They taught us the militancy we needed to get the courage to fight back … I used to think activists and protesters were really crazy. I guess you're never too old to learn."[23] Reverend Bob Nakata, a former state representative, senator, and long-time community advocate, also recalled the role of the RCP in the Waiāhole-Waikāne struggle. "The people were feeling so isolated by the power structure that many of them said, 'If this is what communism is, I want it too.' (Or something to that effect.)" He added that, after the victory, the RCP had "tried to use this Waiāhole-Waikāne struggle as a launching pad for other struggles … and that's when they alienated themselves from the community."[24]

David Palumbo-Liu connected the historical dots between the redevelopment struggles of the 1970s and the alien land laws that prohibited Asians from owning land in the early 1900s, as well as the forced incarceration of Japanese Americans during World War II and concluded that the recurring policy of exclusion was aimed at preserving a national space that separated America from the remnants of Asia. He argued that preventing "aliens" from owning land was a way of deliberately blocking the formation of Asian America. He quoted the author of California's alien land law, who had asserted that aliens "will not come in large numbers and long abide with us if they may not acquire land." In this tradition, Palumbo-Liu determined, "Urban redevelopment was … designed to rescue America from the Third World."[25]

### "If You're not Afraid": Labor Campaigns

Labor has been the bedrock of the history of Asians in the United States, as successive waves of Asian workers were originally brought in as sources of cheap labor. Victims of overlapping working-class as well as immigrant exploitation, early Asian American laborers—largely shut out of traditional labor unions—organized for better wages and working conditions. As early as 1880, Chinese fruit pickers struck for higher wages in Santa Clara, California. In 1903, Japanese and Mexican farm laborers joined forces in Oxnard, California. In 1909, Japanese workers organized the first large-scale labor strike in Hawai'i, in which roughly 70 percent of Hawai'i's plantation workers participated. In 1920, some 10,000 Japanese and Filipino plantation workers went on strike. In 1933 Filipinos started the Cannery Workers' and Farm Laborers' Union and the Chinese Hand Laundry Alliance was formed. Whereas the Marine

Stewards and Cooks Association was initially intent on "replacing the Chinese and Japanese now on the Coast by American citizens," Black and Asian workers fought their way into the union and by the 1950s the majority of the members and leaders of the National Union of Marine Cooks and Stewards were people of color.[26]

At the height of the Civil Rights movement, when the Immigration Act of 1965 finally revoked undue restrictions on immigration from Latin America, Asia, and Africa, the resulting waves of immigrants became new sources of labor—both blue and white collar. This time supported by a generation of Asian American activists, labor struggles in various areas of industry proliferated, in many cases including arrests and violence, and sometimes even death.

### The Alaska Cannery Workers Association, Seattle

In 1951, when Bob Santos, the unofficial mayor of the International District in Seattle, was a high school student, he took his place as an "Alaskero"—a term for the mainly Filipino men who did seasonal work in the Alaskan fish canneries.[27] There, Bob and other young workers faced the same run-down bunkhouses and inferior food, in addition to long hours and dangerous working conditions, that their fathers and uncles had endured. Bob recalled:

> On top of the hill was this white house where the superintendent lived. Then there was a row of cabins where the white machinists lived. Further down there's the sled dogs—they got their own little houses there. And at the very end was the bunkhouse for the Filipinos. We were separated on the other side of the dogs! We were eight in a room—two double-bunk beds with two feet of aisle space down the center. While the white workers ate T-bone steaks and baked potatoes, we had fish heads and rice. Us second-generation guys said, "This is a bunch of bullshit." We tried to make it an issue, but it didn't go anywhere.

Twenty years later, still faced with the same discriminatory working conditions, it was time to make it an issue. In 1972—at only twenty years of age but already a five-year Alaskero veteran—Gene Viernes discovered a warehouse stocked with fruit and vegetables that had been withheld from the Filipino workers. When he made this stockpile known, and his request for better food was rejected, Viernes refused to eat for two days. Soon half the crew joined him in boycotting the mess hall, and Viernes became a spokesperson for the group, taking their complaints to the union representative. Another tactic Viernes and his cohorts tried was eating twice the usual portion at each meal, causing the mess hall to run out of food, and then refusing to eat the next meal. One Alaskero commented, "It was just about the only way you could fight back."[28]

The following year, Viernes found a better way to fight back. In 1973, along with Silme Domingo and others, he formed the Alaska Cannery Workers Association to direct three lawsuits against major Alaska canneries for discriminatory practices in employment and housing, two of which ultimately succeeded. When Viernes and Domingo learned that their largely corrupt and ineffective union had once included a large contingent of Filipino American laborers who had adamantly opposed colonial control of the Philippines, they became determined to reform the union and restore its progressive stance.

During the same period, KDP formed in opposition to the dictatorship of Philippine President Ferdinand Marcos, as well as to advocate for socialism in the United States.[29] Recalling the prominent labor organizing of Filipino Americans in the 1920s and 1930s, KDP worked to re-instill progressive politics among the Filipino American community, and Viernes and Domingo became active members. Their friend Ron Chew, who authored a book about their struggle, wrote that they "saw the fight within the union as part of a larger ongoing international battle against economic repression."[30]

That fight culminated in a fatal shoot-out in 1981. In April, Viernes went to the Philippines to meet with leaders of anti-Marcos groups and then to the International Longshore and Warehouse Union's international conference in Honolulu. When he returned to Seattle, Viernes became the new union dispatcher, and his modifications angered those who prospered from the old, corrupt system. While many complained, no one could have predicted that union reform, coupled with anti-Marcos activity, would soon turn deadly.

On the afternoon of June 1, two gang members made their way into the Local 37 union hall, where they gunned down Viernes and

Domingo. Gene Viernes was killed on the spot. Silme Domingo died hours later, after he had been able to identify the killers. Both of the gunmen, in addition to the head of the gang who ordered the murders, were sentenced to life in prison without parole. The Committee for Justice for Domingo and Viernes, which had formed immediately after their deaths, prevailed.

After years of unremitting investigation, the murders were eventually traced to the president of their union who, it turned out, had been hired by an ally of the Marcos regime to have Viernes and Domingo killed. In 1989, a federal jury found Marcos liable for the murders and awarded $15.1 million in damages to the Domingo and Viernes families. In 1991, the former president of the union was sentenced to life without parole. Ron Chew concluded:

> Silme Domingo and Gene Viernes believed—as most activists of their generation did—that if social change was to come to the United States, it had to come from many people pooling their efforts and forming a collective voice of defiance against the status quo.[31]

## Confucius Plaza, New York City

Although the Civil Rights Act of 1964 mandated equal opportunities in employment, compliance was not always enforced. The construction industry in particular had long been known as a bastion of white male advantages and Asian Americans had long fought for equal opportunity employment in the field. In 1963 Yuri Kochiyama met Malcolm X after demonstrating for construction jobs in New York. In 1969, members of the Asian Coalition for Equality in Seattle protested discriminatory hiring practices on publicly financed construction projects. Legal scholar Karen Tani pointed out that, although New York City construction workers were notorious for their violent attacks on anti-war protestors, it was Asian American activists' experience as anti-war protestors that helped them come together as Asian Americans for Equal Employment (AAFEE), to lead a massive fight to hire Asian American construction workers at the Confucius Plaza development in Chinatown.[32]

In May 1974, construction began on Confucius Plaza, a federally funded high-rise development project that included over 600 apartments, a school, a day care center, and commercial outlets in the heart of New York's Chinatown.[33] In the middle of their Chinatown village, amid the high poverty and underemployment of its residents, when Chinese Americans were denied employment by the construction firm, AAFEE sprang into action. According to Takashi Yanagida, one of the leaders of the AAFEE campaign, AAFEE was formed by construction workers who were joined by students and community members.[34] Others indicate that AAFEE was formed as the mass organization of the revolutionary Asian Study Group.[35] Regardless of its origins, AAFEE took the lead in organizing the immense struggle to win the right to work on Confucius Plaza.

After failing to resolve the issue by going through established channels—organizing workers to apply for construction jobs, reporting to the city's housing office that the contractor was out of compliance with the city's affirmative action plan, and meeting with the construction company directly—AAFEE launched a large-scale public campaign to pressure the construction company to hire Asian American workers. AAFEE distributed leaflets and petitions throughout Chinatown to raise awareness of the discrimination that was happening in its own backyard. On May 16, hundreds of demonstrators converged on the construction site, bringing work to a halt. When the police were called and ten demonstrators were arrested, in Yanagida's words, "The war was on." Their slogan was "The Chinese built the transcontinental railroad, they can build Confucius Plaza."[36]

During the ensuing two-and-a-half weeks of major demonstrations, fifty-seven arrests were made. Television audiences saw a Chinatown they had never known, and community support for the campaign swelled. After several more marches and demonstrations, a settlement was reached calling for the hiring of twelve Asian American journeymen and twenty-seven trainees. Yanagida summarized the significance of the struggle. "Once the idea of fighting against racial oppression was grasped by the community, sweeping changes and powerful forces were set in motion."[37]

### The Jung Sai Garment Workers' Strike, San Francisco

A few months after the Confucius Plaza struggle, across the country in San Francisco's Chinatown, workers at the Jung Sai garment factory waged a massive protest for better working conditions, higher wages, unionization, and job security. Their slogan: "If you're not afraid, join us. If you are afraid, this isn't the place for you."

By 1970, five years after restrictive immigration quotas had been revoked, the population density of San Francisco's Chinatown was eleven times higher than the rest of the city. The only place in the United States with a denser population was New York's Chinatown.[38] In the history of Chinatowns, English-speaking female immigrants were quickly absorbed into the garment industry, which had historically supplied itself with a steady flow of underpaid, nonunion immigrant workers. In San Francisco, Chinese workers had been the dominant labor force in the garment industry since the late 1800s.[39]

At the time of the strike, the Jung Sai workers barely made $2 per hour, often worked overtime without additional compensation, and were promised health insurance and sick leave they never received.[40] To improve their situation, workers attempted to unionize. After their first attempt on July 4, 1974, the owner offered a pay raise of 25 cents per hour if they would cancel their demand for unionization. On July 15 the strike began. Two days later, claiming financial losses, the plant closed, and the protesters moved their demonstration to the company's headquarters, where thirty-eight workers and two supporters were arrested. In a press conference the next day, the workers were appealed for community support and was joined by a group of LeeMAH Electronics workers who, like the Jung Sai workers, were mostly Chinese immigrant women who had also been locked out of their jobs due to their union activity. The emotional testimonies offered at the press conference made mainstream front-page news, with the *San Francisco Chronicle* noting, "Any warmed-over stereotypes about Oriental impassiveness were convincingly shot down yesterday."[41]

Like the struggle for the International Hotel, the Jung Sai strike was fueled by supporters from the revolutionary groups IWK and WMS, which, while united in their support for the workers, advocated divergent strategies. Daryl Maeda writes that IWK saw the workers as suffering from both national oppression and class exploitation, while WMS portrayed the strike primarily as a class struggle.[42] According to Harvey Dong, there were also key strategic differences between IWK and WMS over how to build rank-and-file leadership, with WMS disagreeing with IWK's focus on obtaining union leadership positions.[43]

After almost a year of strike activity that included sixty-four arrests, the workers brought a suit before the National Relations Labor Board, which eventually ruled in their favor. Harvey concluded that, although corporate strategies to minimize financial loss and the capitulation of the union prevented the strike from realizing its maximum potential, the Jung Sai strike was significant for many reasons. Representative of the post-1965 wave of Chinese workers, the strike demonstrated the strength of labor activism and energized other immigrant workers, who faced similar unfair labor practices. Perhaps more importantly, Harvey noted, it transformed both the workers and the Chinatown community itself, dispelling stereotypes of Chinese immigrant women and empowering them both as individuals and as a community. As an editorial in the July 24, 1974, issue of the conservative *Chinese Times* reported, "Unexpectedly these once subservient sewing factory aunties … are crying out angrily for their rights [and] created a new page in Chinatown history."[44]

### The Third World at Home and in the World

Coalition building across ethnic, racial, ideological, and state lines for a common cause was a conscious strategy during the Asian American movement. As Asian America was inextricably part of the larger project of the Third World, activists participated in Third World campaigns both around the block and around the world.

Across the United States, Asian American activists supported a variety of people of color campaigns. On December 21, 1969, the Japanese American Citizens League's National Committee to Repeal Detention Camp Legislation sponsored a food lift to the encamped Indians of All Tribes during their eight-month occupation of Alcatraz Island in San Francisco. Nisei fishermen volunteered their boats to transport fresh meat, produce, and fruit, as well as rice and canned food, citing the common bond of their having also been incarcerated by the US government during Word World II.[45]

In May 1970, Yale University's Asian American Student Association supported Black Panthers Bobby Seale and Erica Huggins during their trial in New Haven. Bill Lann Lee wrote a statement of support that was read at a major press conference. Rocky Chin recalled the morning of one of the rallies: "The tanks, National Guard troops, and helicopters all amounted to an incredible display of raw excessive military force … On that one day, it became all too clear how fascism might come about in a country where the real power is not in the hands of the people."[46]

On August 29, 1970, the National Chicano Moratorium march against the war in Southeast Asia drew an estimated 25,000–30,000 participants from around the country to East Los Angeles, including many Asian Americans. The event was a political watershed in the Chicana/o movement not only for its show of force, but because the rally was broken up by police, tear gas was dropped from police helicopters, more than 150 were arrested, and four were killed—including *Los Angeles Times* journalist Rubén Salazar. Duane Kubo, a film student at UCLA at the time, accompanied fellow student David García to cover the event. He said that while he had seen the violence of the Black Liberation movement played out on television, this was the first time he found himself in actual physical danger. "I was scared. There was group panic when the shooting started. People were scattering all over the place, cops were beating up marchers."

On April 20, 1973, fourteen Asian Americans surreptitiously left Los Angeles to support and bring attention to the Native American struggle at Wounded Knee in South Dakota. On Easter Sunday, representatives of the four races led a march from Crow Dog's Paradise, the home of spiritual leaders Leonard and Henry Crow Dog, to Wounded Knee. Tatsuo Hirano (seen in the middle of Figure 8.3) was selected by the Asian American contingent as their delegate. The accompanying press release indicated, "According to the traditional medicine men of the Oglala Sioux, it fulfills the prophecy that when the four races get together, they will purify the land." The release also pointed out the similarities of their histories: they too had been corralled into reservations euphemistically called "relocation centers" during World War II and watching their people shot on TV in old war movies and in present-day Vietnam.[47]

Fig. 8.3: From a press release about the Asian American
contingent to Wounded Knee, Tatsuo Hirano in center

Mo Nishida, who traveled ahead as part of an advance party, expanded
the Vietnam analogy, saying that the route used to bring supplies into
the besieged encampment in Wounded Knee was so dangerous it was
called the Ho Chi Minh Trail. Kathy Nishimoto Masaoka said that,
for security purposes, they had taken separate cars and different routes
to get there from Los Angeles. Dennis Kobata recalled that as they
approached the Pine Ridge Reservation they were stopped by a swarm
of law enforcement and military forces. "A tremendous overkill," he
said, "it confirmed the perception of the American Indian Movement
and other locals that it was like a war zone."

The warriors of the rainbow on that Easter Sunday never made it to
Wounded Knee. As the press release indicated, "The march was termi-
nated on Wednesday, April 25, when 75 BIA men, Federal Marshalls
and vigilantes confronted the group of 150 peaceful marchers with
M-16s, sub-machine guns, grenade launchers and one helicopter."
Within the week, Cherokee supporter Frank Clearwater and "Buddy"
Lamont, a local Oglala Lakota, would be shot and killed. After their
deaths, seventy-one days of occupation, and reports of between 400 and
1,200 arrests, the siege ended.

As part of a concerted commitment to internationalism, Asian
American activists also rallied against imperialism around the world,

especially when their ancestral countries were involved. Asian Americans protested rising Japanese militarism and imperialism, specifically objecting to the complex and related issues of Japan's 1969 takeover of the Tiao-yu Tai islands, the 1970 renewal of the US-Japan Security Pact, and the 1971 reversion of Okinawa to Japan. When Marcos declared martial law in the Philippines in 1972, the event elicited both outrage as well as support from the Filipino American community, which comprised both US-born Filipino Americans who had no direct connection to the Philippines as well as post-1965 immigrants who had close, continuing links to the islands. Most offensively, what was commonly called the "Marcos Black List"—a list of Filipino American activists, some of whom had never been to the Philippines like Florante Ibanez nor been involved in anti-Marcos activities like Fred Cordova—was widely circulated throughout Filipino communities in the United States, causing pervasive alarm and suspicion.[48]

These and many other battles demonstrate the breadth and intensity of Asian American activism in the 1960s and 1970s. Some were victorious; others were not. Some caused internal strife and intense ideological battles; others brought people from all walks of life together. Through it all, as Takashi Yanagida and Harvey Dong concluded, the idea and the experience of fighting against oppression transformed and empowered the people involved, their communities, and Asian America at large. Just as previous involvement in protesting the Vietnam War and fighting for ethnic studies had prepared activists to take on these challenges, participation in each campaign sharpened individuals and their tactics for the next.

# ACT III: FINDING OUR TRUTH

*Each generation must, out of relative obscurity, discover its mission, fulfill it or betray it.*

Frantz Fanon

# NINE

## Self-Appraisals and Evaluations

*It is time for self-appraisal and evaluation, not only as an organization, but for many of us as individuals. There is a shared feeling, a premonition if you will, that now is somehow a good time to sum up our experiences.*

Mike Murase, in the last issue
of *Gidra*, April 1974

Having come into its own in 1968 when the empire was teetering, the masses were revolting, and global change was ubiquitous, the Asian American movement started to wind down in the mid 1970s. The loss of faith in the ideals of American democracy that resulted from the duplicitous behavior of the United States during the Vietnam War, followed by the scandal of Watergate a mere heartbeat after Nixon's landslide victory the year before, demoralized the nation. For Asian Americans in particular, the Vietnam War, which had a galvanizing effect on the Asian American movement, had a correspondingly deflating impact when it ended. We had come of age during the Vietnam War. An unholy alliance of racism and imperialism, like nothing before or since, the war united Asians in America who, regardless of our various ethnicities, looked more enemy than American. While relieved about the end of the carnage and gratified by the achievement of the anti-war effort, the war's end neutralized what had been a major impetus for Asian American activism.

## From Community Building to Party Building

In addition to the end of the Vietnam War, another factor in the major shift in the Asian American movement as a whole was, as Helen Toribio had pointed out, the turn from Serve the People to party building. In an article called "Where Do We Go From Here?" published in the last issue of *Gidra* in April 1974, Mo Nishida elucidated Toribio's conclusion.

In a summary of the Asian American movement to date, making clear that it was written from a Japanese American perspective grounded in Los Angeles activism, Mo contextualized his evaluation within the major international and political trends of national liberation and working-class consciousness.

Mo asserted that in the Sixties, in our thrust for dignity and equality, people of color tested white America "to see if the principles in the Declaration of Independence and the Bill of Rights were for real." Finding that integration and affirmative action plans were "smoke screens which did not deal with real justice," African Americans, Chicanas/os, Native Americans and Asian Americans realized they could not rely on the policies and practices of the US government and, instead, earnestly engaged in community-nation building.

The other major trend was the development of working-class consciousness and the struggle to gain dignity and some power over their own lives. However, Mo assessed that in the late 1960s, this trend was restricted to intellectuals, the student movement and the general rebellion of white youth. He concluded that the oppression felt by youth was channeled into two paths. One was social change such as the free speech movement and opposing the draft. The other was to escape, "exemplified by Leary and the acid culture, commune experiences and the youth culture in general: 'change yourself' without dealing with the oppressive social system."

Within the Asian American movement, Mo contended that these two trends were manifested—by politicized Japanese Americans in Los Angeles in particular—in the two arenas of identity and Serve the People programs. "Therefore this period [1968–69] saw activists from diverse areas and life experiences coming together and united by the general line of fulfilling one's identity by Serving the People." The next period of 1970–72, Mo surmised, was a time of development and pro-liferation of community building which also brought about "a more sophisticated political understanding of capitalism and imperialism and how our lives were affected by them." In this way, Mo concluded, "The general call of Identity through Serve the People has run its course. A furious development of institution building has taken place with a deeper understanding of the political nature of the work ahead."

### Left Turn

In *Legacy to Liberation: Politics and Culture of Revolutionary Asian America* (2000), Fred Ho provides a number of diagrams mapping out the genealogy of Asian American revolutionary organizations. The Red Guard merged with I Wor Kuen (IWK) in 1971 and later with the East Wind Collective and the August 29th Movement to form the League of Revolutionary Struggle in 1978. The Kalayaan Collective and the National Committee for the Restoration of Civil Liberties in the Philippines became Katipunan Ang Demokratikong Pilipinos (KDP) in 1973. The Asian Community Center (ACC) formed Wei Min She (WMS) in 1971, which dissolved in 1975, with most joining the Revolutionary Community Party.

Another lineage was the Progressive Labor Party that led to the Asian Study Group, which became the Workers Viewpoint Organization that transitioned into Communist Workers Party and then to the New Democratic Movement. Other left groups, however short-lived, included the Garbagemen, Fandi, and Community Workers Collective in Los Angeles; Yellow Seed in Philadelphia; the Japan Town Collective in San Francisco; and the Pacific Rim Collective and Third Arm, which evolved into People Against Chinatown Eviction in Honolulu.[1]

While each group was anti-capitalist and anti-imperialist, as was described in Chapter 8, they often clashed vehemently. The rivalry between IWK and WMS has been particularly well documented in primary documents issued by both organizations. In September 1974, Wei Min She issued a booklet called *I Wor Kuen's Reactionary Line on May Day and the Worker's Movement*, with the subtitle *Wei Min She*

*Reply to IWK Criticism of 1974 May Day Asian Contingent Statement.*[2]

More widely accessible via the internet are IWK'S three journals produced in 1974, 1975 and 1976. In the *I.W.K. Journal*, no. 2 (May 1975), a six-part article was titled "Opportunism in the Asian Movement—Wei Min She/Revolutionary Union."[3] Stating that the WMS had been influenced by the Revolutionary Union from its beginning, in contrast to IWK's stance that "revolutionary minded individuals and organizations should integrate themselves with the masses, transform their thinking and promote revolution," the article indicated that WMS's tendency "maintained that the masses were 'too backward' and 'ignorant.'" "The revolutionary tendency [IWK] and the rightest tendency [WMS] were two fundamentally different outlooks and stands and came into constant clash over the years over practically each and every issue of the revolutionary movement."

The third and last newsletter, dated January 1976, included an article titled "Some Criticisms of Workers Viewpoint Organization on Party Building." Its four parts explained how WVO "Undermines the Theoretical Foundation of Marxism-Leninism-Mao Tsetung Thought," and their deviations on "the Role of Experience in the Theory of Knowledge," "on Theory and Practice," and "on the nature of the Vanguard Party."[4]

### Political Jabberwocky

*Gidra*'s last issue, dated April 1974, took journalistic pause to consider the moment. Mike Murase evoked Mao's polemic on self-criticism that dust will accumulate if a room is not cleaned and faces get dirty if they are not washed.

Bruce Iwasaki, one of *Gidra*'s most prolific writers, prefaced his summation by saying, "A political work in media implies a recognition of the ability to use words as tools, lenses or traps. So I want to meditate on the Asian American movement as I've seen it from my own toadstool in the well."[5] In his essay "The Final Venomous Jabberwocky: Feverish Grunts on the Movement and the Word," Bruce expressed exasperation with the exudation of "antique certitudes of pre-1917 Lenin or truistic

Mao; the imposition of pre-industrial theories of revolution on our own vastly different situation; and the conceptualization of social class—and revolution itself—as 'things' rather than processes." He also voiced his annoyance with "land oriented nationalism imbued more with literary romance than realistic analysis." Jabberwocky, from Bruce's toadstool. But, rather than deconstructing these two theoretical thorns in his side, the focus of his criticism was "the mode of thought that has set them loose," namely "imprecise conceptual tools." Acknowledging the importance of words for communication, he wrote:

> This parroting of theory looks neither far nor deep, and arises from an absence of a *historical* sense and *literary* consciousness … Without a historical sense we wax ultra-left, fail to read historical circumstances, get discouraged when the action lulls, lose patience and perspective, and drop out. Worse, absence of literary consciousness hinders dialogue with people not yet in motion. How can we raise awareness when we can't even talk to those who don't share our assumptions?[26]

Others—from their own toadstools—articulated similar earnestly felt self-appraisals. Warren Furutani, who had found his voice during the movement and traveled the country spreading the word, sadly commented, "The movement was going so far left, it started turning right." Walter Morita, a grunt on the ground, noted, "if you did not share the same opinion, you could get publically blasted for not taking a stand, or taking the wrong stand." Alex Hing, who was arguably the most well-known revolutionary of the day, reflected:

> The one big criticism I have of the early movement is the sectarianism. On all sides we spent an inordinate amount of time fighting each other and our sectarianism did not help us win the hearts and minds of the people. There were actual differences in perspective, but in retrospect they were not that important.

Even in the moment, this premonition was there for the learning. On the cusp of the movement, in 1969, the article that prompted the *Los Angeles Free Press*'s front page headline "Yellow Power Arrives!" warned

that "the majority of Asian Americans are not yet ready for revolutionary ideology [and] cannot be expected to change into revolutionaries
overnight."[7] Toward the end of the movement, in 1977, an editorial
in *Bridge* magazine addressed the internal discord that was running
rampant. Recounting the advances that had been made in the past
decade, it reminded readers that these giant steps were the result of hard
work, persistence, and cooperative effort and that there was much work
yet to be done. Warily, the editorial posed, "Nowadays in the communities there is talk of 'factions,' 'internal squabbles,' 'power struggles.'
Are they just growing pains, or are they serious problems which might
disrupt the progress that we've made in the last ten years?"[8]

Although revolution was in the air, so was paranoia. And for good
reason. For years it was rumored that governmental agencies were using
underhanded and often illegal surveillance tactics to harass, discredit,
and/or infiltrate groups that had been considered subversive. In 1975
the Church Committee investigation of the Central Intelligence Agency,
Federal Bureau of Investigation, and National Security Agency confirmed those fears. In the mounting oppression, elements of the left
became more insulated and self-reinforcing, prompting Jack Tchen to
comment, "People were accused of being lesbians, of being psychotic, of
being bourgeois artists. Groups started fighting each other, literally with
fisticuffs, beating each other up over who was going to be the vanguard."[9]

On the West Coast, Dale Minami, one of the founders of the Asian
Law Caucus, commented, "The arrogance of leaders who thought a revolution was around the corner alienated well-meaning people who would
have contributed a lot more." Dale was part of a group of young progressive attorneys in the early 1970s who were affiliated with the Asian
American left. "We defended them, we helped create their organizations, we showed up when the police had warrants." But the haughtiness
of some of its leaders was vexing:

> There was one leader who was so abusive and sanctimonious, it actu-
> ally was a turning point in my life because I realized if people like this
> were going to lead us, then the current system is better—or just as
> good. Self-righteousness was so prevalent and oppressive, it mirrored
> the system we were trying to change.

When Dale related his frustration to an older leftist lawyer, "he said we were lawyers. Our role was not to organize, our role was to support left organizations—whether we agreed totally with them or not. If you want to lead, don't be a lawyer because that's not your role."[10] Dale continued to defend revolutionary organizations. "When socialism started to break down in other countries, we realized how strong capitalism was. One of the groups decided they were all going to get MBAs and subvert the capitalist system in the belly of the beast. Well, they all got MBAs and now they own businesses, they sell real estate." Dale went on to be a key player in landmark decisions such as *Korematsu v. United States*, a lawsuit to overturn a forty-year-old conviction for refusal to obey exclusion orders aimed at Japanese Americans during World War II, originally upheld by the US Supreme Court (*United Pilipinos for Affirmative Action v. California Blue Shield*), the first class action employment lawsuit brought by Asian Pacific Americans on behalf of Asian Pacific Americans; and *Nakanishi v. UCLA*, which resulted in the granting of tenure after several hearings and widespread publicity over discrimination in academia.

## New Shackles

Internal political discord was by no means exclusive to the Asian American movement. There were parallel disagreements in other movements of the Sixties as well, over questions of nation and class, party building, mass organizing, and united fronts—as well as over China and the USSR, not to mention Vietnam, North Korea, Cuba, Algeria, and Albania. And certainly, disharmony and dissension are also part and parcel of mainstream politics. As activist and filmmaker Eddie Wong pointed out, "The worldwide march toward orthodox Maoist, Marxist, Leninism modes inspired by the efforts of Chinese, Vietnamese and Cuban revolutionaries was complex."[11]

"In the '60s," Audre Lorde wrote, "political correctness became not a guideline for living, but a new set of shackles," noting that newly awakened anger was often expressed, not vertically against the true sources of power, but "horizontally toward those closest to us who mirrored our own impotence … When we disagreed with one another about the solution to a particular problem, we were often far more vicious to each other than to the originators of our common problem."[12] Fay Chiang's experience is a case in point. Fay was the executive director of Basement Workshop. The only pan–Asian American community organization in New York at the time, it was an attractive grassroots organization ripe for political takeover:

> During 1974–75 there was a deep political schism within the organization in terms of the organization's purposes and direction. One of the two camps was for community arts and resources; the other was for partisan political organizing using Basement as a front. Friends, families and former co-workers were split and the organization was on the verge of exploding. In June 1975, I attended a meeting where a position paper drafted by the members of the partisan group was read to me accusing me of selling out the community to the federal and state government by accepting arts funding.[13] I demanded, "How can you do this? Talk to me!" It was pretty ugly. I screamed so much that four guys pinned me to the ground. I kept screaming so they finally let me go and I ran into the stairwell. "If you want theater, you're going to get it!" And I just howled non-stop in the stairwell. Up and down the sound went. People later told me the tension was so great people left the meeting sobbing. For several months afterwards, I was harassed and followed in the streets of Chinatown as this group tried to break me—"Aren't you tired today? Don't you need a vacation?"

The lessons? "Hopefully," Audre Lorde wrote, "we can learn from the '60s that we cannot afford to do our enemies' work by destroying each other."[14] Another lesson lies in Fay herself. The experience was appalling, made crueler because "they were people who I thought were my friends." Despite being hijacked, Fay did not succumb to the psychological extortion. Instead, she persevered. A few months after the incident, she formalized a compromise and consolidated the organization, paying off back rent, giving up some spaces, and acquiring another. Within a year, Basement not only survived the attempted coup but had grown in scope and strength. Fay ended up working at Basement Workshop for many years. When she had begun, she was all of nineteen. When she left, she was thirty-four.

## Bourgeois Decadence

Another factor that, no doubt, played a part in Fay's attempted purge was the misunderstood role of arts and culture in the social movements of the era. As the last chapter discussed, art was neither a luxury nor entertainment; at its best it was revolution. Yet in the days of ultra-leftism, as Jack Tchen noted, artists were often considered bourgeois, individualistic, and counterrevolutionary. Besides being a woman, Fay was also an artist.

Fay's fellow artist Arlan Huang, who, with Takashi Yanagida, took on the challenge of overseeing the development and production of "Yellow Pearl," the innovative box collection of poems, songs, and graphics produced out of Basement Workshop, felt the rumbles of political correctness threatening Basement Workshop before Fay was assaulted:

> There were these artists' meetings but what they really were were disguises for political recruitment. And at a certain point you say, "What is this!?" I remember Amiri Baraka saying something like art is the anarchistic cog in the wheel of capitalism. There is a place for art in a capitalist system, you get to be an anarchist. But overall you're still a capitalist. You get caught up in having to be politically correct, say the right thing, draw the right thing, and your art becomes just a political tool. After the big split in the movement, I just said, "Forget it—all you guys—I'm out of here." It was art that saved me. I just hid in my art until I could come back out.

Nancy Hom, who could have had a promising future as a fine artist but instead chose to become a community artist, curator, administrator, and activist, reflected that, during the period when the movement was engulfed in dogmatic self-righteousness, "People didn't understand the significance and role of art in the movement, and treated artists as cultural workers who were to provide illustrations for propaganda or as lightweight activists who were not central to the movement."

A more emphatic zone of "bourgeois decadence" was the issue of homosexuality. While revolutionary in many ways, the left was woefully reactionary when it came to the realities of gay and lesbian life. The conventional communist view on homosexuality was that it was a product of bourgeois decadence—a point that most Asian American left groups accepted without question. Don Kao, who publicly came out at the second Midwest Asian American Conference at the University of Wisconsin, Madison, in 1974, recalls hearing that, although he did good work, because he was gay he could never be a true communist. This despite Huey Newton's statement as early as 1970 that "there is nothing to say that a homosexual cannot also be a revolutionary,"[15] which activist Sherry Wolf indicated was the "first openly pro-gay statement by a major heterosexual movement activist of any race."[16]

Activist and scholar Daniel Tsang wrote the first published essay on Asian American homosexuality in the February 1975 issue of *Bridge*. In it he quoted an earlier letter to *Bridge* that read, "I am Asian, a male and gay. For the past year since I've gotten involved with the Asian American Movement, or at least tried, I've been scorned, ridiculed, and rejected by many so-called sincere Asian Movement people, especially the males."[17]

Filmmaker and writer Richard Fung, a fourth-generation Trinidadian Chinese who lives in Canada, said, "I learned I was 'gay' before I learned I was 'Asian.'"[18] Regarding his dual identity, he wrote, "The homophobia of our 'ethnic' communities and the subtle racism of the gay community combine to isolate us and produce a kind of cultural schizophrenia."[19]

Writer Helen Zia, who at the time had not come out to herself as a lesbian, was in essence tried before a court of her comrades:

> The official position of almost all of the Marxist-Leninist-Maoist groups was totally anti-gay. At meetings they would say, "Homosexuality is a disease. It's a disease of decadent bourgeois society and harmful to the working class." It would be really vile, just as bad as the Catholic or Mormon church. I mean really. It was the same kind of homophobic, close-minded vitriol but it would be masked in all this scientific Marxism, Leninism, Mao Zedong language.

One day Helen was called to a meeting of the study group she was a part of in Boston, consisting of African and Asian Americans. Since there were meetings all the time, she thought nothing of it until she got there. But when she arrived, everybody was sitting in a semi-circle. Helen was then seated in front of them:

> They didn't waste any time. The African American leader began, "Basically, Helen, we've noticed that you have been hanging around with a lot of lesbians. The African American community does not accept homosexuality. This is a white disease. So if you are a lesbian, we would have to break off ties with you and other Asian Americans." The Asian Americans in attendance all nodded in agreement, and the Asian American leader commanded, "So Helen, tell us, are you a lesbian?" I was all of twenty-three then. I had never dated a woman. I thought, "Am I a lesbian?" I didn't know. But I was certain of one thing: my Chinese upbringing had taught me to value family above all. Suddenly, my extended family, my community, was threatening to disown me. So I said, "No, I'm not a lesbian." And then the meeting was over. Everybody was happy. It was like I said the magic words, and it was all done and it never came up again. Except for me, it was the equivalent of stepping in the closet and slamming the door shut.

Four decades after her lesbian trial, having been in touch with her Asian American inquisitor over the years through their continued activism, one day Helen asked him if he remembered the incident and his role in it:

> He said, "No, can't say that I do." It was as though I had asked him if he recalled the fly that landed on his sleeve forty years ago. I was struck by how such a significant event in my life was nothing to him. It was a clear example of heterosexist privilege in action. But to his credit, he added, "But I don't doubt that it happened—we were very homophobic then." Indeed.

## Half the Sky and Most of the Room

Basement director Fay Chiang felt that another factor in her being the target of an attempted political coup was that people had a problem with a woman in leadership: "Some days it felt like I was battling both men and women who found shifting from very traditional, ingrained roles very difficult and challenging." Similarly, Mary Uyematsu Kao wrote that women and men "came into the Movement with gender role baggage from our 1950s upbringings. The struggle to let go of this baggage for both women and men embodied the struggle against male chauvinism."[20] Unlike white feminists of the time, Asian American women, like other women of color, understood the centrality of race to their lives and, more specifically, the simultaneous and interlocking forces of "triple jeopardy"—racism, imperialism, and sexism. Tracing the roots of intersectionality to the notion of triple jeopardy—which was also the name of the Third World Women's Alliance[21] newsletter—feminist writer Delia D. Aguilar emphasized that its conceptualization was "honed in the intensity of revolutionary struggle by women-of-color organizations."[22]

Organizational consultant Evangelina Holvino identified four major lived differences between white women and women of color. Because women of color have always worked, white feminists' demands for recognition of the role of housewives and access to work were not priorities. Because both men and women of color are subjugated by racism, women of color did not define men as the oppressor. Because race is a major dynamic, there is a tendency for white women to be complicit with white privilege, colluding with white men in the private sphere while fighting the "male oppressor" in the public sphere. And because of the distinctive set of experiences that arise from their lives in the interstices of race, class, and gender, women of color mix genres to make feminist theory in the form of poetry, short stories, and memoirs, producing knowledge that is less tied to the academy.[23]

An example of this radical feminine way of knowing is the poetry of Janice Mirikitani. Named San Francisco's second Poet Laureate in 2000, in 1972 she was one of the editors of *Third World Women*, an early anthology of poetry and essays by African American, Chicana, Native

American, and Asian American women. In that collection, her poem "Ms" confronted the peculiar brand of racism that was at the heart of the deep chasm that existed between women of color and the white feminist movement. Having been accused of being a victim of sexism by a white feminist for using the title "miss" instead of "ms:"

> I said,
> White lace and satin was not soiled by sexism,
> sheltered as you were by mansions built on Indian land
> your diamonds shipped with slaves from Africa
> your underwear washed by Chinese laundries
> your house cleaned by my grandmother
> so do not push me any further.
> And when you quit
> killing us for democracy
> and stop calling ME *gook*,
> I will call you
> whatever you like.[24]

*Gidra* published two issues focusing on Asian American women. In its first woman's issue, in January 1971, the editorial by the special collective of women editors placed the Asian American women's movement firmly within the framework of the larger Asian American movement by declaring opposition to capitalistic society and resistance to degrading media images, while acknowledging the shared struggle with "our brothers against male chauvinism" and constructing new definitions of self-determination.[25]

Expanding on the point of men and women struggling against sexism and constructing new definitions of self, Vietnam veteran and newly appointed attorney Mike Yamamoto wrote an article titled "Male Perspective," in which he concluded, "The women's struggle is the liberation of MEN." He argued that, as women became able to shed their stereotypes, so too would men: "A man won't have to be tall, dark, strong, aggressive, competitive, rugged or independent any more than women will have to be small, delicate, passive, artistic or dependent … The old order will be destroyed for the creation of a new, emancipated order."[26] Thirty years later, Yamamoto emancipated his own self, transitioning from male to female, and emerging as Mia in 2003. Coming full circle to the early days of making Asian America, she wrote:

> It's reminiscent of when I was first coming up as a Japanese American litigator and had something to prove. People didn't believe that an Asian litigator could be as assertive or effective as other attorneys, especially in the courtroom. In some ways, that chip on my shoulder prodded me to do well. Once again, I'm feeling that I have something to prove: People must understand that a transgender woman can do as good a job as anyone else.[27]

Occupying the space of gender privilege, men in general understandably have a harder time comprehending sexism. So when they do, it is profound. A case in point is Steve Louie, who spent almost two years traveling and working through Asian America in the early 1970s. When I asked Steve what some of his epiphanic experiences had been, he replied by telling me about a particular meeting in Boston. He had been helping out at an anti-war newspaper where "the typists were all women, and the leadership was all men." At one meeting, one of the women typists—"and that's what I thought of her as, one of the women typists"—addressed the male leadership in a rage of frustration. "'You assholes aren't listening to us and we're changing the way this organization works right now. If you don't like it you can leave.' She added, 'We know how to put the paper out, you don't.'"

Steve remembered just sitting there agape. And then the light went on:

> I related it to race, that just because you're black, brown, Asian, whatever, you're not as good or as capable. For me it wasn't so much a woman's issue, it was more ideological. Just like putting black or Asian people down, if you're going to put women down, you're cutting out half the sky and most of the room. That incident crystallized a lot of things for me politically. That it happened to involve women was part of it. The larger lesson was that you better include everybody in the room and you better figure out what your blinders are. At that time I realized I had blinders on, and I didn't even know it.

Fig. 9.1: Asian American women react to leaflet on "how to meet girls and ladies right here in America." From *Gidra* 3: 1 (January 1971).

### *"We All Haole Now"*

When US business and government interests wrested control of Hawai'i in the late 1800s, despite a petition against annexation signed by over half of all native Hawaiians, Hawai'i became a territory of the United States. In 1959, Hawai'i became the 50th state of the union, prompting a local newspaper headline to announce wryly: "We All Haole Now."[28] Used either as a slur or simply a statement of fact, depending on the context, in light of the missionization and corporatization of Hawai'i, being *haole* also meant having the rights of a first-class citizen. The headline "We All Haole Now" thus implied the conflation of "American" and "white," entailing the underlying notion of whiteness as an accomplishment and a basis of social status.

The transition of the Islands from colony to state was considered progress by some and cooptation by others. In a similarly contested shift, by the end of the 1970s the mainstream had begun to absorb minority standpoints even as Asian American organizations adopted mainstream policies and practices. The same social commentary inherent in the headline "We All Haole Now" was now implicated by the headlines: "Are Asian Americans Becoming White?"[29] "Forever Foreign or Honorary White?"[30] and the many variations of "Are Asians the New Jews?"[31]

Asian American Studies scholars Michael Liu, Kim Geron, and Tracy Lai commented that, as service agencies adopted more professional approaches, "the 'social service activist' became 'the social service professional,'" adding that what had begun as law collectives became public-interest law firms, while housing and tenant programs often mutated into development corporations.[32] Using as an example the institutionalization of Asian Americans for Equality, which had begun as grassroots organization, Liu and Geron noted that, "Having built its reputation through a militant mobilization for construction jobs and its open association with a Marxist organization, over time it has become a multi-million-dollar community development corporation. Rather than being critical of the system, its growth has been predicated on working closely with local and state government, becoming dependent on foundations and public funds."[33]

The discipline of Asian American Studies is now over thirty years old and can claim national conferences, fields of specialty, and advanced degrees; but in 1968 there were no classes, no instructors, no curriculum, no textbooks. While the discipline has now become its own academic complex, presided over by, and churning out, PhDs, it began as a DIY project that was initiated and implemented by students who had no infrastructure, no budget, and no power in the university system.

Psychologist Chalsa Loo noted that Asian American Studies was born not in infancy but in adolescence—a time of fierce independence and rebelliousness against authority and conservatism. "The field of ethnic studies symbolized a rebellion against the traditional, unidimensional, minority-negating perspective of Western-based history and experience."[34] As others have also done, Loo pointed out that the field's acceptance—and survival—within the academy required a curtailing of its inaugural revolutionary spirit, resulting in Asian American Studies having to "assimilate" into the white-dominant values and traditions of the ivory tower. Students now are more caught up in theory than practice. Pioneering filmmaker and teacher Spencer Nakasako challenged:

Now there's people of color everywhere, in all walks of life, even in high places, but is this a good thing? You have to ask, for what and for whose benefit? At UCLA, for example, there are dozens of Asian American organizations, but is this progress? They're still doing the equivalent of Miss Chinatowns. Asian American Studies is now more professional and institutional than community-based. They [professional Asian Americanists] have become like who they replaced, and the irony is they relate better to today's students than we do.

Activist-scholar Glenn Omatsu wrote that, in the mid 1990s, he sat in on an Asian American Studies class. Although the lecture on the period between the late 1950s and early 1970s was cogent, tightly organized, and even well received by the students, "there was only one problem: the reinterpretation was wrong on every aspect."[35] Omatsu went on to explain that, contrary to what the instructor claimed, the leading influence had been not MLK but Malcolm X; the movement had not been centered on racial identity, but embraced fundamental questions of oppression and power; the main thrust had not been to seek legitimacy and representation within American society, but to pursue the larger goal of liberation.

Theodore L. Gross, dean of humanities at the City College of New York during the college's open admissions policy in the mid 1970s, stated:

The creation of ethnic studies departments at the City College and throughout the nation represented an educational capitulation to extreme political pressure by minority groups … Each ethnic group raises its own consciousness at the expense of general education.[36]

But relevant education could not have been accomplished any other way. Following in the footsteps of the Little Rock Nine, who dared to integrate Central High School in 1957; of the four North Carolina Agricultural and Technical College freshmen who had the gall to sit at a Woolworth's lunch counter in Greensboro in 1960; and of the 15,000 Chicano/a high school students who walked out for better education in East Los Angeles in 1968, Asian American student activists became part of the larger student movement of the Sixties, which in turn was part of an overarching movement for social change and self-definition.

In opposition to Theodore Gross's view that the rise of ethnic studies represented an unfortunate surrender to political force that compromised the quality of education, Gary Okihiro argued that the academy's opposition to the strike's demands was not a product of pedagogical concerns that community relevance or affirmative action would compromise standards of teaching or scholarship. "Rather," he said, "the conflict was over power—continued hegemony or liberation."[37]

### Lessons?

Mao Zedong's dictum on criticism instructed that we should "learn from past mistakes to avoid future ones." Certainly this is true. And yet we know that past mistakes do not always prevent future ones.

The redress-and-reparations campaign of the 1980s that sought restitution for the wrongful incarceration of 120,000 Japanese Americans during World War II was not driven by the redemptive quality of an official apology, nor by the nominal monetary compensation that might accompany it, but in the hope that both would reinforce the lesson that it should not happen again, that the government—the country—would learn from its mistake. Then, after September 11, 2001, the racial profiling and hysteria that ran amok after December 7, 1941, prevailed again.

Appalled, Asian Americans and in particular Japanese Americans who had been targeted during World War II were among the first to speak up on behalf of beleaguered Muslims, South Asians, Sikhs, and anyone else who now looked like the enemy. While Chairman Mao emphasized the dialectical unity of knowing and doing, knowing usually isn't the problem; it's the doing that gets us every time.

In hindsight, Fay Chiang offered another version of Mao's maxim to learn from past mistakes when she said, "We learned by making mistakes." Mike Murase concurred, "We floundered and blundered. We stumbled and grumbled. We screwed up many times." Yet, he reminded us, "Despite it all, we had an impact."

TEN

Generations to Come

> *What is important is that the action took*
> *place … If it took place, it can happen*
> *again.*
>
> Jean-Paul Sartre

*P*uckyoo sunn-obbaa-bit, muderrpuckkerrrrr!!*[1] Those were the
first words we uttered when we found our voice. After growing
up alien in a black-and-white world, we founded the home/land
we never had and gave birth to ourselves as Asian Americans—a political identity based in the alternative universe of the Third World. As part
of the worldwide revolution, we said *puckyooo* to racism, to imperialism,
to assimilation, to white standards, to a failed democracy, to our own
internalized boundaries and barriers, to everything that had kept us distanced from the sovereignty of our communal selves. And with this new
voice we created a new world. With the power of new consciousness
and new language, and ample doses of audacity as well as naiveté, we
created a new sense of community and culture with few resources and no
experience—because until then we had nothing to lose.

As scholar and activist L. Ling Chi Wang noted, the Asian American
movement of the 1960s and 1970s was the turning point in our history
in this country. It marked the end of our being sidelined as "Orientals"
and the emergence of a homeland we called Asian America. It was a
time, as Ron Chew remarked, "of fierce idealism, radical politics, and
boundless optimism."[2]

As central as the Asian American movement has been to both our history as well as our individual lives, it has scarcely been acknowledged in the canon of US history and culture. Residing outside the power structure that determines what becomes official history, Asian Americans and other disenfranchised groups have always relied on oral histories to recover and reconstruct our collective pasts against the hegemony of dominant narratives. In that tradition, to help fill these gaps as well as to help me better understand how and why I had been so transformed, I turned to those who were among the first to find the oppressor out and become involved in the struggle for their—which was our—liberation. Their stories are the mainstay of this book.

### Collective Memory, the Politics of Nostalgia, and the Making of Asian America

Not that memories are always accurate depictions of what has transpired. The past is not fixed, and memories are not videotaped archives that can be retrieved from the hard drives of our lives. All memory is reconstructed, and we infuse our memories with meaning. Like the parable of the blind men each describing the elephant differently depending on whether they were feeling its long trunk, its broad side, or its thin tail, there are conflicting memories, analyses and conclusions about the making of Asian America. There is no single correct interpretation, just as there was no single correct political line because, as Winifred Breines said of the New Left, "no unified center could have represented the multiplicity and variety of perspectives and activities."[3]

From this multiplicity and variety emerged the take-home messages that constitute the legacy of the Asian American movement: that Asian Americans were not born but made; that, even as silence was a strategy of self-preservation in the face of abject racism for our grandparents, for us it was a recipe for erasure; that, while there is now a plethora of Asian Pacific American organizations and institutions, nothing was handed to us—we had to fight to create what is now taken for granted, and we did so on the shoulders of generations before us, whether we knew it or not; that, despite sincere beliefs in various political lines, there were no magic bullets; that, despite criticism by contemporary Asian American scholars regarding the cultural nationalism of the movement, as social bandit-turned-state assembly person George Nakano said, given the times "it was the only thing you could fall back on in order to maintain your self-dignity and pride"; that, despite the many frustrations and setbacks, mistakes and misunderstandings, making Asian America was probably when we felt most alive. It is no wonder we feel downright nostalgic; there is much to be nostalgic about.

When I interviewed Chris Iijima about his extensive experience in the movement, he began by declaring, "I hate this nostalgia stuff!" Simultaneously refusing and expressing nostalgia, he proceeded to reminisce for over three passionate hours.

Despite its reputation as overly sentimental, as political scientist Kimberly K. Smith argued, nostalgia is "a weapon in the debate over whose memories count and what kinds of desires and harms are politically correct." Since minoritized viewpoints are too often discarded as merely anecdotal rather than of value, Smith maintained that nostalgia has the capacity to "counter historical narratives that misrepresent the experiences of oppressed groups."[4]

Derived from the Greek *nostos* ("homecoming") and *algos* ("pain"), nostalgia was originally considered a medical disease afflicting people living, working, or fighting in foreign countries. Nostalgia was literally a case of homesickness—a condition, I suspect, that led to the making of Asian America in the first place. Continually asked where we came from and told to go back to wherever that was, Americans of Asian descent yearned for a place to which we belonged. When many of our parents and grandparents immigrated to the United States in the late 1800s and early 1900s, they embraced the United States as their home, although they were not allowed to become naturalized citizens until half a century later. They lived out their lives here while no doubt homesick for their home country.

By the time we came along, two, three, four, and even five generations later—many of us never even having visited our so-called motherland, and being treated as foreigners in the country of our birth—we too became homesick for a place to call home. So, during the cultural revolution of the Long Sixties, when anything seemed possible, fed up with the long history—as well as day-to-day reality—of white supremacy, we were pushed by the atrocities of the Vietnam War, pulled by the inspiration of the Black Liberation movement, and bolstered by the proposition of Third World solidarity to take it upon ourselves to found the homeland we had never had.

## Careers, Personalities, and Pleasures of Asian American Activism

In periodizing the 1960s, Frederic Jameson concluded twenty years later that the sense of freedom and possibility of the period had been "a momentary reality," and in hindsight "a historical illusion."[5] If the Asian American movement has outlived its momentary reality, and yet is not a mere historical illusion, more than the institutions that it gave rise to, its greatest impact has been the metamorphosis, both personal and political, of its innumerable participants. Studies of social movement participants show that, despite the demise of organizations and long after the movements themselves have subsided, individuals continue to be involved in a variety of social changes over several decades, making personal and political decisions in light of their identity as activists.[6] During the low points of protest cycles, they act as keepers of the flame, nourish the traditions of activism, and nurture new generations of activists. The majority of individuals featured in this book have done just that. They have embodied, in James M. Jasper's words, careers of protest, personalities of protestors, and pleasures of protest.[7]

### Careers of protest

Ron Chew, who wrote that his slain friends Gene Viernes and Silme Domingo were "trailblazers in a generation that yielded many pioneers,"[8] was himself a trailblazer and pioneer. He started his career of activism in 1972 when he filed a discrimination complaint that became a highly charged public controversy. A child of Seattle's Chinatown–International District, he worked as a busboy from the age of thirteen throughout college, in the same restaurant in which his father had been a waiter for some thirty years. Ron was fascinated by the stories he heard working in the restaurant, which whetted his interest in oral history and journalism. He attended the University of Washington, majored in communications, and wrote prolifically for the school newspaper, often helping his colleagues edit their work. When Ron applied for the position of news editor, despite his extensive experience—and despite being the only one who applied for the job—he didn't even get an interview. Instead, the editor gave the job to his handpicked recruit, a white person with far fewer credentials and experience.

Feeling that he was well qualified and had been treated unfairly, Ron filed a discrimination complaint, which was found in his favor. In the meantime, however, his case had become a highly controversial public issue when a professor in the communications department, brandishing the First Amendment, claimed that the right of journalism to operate unfettered was being attacked. Despite the broad show of support Ron received from the Native American, black, and women's journalists' organizations—as well as the Society of Professional Journalists—the publications board determined Ron's complaint invalid on the grounds that it represented an intrusion from an outside party (the university) into the realm of journalism. The university negotiated a settlement that included back pay and the creation of an affirmative-action plan, as well as revising hiring and firing policies; yet when the mainstream press billed the story as a dispute between "freedom of the press" and "affirmative action," Ron was widely branded a troublemaker. The final blow came when Ron was declined the reporting hours that he needed for his degree because he had earned them working for the *International Examiner*, which, as a community newspaper, was not considered a legitimate news outlet.

With his journalism career mired in protest, Ron turned it into a lifelong career of community activism, going on to become the editor of the *International Examiner*, the executive director of the Wing Luke Asian Museum and, at the time of writing, the executive director of the International Community Health Services Foundation, all the while playing a key role in a number of labor and social justice organizations, including the Alaska Cannery Workers Association, the International District Economic Association, Seattle Rape Relief, and the Organization of Chinese Americans. Thirty years after filing his complaint, due to the inquiry of a prominent community member, the

University of Washington belatedly gave Ron his degree and a formal apology. A year later, Ron was asked to give the commencement speech for the very school that had denied him his degree and a career in mainstream journalism.

Ron is just one example of the many who have parlayed the activism of their youth into a lifetime career of community service and working for social justice. David Monkawa, the artist who no longer wanted to "just do *Gidra*" but instead be a soldier on the front lines, has been a career warrior in many battles between, as he says, "the few haves and the many have-nots," operating from the inside as a worker and from the outside as a union official. During the recession of the early 2000s, almost forty years into his long career as an activist, David experienced what he called a "second politicization":

> Before it was just me that was feeling oppressed, if you will. But now I see it in my kids, and it's much worse than when I was young. It's given me a second wind, so now I'm just as pissed as I ever was about the system and I want to change it. I'm going to be retiring in sixteen months, so then I'll have time—that's what I'm going to be doing full-time.

David was a member of the East Wind Collective, a founding member of the National Coalition for Redress and Reparations, and an organizer for the Teamsters for more than a decade. He recently retired as an organizer for the California Nurses Association.

Nancy Hom forsook a promising career as a conceptual artist to become a community-based artist, and eventually the executive director of Kearny Street Workshop (KSW). She was born in China and was part of the mass exodus to Hong Kong in the 1950s: "When I saw the beginning scene of the *Joy Luck Club* I started to cry uncontrollably for seemingly no reason. Later I realized that my experience must have been like that."

At KSW, Nancy deliberately orchestrated a multiyear plan to turn over the reins to the next generation of artists and administrators. Being one of only two part-time paid staff at the time, Nancy wanted to grow the organization but found that most young people tended to come and go. So Nancy came up with a program that would be run by young people themselves, basically telling new recruits, "You guys take charge. You decide what issues are important to you, and I'll be right behind you. I'll provide whatever training or mentorship you need, or find the people who can."

The first year, Nancy sat in on all the meetings and was there to help when needed. The second year, her young assistant was more hands-on, and Nancy stayed in the background. By the third year, Nancy says, "they managed it themselves with a little oversight from the office. The theory behind this is that if you give people ownership where they really feel like their opinions matter and they're not just volunteering for you, they'll stay." And they did. Founded in 1972, KSW is now the oldest Asian Pacific American multidisciplinary arts organization in the country. Having stepped down as director, Nancy has carried on her career of service to the community in the area of arts management and exhibitions and remains a prolific artist whose work has been exhibited around the United States and internationally.

## Personalities of protest

Early signs of leadership were evident in the significant number of activists who had held student body or student club offices while they were in high school. Peggy Saika lost the first several times she ran for office at her all-white high school in Sacramento. When I asked if that didn't discourage her, she replied that it was probably just a "personality thing … I'd think, 'Oh, this is so sad, nobody wants to vote for me.' But then I would just start thinking, 'Okay, what else can I do?'"

In addition to conventional areas like organizational leadership, others showed personality traits of determination, and downright daring, that were manifested in a variety of nervy ways.

When Steve Louie—the Presbyterian minister's son who refused to turn the other cheek when he literally had to fight his way through school—was in the seventh grade, unbeknownst to his minister father, Steve made a surprise appearance before a session of their church and renounced his membership. This, of course, caused a big uproar. Steve says that his mother cried for three days but that his father, who sat through Steve's bombshell of a presentation, said, "He's thought it through. I don't agree with his arguments, but this is his decision." Being the son of a minister and having grown up as a gold-star pupil at Sunday school, Steve knew his Christianity. "But then I really started thinking about it. I had done my homework, researching atheists' and agnostics' reasons for not believing in God. I quoted St. Thomas Aquinas and all these other folks. I felt to be consistent with myself I had to go through with this."

When I asked Steve if he has ever regretted this decision, he replied, "No, never." His siblings did, however. "They thought I was crazy. They said, 'You're bringing more trouble on yourself and you're making trouble for us.' … That was actually my first experience with being out in front of something and fighting for what you believed in." Two years later, when Steve watched the Civil Rights movement unfold on television, he remembers thinking to himself, "Yes! These people are fighting back! This is what I need to be doing"—wishing he was old enough to go to the South to join the protest.

In 1965, when Watts went up in flames, his father urgently tried to set up liaisons between white churches and black churches in the area. Steve recalled, "He really felt the church had a role to play." Eventually, Reverend Louie too decided to leave the church because, as Steve said, "he felt the church was too conservative." After fifteen years as a minister, Reverend Louie went to work at the Los Angeles County Human Relations Commission as Paul Louie, where he worked for another fifteen years until he retired.

Over 2,000 miles away, after having grown up in Appalachia where his father taught in the small town of Berea, Kentucky, and attending an elite prep school in Massachusetts where he received his first lessons in classism, Rocky Chin attended Lehigh University in Bethlehem, Pennsylvania—still one of the few Asians for miles around. If that wasn't enough, at this fairly conservative university in the mid 1960s Rocky took on the heralded tradition of fraternities, blasting the system for being racist and sexist. His essay was published, of all places, in the alumni journal. Shortly after its publication, along with other student leaders, Rocky was invited to a social event where students met alumni. "And those alumni hated me!" Rocky recalled. "They actually came up to me and said, 'How dare you write such a thing!'" Rocky went on to earn a master's degree in city planning and a law degree. He has been active in labor and community rights, as well as civil rights, ever since.

## Pleasures of Protest

In the midst of the demonstrations and demands, alongside the anger and the angst, there was a lot of gratification, pride, and downright fun. Bea Tam, who began as a volunteer at the Chinatown Cooperative Garment Factory, ended up working in the garment industry for the next five years and was one of the supporters who was arrested with the Jung Sai workers. She wrote about the camaraderie among the women and their high spirits.: "To our increasing admiration, the Jung Sai women went to jail in the paddy wagon, singing and chanting all the way through booking, fingerprinting and being locked behind bars." When Bea married fellow activist Harvey Dong in between picketing, she

> bought a new dress and we went down to City Hall for the ceremony. Immediately after, my husband and I ran back to join the picket line again. The Jung Sai workers congratulated us and then teased me mercilessly. To my embarrassment, I had bought a scab dress from Macy's in my hurry to get a wedding outfit. The strikers immediately recognized it as one of the styles they had sewn.[9]

Norman Jayo is a poet and musician who was part of the Kearny Street Workshop in San Francisco; she cannot help but speak in poems. With fellow musician and radio producer Tarabu Betserai, he broadcasted directly from the I-Hotel on the night of the eviction.[10] Speaking of the I-Hotel struggle, Norman recalls:

> People sang, did poetry, talked, and fought because it was being threatened. And what was being threatened? The wood, the bricks? No, it was the bond that people have when they express themselves. And it wasn't just saying no to the eviction, it was saying, "Yes to, oh man, I hear what you're doing, that's really—wow! I'm moved by the way you do that poem. Oh wow, do that again. Let's drink some wine, and laugh, and love, and create, and say, 'Wow.'"[11]

Bob Santos has been called "the Asian American community's elder statesman and enduring rabble-rouser,"[12] "an advisor, mentor, confidante, and drinking buddy for a generation of our community's Jedi Knights,"[13] and "a hero in an urban hamlet called the International District"[14] for his lifetime career of activism in Seattle. He started his career as a fringe activist until he got busted. "After the first couple of times, I said, Shit, I might as well go full force."

In 1968 he became assistant manager of the St. Peter Claver Center. Because it had a kitchen he was approached by Aaron and Elmer Dixon to open up a Black Panther breakfast program there:

> I was new, I didn't know what was going on, so I looked around and said, "It's okay by me." Then the archdiocese said, "Bob, we're not seeing any rent money coming in from them." So I go to Elmer and Aaron, and they're each about ten feet tall and I'm looking up at them, and I say, "Uh, good work, guys." And I go back to the archdiocese and report, "They're doing the Lord's work."

When one of the sisters told him young Indian kids were starting to smoke the sage, he replied, "It's okay, as long as they don't inhale."

Bob collaborated regularly with Bernie Whitebear of the United Indians of All Tribes, Roberto Maestas from El Centro De la Raza, and Larry Gossett, one of the founders, with the Dixon brothers, of the Seattle chapter of the Black Panthers, who later became a councilperson. They became known as the Gang of Four. Bob recalls, "We would bring each other's forces to each other's demonstrations. When the press saw this they thought, wow, two hundred people here, two hundred people there, this movement is really growing. But it was the same two hundred people! It was us!" After each campaign Bob told me about—like the time they shut down several flights out of Seattle-Tacoma Airport to protest the nonhiring of minority construction workers—he would routinely conclude the story with, "And that was fun."

Chris Iijima, our beloved griot and astute activist, was terminally ill when I interviewed him about his experiences in the Asian American movement. I had been talking to him about this project, and when he took a turn for the worse, my husband, son, and I flew to Honolulu, where he lived, to interview him on videotape, knowing he might be too weak to talk for long, or at all. Instead, he talked nonstop for hours.[15] Just as we were about to wrap, he suddenly said:

> I know what I want to say. Can I say one more thing? I think what gets lost is that, in the midst of all of this, it was a tremendous amount of fun! When your life is changing, when things are alive and vibrating and popping all over the place, being a part of that is just fun! Part of the reason people were attracted to the movement may not have been the politics, but it's where it was happening. It was where the party was! It was a blast! And I think that's what we never talk about—what a great amount of fun it was! That gets lost sometimes, and we have to remember that.

### The Long View: Recovering the Past, Negotiating the Present

While in the moment, revolution seemed just around the corner. Yet real social change is a long-term, protracted struggle that begins in the past and extends into the future. It's a continuum that requires an historical sense and provides not only shoulders upon which to stand but also the knowledge that although history repeats itself, we cannot rely on political solutions of the past.

### Recovering the past

Historical recovery was one of the major themes of the Asian American movement. Like so much else in those days, it began as a do it yourself project that had no handbooks, textbooks, maps, or curricula. Although not as grand as fighting the evil twins of racism and imperialism, it was nonetheless one of the movement's primary ventures that has left a tangible legacy. Recovering history was not just an intellectual pursuit, it was critical for political longevity. Without an historical understanding, every generation of activists thinks it is the first. We did. We had no idea of the legacy and long history of Asian American resistance.

We did not realize that early Asians in America had already put our thoughts into words. Between 1910 and 1940, the Angel Island

Immigration Station was essentially a detention center obstructing the entry of Chinese and Japanese into the United States. Confined there for months, our soon-to-be grandparents and great-grandparents carved and ink-brushed more than 135 poems on the walls that bear witness to their plight. As if directing us to redress their abuse, one reads:

> Dare to conquer America
> and avenge past wrongs.[16]

In 1938, Happy Lim, who helped organize the Chinese Workers Mutual Aid Association in San Francisco's Chinatown, wrote a poem titled "Song of the Chinese Workers," in which he declared:

> We are already a people with consciousness and organization,
> we've already learned how to live, how to struggle, to unite for
> survival,
> from today on, we are no longer docile slaves,
> we will unite with American workers to build a link that is
> inseparable![17]

In the 1940s, from within one of America's World War II concentration camps for Japanese Americans, Kikyo Sanada, an Issei woman, wrote:

> Enduring
> and still enduring
> the color of my skin.[18]

And Carlos Bulosan wrote, in *America Is in the Heart*:

> The old world is dying, but a new world is being born.
> It generates inspiration from the chaos that beats upon us all.[19]

As we recovered our history, our ancestors told us we were not, and never have been, the complacent minority. Beginning in 1905, Japanese sugar plantation workers in Hawai'i repeatedly struck for better conditions and pay. As early as 1914, the Chinese Socialist Club was formed in San

Francisco. Throughout the 1930s, Filipino American farmworkers and cannery workers along the West Coast organized major labor struggles, and in the same decade there were nearly 200 Japanese Americans in the Communist Party USA—a higher proportion (1 in 650) than in the United States as a whole (1 in 5,000).[20] In the early 1940s, Kazu Iijima, cofounder of Triple A, was a board member of the Japanese American Committee for Democracy, an anti-fascist civil rights organization in New York City, of which Pearl Buck, Carey McWilliams, and Adam Clayton Powell were advisory committee members. During World War II, four Niseis took the matter of the undemocratic practices against Japanese Americans all the way to the Supreme Court; feeling betrayed by their native country, Nisei draft resisters said they would go to war if and when their rights as citizens were restored; and the Women's Federation of Amache voiced its "demands and dissatisfactions" to the camp administrators, presenting issues that "men councilmen think superfluous."[21]

## Negotiating the present

On the long road of social change, sometimes you take one step forward, only to go back two steps. As Bernardine Dorhn commented, "The Sixties began in 1954 and they're not over yet."

On June 25, 2012, an editorial in the *Los Angeles Times* declared, "It's official! A new study by the Pew Research Center proves the old trope true: Asians are the new Jews."[22] Reprising the model minority myth we had tried to get rid of during the Long Sixties, the Pew Report concluded that Asian Americans were the wealthiest, best-educated, fastest-growing, hardest-working, most assimilated, most career-oriented, most out-marrying, and most "satisfied" racial group in the United States.

On August 20, 2012, one of the biggest badasses of the Asian American movement was accused of being a snitch for the FBI. The suspect, Black Panther and Third World Liberation Front strike leader Richard Aoki, had died three years earlier, so he could not respond to the allegation or the avalanche of questions. As Belvin Louie and Miriam Ching Yoon Louie, comrades of Richards on the frontline of the Third World Liberation Front strike, exclaimed, "Damn it, Richard, what the f***?!"[23]

On December 15, 2013, the tweet "Nobody will GIVE us a space. We need to MAKE a space to use our voices, build community and be heard" launched the hashtag #NotYourAsianSidekick, calling for a global discussion of "Asian American feminism, stereotypes, myths and more." The tweet attracted the attention of mainstream news outlets around the world that never gave Sixties activists the time of day. Inspired by the rejuvenation of youthful engagement powered by hashtag activism but reflecting the exasperation of a generation who lament that young people are estranged from their political heritage, founding critical race theorist Mari Matsuda tweeted back, "We theorized #NotYourAsianSidekick ideas since the 70s but kids gotta learn it from a damn hashtag. Still no as am studies at most U's."

News reports like these make the as yet short 2010s sound like the Long Sixties, reminding us that, despite the achievements of the Asian American movement, it's not over yet. The Pew Report touting the model minority theme, which resurrects itself like a remake of a bad movie, shows how the United States is plagued by a bad, maybe terminal, case of historical amnesia. Outraged by this remix of a worn-out tune, more than thirty Asian Pacific Island organizations issued statements criticizing the Pew Report's biases, incomplete analyses, misleading interpretations, and imprecise conclusions.

In 2012, when journalist Seth Rosenfeld, obtained FBI files through the Freedom of Information Act and made the accusation that Richard Aoki had been an FBI informant, Asian American activists, hard-bitten by FBI duplicity throughout the Long Sixties, reacted to the revelation with suspicion and outright denial. Miriam and Belvin Louie, after conducting their own study of the available evidence, wrote that they "had to accept the fact that our friend had worked as an FBI informant over a span of some sixteen years," and added, "we believe our movements unknowingly flipped him in the late Sixties."[24]

The tweet that vented a need for a space to deliberate concerns we had grappled with forty years ago was apparently newsworthy enough to have gone viral in less than twenty-four hours, attracting mainstream media attention around the world. But, to those of us who had made such a space in the Long Sixties—or so we thought—it was déjà vu.

Tremors such as these shake up neat nostalgias of the past. Spencer

Nakasako challenged, "So was Richard a hero or a rat? Why can't he be both?" To Spencer, the bottom line was the work that you did. Leery of supermen and partial to underdogs, Spencer makes award-winning films whose subjects are drawn from the margins and are both good and bad. About the legacy of the Asian American movement, he advised: "Young people should realize it wasn't about being a hero but working hard for a common cause. In the day there was no work beneath us. We were used to working hard because our parents were, like, gardeners. We got things done because we just jumped in—often leaping before we looked. Naiveté is a great thing. Young people now are more hesitant. They're wary of drinking the Kool-Aid, because the stakes are higher."

From her vantage point, after over seventy years of activism, Grace Lee Boggs remarked:

Most Americans have a very short-range idea of history. They don't realize there's been a huge evolution of culture and paradigm shifts in everything … and it is this lack of the long-range view that can make you think that, when change happens, when you see ruins and disintegration, you see collapses, it's the end of life."[25]

© Karen L. Ishizuka

Fig. 10.1: Grace Lee Boggs with youth activists,
June 15, 2013, Los Angeles

If the content hasn't changed much, the context has, and the form of response must adjust accordingly. Although each generation of activists will ultimately make its own mistakes, we would be remiss in fulfilling our generation's mission if we did not try to prevent what Diane Fujino calls "intergenerational discontinuity"—the disruption of information between generations.[26]

Even in the moment, we understood that. In 1974 Mike Murase wrote that along with the expansion of consciousness and possibilities comes an enlarged responsibility, "the responsibility of preserving the movement's past, its sequence of ideas, its different experiences, its changing spirit."[27] Going into the twenty-first century, Harvey Dong stated, "We have looked into the past not out of nostalgia but because remembering it can provide a vision for the future. In many ways, the struggle for control over the past has been a struggle for the future."[28]

## Toward a Radical Nostalgia

Building on the traditional Marxist concept of dialectical materialism that declared "It is not the consciousness of men that determines their existence, but their social existence that determines their consciousness,"[29] Grace Lee Boggs and her husband Jimmy promoted "dialectical humanism." At an Asian American conference in 1973, in the closing speech titled "Asian Americans and the US Movement," Grace stated that fixed Marxist dialectics were no longer effective in the contemporary context and advocated "the revolutionary transformation not only of social institutions but of oneself."[30]

Nearly forty years later, she reiterated this point: "In order to change/transform the world, you must change/transform yourself."[31] Veteran scholar, activist, and mentor Glenn Omatsu added, "Otherwise, greater political awareness promotes an attitude of arrogance marked by impatience and disdain for others and a belief that political change can be created and managed by an elite."[32] Rather, Omatsu maintained that political consciousness did not arise from study groups but from "involving people in the process of social change—through their confronting the institutions of power around them and creating new visions of community life based on these struggles."[33]

Projects of history and memory are haunted by the specter of nostalgia. Connected to loss and estrangement—ontological homelessness—nostalgia is endemic in capitalistic society, a collective rather than individual phenomenon. The dialectic, however, is that in the sense of loss over the past lives the promise of hope for the future. Using the battle of Wounded Knee as an example, investigative reporter Jim Hougan argued that a radical nostalgia does not merely mourn the loss of old values and ways but takes action to have those values and ways reinstated.[34] Anthropologist Maureen McKnight similarly argued that a critical nostalgia can recast the inequities of the past as fuel for the pursuit of justice in the present and future, quoting Frederick Douglas: "The colored people in this country are bound to keep the past in lively memory til justice shall be done them."[35]

The Asian America of the late 1960s and early 1970s no longer exists. Nor should it. Young Asian Pacific Islanders activists now are more naturally pan–Asian Pacific than our generation ever was, being more comfortable in their yellow-brown skins. They take greater ownership of the world around them than we ever dared, most likely a result of having grown up in an Asian America that we helped create. And they are, as we were, fortified by generations of activists whether they know it or not. As for me, I rest in the summation of our poets who, as Russell Leong said, can "nail down the times," and, as Audre Lorde claimed, lay the "foundation for a future of change, a bridge across our fears of what has never been before." When the Asian American movement was winding down in 1976, poet Lawson Inada proclaimed that "whatever anyone may say about 'The Movement,' our work is tangible proof of our accomplishments, of who we are, of who we've been all along, and transcends all of the ignorance and garbage, even our own."[36] Our cherished Al Robles murmured, "Ah Pilipinos, if you only knew how brown you are." The unknown poet of Angel Island challenged: "Dare to conquer America, and avenge past wrongs."

We were the generation for whom the Long Sixties—a time of unrestrained possibilities—was our initiation into adulthood. In that explosion of human capacities, we aspired to make the world a better place. Seeking an understanding of how the political project of Asian America came into being does not imply a desire to resurrect it, but rather to build upon it. Every generation must create its own nostalgia worth remembering.

## Acknowledgments

Acknowledgments is a wily genre. In the world of community-based film where I've resided, for example, the end credits often seem longer than the film itself. The "Thanks to" section typically incorporates everyone who contributed to the making of the film including family and friends who both put up with and nourished you during the extended process—not facile tasks and not merely gratuitous recognition. Then there's the "Special thanks to" portion to somehow highlight those without whose participation and input the project could not have been completed. Never included is a "No thanks to" credit roll to acknowledge those who were a pain in the ass and thereby made you work harder or maybe even better; these contributors, however few or many, are never acknowledged.

The list is long and incomplete. And there are numerous people who played multiple roles and should be thanked repeatedly. We would be here forever. Especially when you're connected vertically through generations and laterally to all sentient beings, it's downright tough and essentially awkward to write an adequate (forget about eloquent) acknowledgment. Even if you generally manage to steer clear of the heedless adverb, in your last-gasp effort to express your profound gratitude, you are wont to splatter superlatives, which in the end, sabotages sincerity.

Having laboriously written and mercifully discarded most of them, with profound apology for inevitable omissions, and as inadequate as it is, I offer the following guileless credit roll, counting on you to appreciate that each name represents a pillar of information, insight, support, and generosity that cannot sufficiently be expressed.

Thanks first and foremost to:

All the builders and architects of Asian America in the Long Sixties who shared the experiences and emotions that informed this book and gave it life, giving me the pleasure and privilege of their time, expertise, emotions, inspiration, camaraderie, and criticism as well as life-saving transportation, housing, meals, bad jokes, and good karma: Chris Aihara, Doug Aihara, Tomie Arai, May Chen, Laureen Chew, Ron Chew, Fay Chiang, Charlie Chin, Rocky Chin, Curtis Choy, Dale Davis, Dorothy Cordova, Emil De Guzman, Stephan Doi, Harvey Dong, Hilma Fujimoto, Richard Fung, Jeff Furumura, Warren Furutani, Estella Habal, Larry Hama, Phil Hayasaka, Lois Hayasaka, Aiko Herzig, Alex Hing, Lane Hirabayashi, Ron Hirano, Tats Hirano, Arnold Hiura, Eloise Hiura, Nancy Hom, Bob Hsiang, Arlan Huang, Florante Ibanez, Chris Iijima, Kazu Iijima, Darcie Iki, Lawson Inada, Frank Irigon, Bruce Iwasaki, Glen Iwasaki, Norman Jayo, Lloyd Kajikawa, Don Kao, John Kao, Mary Kao, Dennis Kobata, Audee Kochiyama-Holman, Eddie Kochiyama, Yuri Kochiyama, Alan Kondo, Masao Kodani, Duane Kubo, Dan Kuramoto, June Kuramoto, Corky Lee, Marlene Lee, Russell Leong, Willon Lew, Paul Liem, Adna Louie, Belvin Louie, Miriam Ching Louie, Steve Louie, Sharon Maeda, Sandy Maeshiro, Mark Masaoka, Kathy Masaoka, Mari Matsuda, Jim Matsuoka, Dale Minami, Janice Mirikitani, Nobuko Miyamoto, Ron Miyamura, David Monkawa, Walter Morita, Mike Murase, Nick Nagatani, Norman Nakamura, Robert A. Nakamura, Don Nakanishi, Spencer Nakasako, Ronnie Nakashima, Penny Nakatsu, Mike Nakayama, Phil Nash, Mo Nishida, Alan Nishio, Franklin Odo, Alan Ohashi, Alan Okada, Tracy Okida, Glenn Omatsu, Alan Ota, Peggy Saika, Bob Santos, Victor Shibata, Al Sugiyama, Rene Tajima-Peña, Janice Tanaka, Ray Tasaki, Alan Takemoto, Jack Tchen, Russell Valparaiso, Eddie Wong, Paul Takagi, Tani Tagaki, Dean Toji, Rene Tajima, Pete Yamamoto, Mia Yamamoto, Qris Yamashita, Takashi Yanagida, Mike Yanagita, Evelyn Yoshimura, Liz Young, Eddie Wong, Legan Wong, and Helen Zia.

Very special thanks to my very smart and incisive editor Andrew Hsaio and all the good folks at Verso Press. Andy's acumen and "massaging," as he puts it, functioned as a magic camera filter that smoothed out the wrinkles and as many imperfections as he could, casting my words in the best light possible. Very special thanks to the very busy and ever brilliant Jeff Chang for taking the time to capture the gestalt of the book in his succinct foreword. I just hope people read beyond it, although I couldn't blame them if they didn't. Much gratitude to Maurine Knighton and the Nathan Cummings Foundation for believing in the idea and promise of the project enough to support my research. I hope it was worth it. Special aloha to the spirit and very realness of my New York *onesans* (older sisters)—Kazu Iijima, Yuri Kochiyama, Michi Weglyn and Aiko Herzig-Yoshinaga—who nurtured a generation to strive to follow their example. You molded a movement. To my brothers Chris Iijima and Victor Shibata for their valued input and inspiration both during their lives and after their deaths. And Louie C. Green, my first brother, who made me see. I miss you guys.

Much appreciation to my much-loved family, friends and colleagues: Katja Antoine, Nancy Araki, Tarabu Betserai, Claudine Brown, Art Chen, Kori Chen, Jane Dickson Iijima, Tom Drysdale, Donna Ebata, John Esaki, Jun and Toshiko Fukushima, Diane Fujino, Lisa Furutani, Neil Gotanda, Sondra Hale, Clement Hanami, Dean Hayasaka, June Hibino, Keiko Higa, Lynne Iijima, Kathy Ishizuka, Janet Ito, Nori Ito, Miya Iwataki, Kenwood Jung, Audrey Kaneko, Akemi Kikumura, Helen Kim, Jimmy Kochiyama, Tommy Kochiyama, Mayumi Kodani, Chris Komai, Shiz Komatsu, Ford Kuramoto, Chuck Lawrence, Margie Lee, Janice Liao, Robert and Jeanie McNamara, Yoko Miyagawa, Wendy Mori, Johnny Mori, Paige Morikawa, Carrie Morita, Janice Nabara, Don Nakanishi, Erich Nakano, Wendy Nagatani, Henry Nishi, Yvonne Nishio, Gary Okihiro, Ets Okura, Tee Okura, Russell Robles, Susan Slyomovics, Supachai Surongsain, Scarlett Sy, Mariko Tamanoi, Ron Tham, Barbara Taniguchi, Suzanne and Bob Toji, Rene' Tomita, Michael Truong, Mayumi Tsutakawa, Roberta Uno, Gary Uyekawa, Bill Watanabe, and Edith and Ken Yamamoto for valued assistance, insight, sustenance, ears and eyes, warnings, reinforcement, rescue, food, shelter and good cheer.

And especially to my children Thai Binh Etsuko Ishizuka Capp Checel and Tadashi Harukichi Nakamura who have been my personal cheerleaders and raison d'etre; daughter-in-law Cindy Sangalang for fathoming the maelstrom of graduate school in overlapping years, and grandchildren Mina Loy Akira Checel and Gus Ishizuka Checel, my safe havens of respite and rejuvenation.

Lastly, and most extensively, to Bob Nakamura who used to say he married me to produce his films. Little did he know that later the tables would be turned.

# Illustrations Credits

Fig. 1.1. Demographics of Japanese, Chinese and Filipinos in the United States using 1970 census figures. *Gidra* 4: 3 (March 1972)

Fig. 3.1. *Los Angeles Free Press*, October 31–November 6, 1969

Fig. 3.2. Royal Morales in front of SIPA office, Los Angeles, c. 1970. Photo courtesy of Visual Communications.

Fig. 3.3. Warren Furutani with representatives of the Republic of New Afrika and El Comite speaking at rally in Harlem, 1971. Photo courtesy of Warren Furutani.

Fig. 4.1. Russell Valparaiso nominated for Optimist of the Year. *Gidra* 2: 12 (December 1970). Photo by Alan Ota

Fig. 4.2. Yellow Brotherhood member Ronnie Nakashima speaking at Optimist Club dinner. *Gidra* 1: 4 (July 1969).

Fig. 5.1. Placard "Stop Genocide" behind Mike Murase in first Asian American anti-war rally in Los Angeles on January 27, 1970. Photo by Robert A. Nakamura. Courtesy of Visual Communication's George T. Ishizuka and Harukichi Nakamura Asian American Movement Collection

Fig. 5.2. Cover, *Gidra* 4: 5 (May 1972). Art by Alan Takemoto

Fig. 5.3. Cover, *Kalayaan International*, July 1971

Fig. 5.4. Mike Nakayama in Nixon mask leading Thai Binh and Van Troi Youth Brigades at Nisei Week parade, Los Angeles, August 1972. Photo by Alan Ohashi. Courtesy of Visual Communication's George T. Ishizuka and Harukichi Nakamura Asian American Movement Collection

Fig. 6.1. Advertisement for Chinatown Cooperative Garment Factory, *Rodan* 2: 4 (November 1971).

Fig. 6.2. Nick Nagatani assisting Mr. Nishioka. *Gidra*, 4: 2 (February 1972). Photo by E. Nagamatsu

Fig. 6.3. Sherrie Chinn, Susan Alfonzo, Reme Bacho Norris Bacho, Bob Santos and Al Sugiyama in march on the Department of Housing and Urban

Development, Seattle, November 12, 1972. Photo by Eugene Tagawa. Courtesy of Eugene Tagawa

Fig. 6.4. Mo Nishida at Little Tokyo Information Day, June, 1971. Photo by Robert A. Nakamura. Courtesy of Visual Communications' George T. Ishizuka and Harukichi Nakamura Asian American Movement Collection

Fig. 7.1. From a retrospective of poster art in *Bridge* 8: 1 (Summer 1982)

Fig. 7.2. Poster for Yellow Pearl by Tomie Arai, Amerasia Creative Arts, Basement Workshop, New York, 1972. Courtesy of Tomie Arai

Fig. 7.3. Poster for Asian American Dance Collective by Nancy Hom, Kearney Street Workshop, San Francisco, 1979. Courtesy of Nancy Hom

Fig. 7.4.a&b. "I Am Yellow…Curious??" by Larry Hama. *Bridge* 2: 4 (April 1973)

Fig. 7.5. "Make This Picture Decent!" by Alan Takemoto. *Gidra* 5: 11 (November 1973)

Fig. 7.6. Cartoon by David Monkawa. *Gidra* 5: 5 (May 1973).

Fig. 7.7. Illustration by Glen Iwasaki. *Gidra* 5: 12 (December 1973)

Fig. 7.8.a–d. Series of four political cartoons by Mike Murase depicting stereotypes of Japanese, Chinese, Filipino and Koreans in the United States. *Gidra* 1: 1–4 (April, May, June, July 1969)

Fig. 7.9. First Manzanar Pilgrimage, California, December 1969. Photos by Robert A. Nakamura. *Gidra* 2: 1 (January 1970)

Fig. 7.10. Nobuko (Joanne) Miyamoto and Chris Iijima performing on Martin Luther King Jr. Day, New York, 1971. © Bob Hsaing Photography

Fig. 7.11. Rally against police brutality, New York Chinatown, May 18, 1975. Photo by Corky Lee. © Corky Lee and the Chinese American Museum of Los Angeles

Fig. 7.12. Alan Ohashi, Eddie Wong, Robert A. Nakamura and Alan Kondo on Visual Communications shoot, c. 1971. Photo courtesy of Visual Communications' George T. Ishizuka and Harukichi Nakamura Asian American Movement Collection

Fig. 7.13. Poster by Leland Wong for the first Asian American Film Festival, produced by Chonk Moonhunter, 1977, San Francisco. Courtesy of Curtis Choy

Fig. 8.1. Police charge demonstrators on the night of the I-Hotel eviction, San Francisco. © Bob Hsaing Photography

Fig. 8.2. Cover, *Gidra* 5: 8 (August 1973). Art by David Monkawa

Fig. 8.3. From a press release about the Asian American contingent to Wounded Knee with Tatsuo Hirano in center, from collection of author

Fig. 9.1. Asian American women react to leaflet on "how to meet girls and ladies right here in America." From *Gidra* 3: 1 (January 1971)

Fig. 10.1. Grace Lee Boggs with youth activists, June 15, 2013, Los Angeles. Photo by Karen L. Ishizuka

# Notes

## Introduction

1. Irene Natividad, ed., *The Asian American Almanac* (Detroit: Gale Research, 1995), p. 282.
2. Al Robles, "A Manong's Language," *Bridge: An Asian American Perspective* 4: 4 (October 1976), p. 37.
3. Chris Iijima, "Pontifications on the Distinction between Grains of Sand and Yellow Pearls," in S. Louie and G. Omatsu, eds., *Asian Americans: The Movement and the Moment* (Los Angeles: UCLA Asian American Studies Press, 2001), pp. 2–15.
4. Arthur Marwick, "The Cultural Revolution of the Long Sixties: Voices of Reaction, Protest, and Permeation," *International History Review* 27: 4 (2005).
5. Fredric Jameson, "Periodizing the 60s," *Social Text* 9/10 (1984).
6. Jeremy Varon, Michael S. Foley, and John McMillan, "Time Is an Ocean: The Past and Future of the Sixties," *The Sixties: A Journal of History, Politics and Culture* 1: 1 (2008).
7. Elizabeth Martínez, "Histories of 'The Sixties': A Certain Absence of Color," *Social Justice* 16: 4 (1989), p. 177.
8. Diane C. Fujino, "Who Studies the Asian American Movement? A Historiographical Analysis," *Journal of Asian American Studies* 11: 2 (2008).
9. Ibid.
10. James M. Jasper, *The Art of Moral Protest: Culture, Biography, and Creativity in Social Movements* (Chicago/London: University of Chicago Press, 1997), p. 215.
11. "Jack Armstrong: All-American Boy" was a popular radio adventure series for youth from 1933 to 1951.
12. Karen Brodkin, *Making Democracy Matter: Identity and Activism in Los Angeles* (New Brunswick, NJ: Rutgers University Press, 2007).
13. Cherrie Moraga and Gloria Anzaldua, *This Bridge Called My Back: Writings by Radical Women of Color* (Watertown, MA: Persephone, 1981).

14. Barbara Christian, "The Race for Theory," *Feminist Studies* 14: 1 (1988).
15. Paulo Friere, *Pedagogy of the Oppressed* (New York: Continuum, 2001).
16. Ibid., p. 54.
17. All quotes in the book that are not cited are from interviews I conducted and discussions I had.
18. Frantz Fanon, *The Wretched of the Earth* (New York: Grove, 1963).
19. Fujino, "Who Studies the Asian American Movement?"
20. Clive James, *Cultural Amnesia: Necessary Memories from History and the Arts* (New York: W.W. Norton, 2007).

## 1. *Growing Up Alien in America*

1. Edward C. Long, "Reflections in a Slanted Eye," *Gidra* 1: 3 (June 1969).
2. Edward W. Said, *Orientalism* (New York: Vintage, 1994).
3. Grace Zia Chu, *The Pleasures of Chinese Cooking* (London: Simon & Schuster, 1962).
4. J. Hector St. John de Crèvecœur, *Letters from an American Farmer*, ed. Susan Manning (Oxford/New York: Oxford University Press, 1997).
5. Israel Zangwill's 1908 play *The Melting Pot* is online at readbookonline.net.
6. Philip Sheldon Foner, *Mark Twain: Social Critic* (New York: International Publishers, 1958).
7. US Department of State, Office of the Historian, "The Immigration Act of 1924 (The Johnson-Reed Act)," at history.state.gov.
8. Carlos Bulosan, *America Is in the Heart: A Personal History* (New York: Harcourt Brace, 1946).
9. Arthur M. Schlesinger, "Our Ten Contributions to Civilization," *Atlantic Monthly*, March 1959.
10. Nathan Glaser and Daniel P. Moynihan, *Beyond the Melting Pot*, 2nd edn (Cambridge: MIT Press, 1970 [1963]), p. 290.
11. US Department of State, Office of the Historian, "The Immigration and Nationality Act of 1952 (The McCarran-Walter Act)," at history.state.gov.
12. National Public Radio, "1965 Immigration Law Changes Face of America," in *All Things Considered*, NPR, May 9, 2006.
13. Irene Natividad, ed., *The Asian American Almanac* (Detroit: Gale Research, 1995), p. 284.
14. Wikipedia entry for "Asian Pacific American," note 14, at en.wikipedia.org.
15. Ibid.
16. Karen Brodkin points out that Bill Levitt built several Levittowns, first in Long Island and then in Pennsylvania and New Jersey, and that it was the state of New Jersey, not the US government, that prohibited discrimination in federally subsidized housing. Karen Brodkin, *How Jews Became White Folks and What That Says About Race in America* (New Brunswick, NJ: Rutgers University Press, 1998).

17. Helen and her brothers had devised a way to fight backhanded racism equally obliquely, but nonetheless unambiguously: "My brothers and I had this thing— we never verbalized it—but if we walked into a place and people started staring at us, we'd all turn and just glare back at them. We would stare them down."

18. When Helen returned, she was written up in the *New York Times* as one of the first Americans to visit China. From that article, she was selected to be on the television program *To Tell the Truth*, in which celebrity panelists were to guess which of three people was the "real" guest. "So they found two beautiful Chinese American starlets to be the impostors. I brought my Mao suits, and they put them on top of their beautiful clothes and coiffed hair and makeup— and guess what? They all picked me."

19. Scott Kurashige, *The Shifting Grounds of Race: Black and Japanese Americans in the Making of Multiethnic Los Angeles* (Princeton, NJ: Princeton University Press, 2008).

20. Japanese Americans traditionally self-identify by generations in the United States. *Issei*, literally "first generation," refer to immigrants from Japan. *Nisei,* ("second generation") refers to a person born in the United States (or any country outside of Japan) whose parents were immigrants. *Sansei* are the third generation. *Yonsei*, the fourth; and *Gosei*, the fifth.

21. This Institute is distinct from the existing Gardena Valley Japanese Cultural Institute, which dates back to 1912 when it was founded as the Moneta Gakuen, a Japanese language school. See Lane Ryo Hirabayashi and George Tanaka, *The Early Gardena Valley and the Issei* (Gardena, CA: Gardena Pioneer Project, 1986), p. 157, fn 36; and "History of the Gardena Valley JCI," at jci-gardena.org.

22. Michi Weglyn, *Years of Infamy: The Untold Story of America's Concentration Camps* (Seattle: University of Washington Press, 1996), p. 42.

23. Jonathan Y. Okamura, "Why There Are No Asian Americans in Hawai'i: The Continuing Significance of Local Identity," *Social Processes in Hawaii* 35: 162 (1994).

24. Wikipedia entry for "Asian Pacific American," note 14, at en.wikipedia.org.

25. Okamura, "Why There Are No Asian Americans in Hawai'i."

26. Jonathan Y. Okamura, "*Aloha Kanaka Me Ke Aloha 'Aina*: Local Culture and Society in Hawaii," *Amerasia* 7: 2 (1980).

27. Robert G. Lee, *Orientals: Asian Americans in Popular Culture* (Philadelphia: Temple University Press, 1999).

28. Mia Tuan, *Forever Foreigners or Honorary Whites? The Asian Ethnic Experience Today* (New Brunswick, NJ: Rutgers University Press, 1998).

29. W. E. B. Du Bois, *The Souls of Black Folk* (New York: Dover, 1994 [1903]). An earlier essay in an 1897 issue of *Atlantic Monthly* became the first chapter of *The Souls of Black Folk*. See Ernest Allen, Jr., "On the Reading of Riddles: Rethinking DuBoisian 'Double Consciousness,'" in Lewis R. Gordon, ed., *Existence in Black: An Anthology of Black Existential Philosophy* (New York/London: Routledge, 1996), p. 49.

## 2. Living in B&W

1. Peggy McIntosh, "White Privilege: Unpacking the Invisible Knapsack," *Independent School*, January 1990, available at amptoons.com.
2. Frantz Fanon, *Black Skin, White Masks*, trans. C. L. Markmann (New York: Grove, 1994).
3. Claire Jean Kim, "The Racial Triangulation of Asian Americans," *Politics & Society* 27: 1 (1999), p. 112.
4. Eric Liu, *The Accidental Asian: Notes of a Native Speaker* (New York: Random House, 1998).
5. Elaine H. Kim, "'At Least You're Not Black': Asian Americans in US Race Relations," *Social Justice* 25: 3 (1998).
6. David Leiwei Li, "On Ascriptive and Acquisitional Americanness: The Accidental Asian and the Illogic of Assimilation," *Contemporary Literature* 45 (2004).
7. Min Zhou, "Are Asian Americans Becoming White?" *CSA Academic Perspective* 3 (2007).
8. Touré, *Who's Afraid of Post-Blackness? What It Means to be Black Now* (New York: Free Press, 2011), pp. 158–59.
9. Karen Brodkin, *How Jews Became White Folks and What That Says About Race in America* (New Brunswick, NJ/London: Rutgers University Press, 1998), p. 30.
10. Cornel West, "The New Cultural Politics of Difference," in R. Ferguson, M. Gever, T.E. Minh-ha, and C. West, eds., *Out There: Marginalization and Contemporary Cultures* (New York: New Museum of Contemporary Art, 1990), p. 29.
11. Edward W. Said, *Orientalism* (New York: Vintage, 1978).
12. Stuart Hall, "The West and the Rest: Discourse and Power," in S. Hall, D. Held, D. Hubert, and K. Thompson, eds., *Modernity: An Introduction to Modern Societies* (Malden, MA: Open University, 1996).
13. Helen H. Jun, "Black Orientalism: Nineteenth-Century Narratives of Race and US Citizenship," *American Quarterly* 58 (2006).
14. Stuart Hall, "New Ethnicities," in K. Mercer, ed., *Black Film, British Cinema* (London: Institute of Contemporary Art, 1988).
15. Jun, "Black Orientalism."
16. Fred Wei-han Ho and Bill V. Mullen, *Afro Asia: Revolutionary Political and Cultural Connections between African Americans and Asian Americans* (Durham, NC: Duke University Press, 2008).
17. W. E. B. Du Bois, *The Souls of Black Folk* (New York: Dover, 1994 [1903]).
18. W. E. B. Du Bois, *W. E. B. Du Bois on Asia: Crossing the World Color Line*, ed. Bill V. Mullen and Cathryn Watson (Jackson: University Press of Mississippi, 2005), p. viii.
19. Recounted in Gary Y. Okihiro, *Pineapple Culture: A History of the Tropical and Temperate Zones* (Berkeley: University of California Press, 2009), p. 68.
20. Luo Lianggong, "China and the Political Imagination in Langston Hughes's Poetry," in Z. Yuejun and S. Christie, eds., *American Modernist Poetry and the Chinese Encounter* (New York: Palgrave Macmillan 2012).

21. Lanston Hughes, "Roar, China!" in *The Collected Poems of Langston Hughes*, Arnold Rampersad, ed., (New York: Vintage, 1994), pp. 199–200.

22. George Lipsitz, "Frantic to Join … the Japanese Army": Black Soldiers and Civilians Confront the Asian Pacific War," in T. Fujitani, G.M. White, and L. Yoneyama, eds., *Perilous Memories: The Asia-Pacific War(s)* (Durham, NC: Duke University Press, 2001).

23. Scott Kurashige, *The Shifting Grounds of Race: Black and Japanese Americans in the Making of Multiethnic Los Angeles* (Princeton, NJ: Princeton University Press, 2008), p. 165.

24. S. I. Hayakawa, who would become the president of San Francisco State College during the 1968 Third World Liberation Front strike and Republican US senator from California, also wrote for the *Chicago Defender* from November 1942 until January 1947.

25. C K Doreski, " 'Kin in Some Way': The Chicago Defender Reads the Japanese Internment, 1942–1945," in Todd Vogel, ed., *The Black Press* (New Brunswick, NJ London: Rutgers University Press, 2001), pp. 161–87.

26. Robeson Taj P. Frazier, "The Assault of the Monkey King on the Hosts of Heaven: The Black Freedom Struggle and China—The New Center of Revolution," in M. L. Clemons, ed., *African Americans in Global Affairs: Contemporary Perspectives* (Boston: Northeastern University Press, 2010), p. 322.

27. Both statements are reproduced in Ho and Mullen, *Afro Asia*.

28. Robin D. G. Kelley and Betsy Esch, "Black Like Mao: Red China and Black Revolution," in Ho and Mullen, *Afro Asia*.

29. Daniel Widener, "'Perhaps the Japanese Are to Be Thanked?': Asia, Asian Americans and the Construction of Black California," *Positions: East Asia Cultures Critique* 11: 1 (2003), p. 148.

30. Widener, "'Perhaps the Japanese Are to Be Thanked?'"

31. Kurashige, *Shifting Grounds of Race*.

32. Mari J Matsuda, "Planet Asian America," *Asian American Law Journal* 8: 1 (2001), 169–86.

33. Yuri Kochiyama, *Passing It On: A Memoir* (Los Angeles: UCLA Asian American Studies Center Press, 2004).

34. Diane Fujino, *Heartbeat of Struggle: The Revolutionary Life of Yuri Kochiyama* (Minneapolis/London: University of Minnesota Press, 2005), p. 148.

35. Ibid., p. 143.

36. Yuri Kochiyama, "The Impact of Malcolm X on Asian American Politics and Activism," in J. Jennings, ed., *Blacks, Latinos and Asians in Urban America: Status and Prospects for Politics and Activism* (London: Praeger, 1994), p. 137.

37. Gary Y. Okihiro, *Margins and Mainstreams: Asians in American History and Culture* (Seattle: University of Washington Press, 1994).

38. Mari J. Matsuda, "Planet Asian America," *Asian American Law Journal* 8: 1 (2001).

39. Lawson Fusao Inada, *Legends from Camp Minneapolis* (Minneapolis: Coffee House, 1992), p. 57.

40. Jun, "Black Orientalism."

41. Karen Brodkin credits Barbara Fields for pointing this out in her *How Jews Became White Folks* (p. 54).

42. Frederick Douglass, "The Myth of 'Yellow Peril,'" in J. Gottheimer, ed., *Ripples of Hope: Great American Civil Rights Speeches* (New York: Basic Civitas Books, 2004).

43. Nami Kim, "Engaging Afro/Black-Orientalism: A Proposal," *Journal of Race, Ethnicity, and Religion* 1: 7 (2010).

44. From *Looking Like the Enemy* (52 min, color, 1996). Directed by Robert A. Nakamura. Produced and written by Karen L. Ishizuka for the Japanese American National Museum.

45. L. Ling Chi Wang, "The Structure of Dual Domination: Toward a Paradigm for the Study of the Chinese Diaspora in the United States," *Amerasia* 33: 1 (2007).

46. William Petersen, "Success Story, Japanese-American Style," *New York Times Magazine*, January 9, 1966.

47. "Success Story of One Minority Group in US," *US News and World Report*, (December 26, 1966). Reprinted in Amy Tachiki, *Roots: An Asian American Reader* (Los Angeles: UCLA Asian American Studies Center, 1971).

48. "Success Story: Outwhiting the Whites," *Newsweek*, June 21, 1971.

49. Vijay Prashad, *The Karma of Brown Folk* (Minneapolis: University of Minnesota Press, 2000).

50. Scot Nakagawa, "The Model Minority is a Lever of White Supremacy," *Race Files*, 2014, at racefiles.com.

51. Charles R. Lawrence III, "Race, Multiculturalism, and the Jurisprudence of Transformation," in K. R. Johnson, ed., *Mixed Race America and the Law: A Reader* (New York: New York University Press, 2003).

52. Paul Takagi and Tony Platt, "Behind the Gilded Ghetto: An Analysis of Race, Class and Crime in Chinatown," *Crime and Social Justice* 9 (1978).

53. Frank Chin and Jeffrey Paul Chan, "Racist Love," in R. Kostelanetz, ed., *Seeing Through Shuck* (New York: Ballantine, 1972).

54. Ibid.

55. Julius Lester, "The Angry Children of Malcolm X," *Sing Out!* October–November 1966.

56. Claire Jean Kim, "Asian Americans Are People of Color, Too … Aren't They? Cross-Racial Alliances and the Question of Asian American Political Identity," *AAPI Nexus: Policy, Practice and Community* 2: 1 (2004), p. 23.

57. Claude M. Steele, *Whistling Vivaldi: How Stereotypes Affect Us and What We Can Do* (New York: W.W. Norton, 2011).

### 3. *Yellow Power*

1. John McMillan, *Smoking Typewriters: The Sixties Underground Press and the Rise of Alternative Media in America* (Oxford: Oxford University Press, 2011), p. 38.

2. Ludwig Wittgenstein, *Tractatus Logico-Philosophicus* (London/New York: Routledge, 2011 [1921]).

3. Geoffrey Nunberg, *Ascent of the A-Word: Assholism, the First Sixty Years* (New York: Public Affairs, 2012).

4. Tom Wolfe, "The New Yellow Peril," *Esquire*, December 1969.

5. Tariq Modood, "The History of Multiculturalism," in *Multiculturalism Bites*, Open University, at open.edu.

6. June Jordan, *Technical Difficulties: African-American Notes on the State of the Union* (New York: Vintage, 1994).

7. John Baugh, "The Politicization of Changing Terms of Self-Reference among American Slave Descendants," *American Speech* 66: 2 (1991).

8. Kwame Turé and Charles V. Hamilton, *Black Power: The Politics of Liberation*, 2nd ed. (New York: Vintage, 1992).

9. Gloria Auzaldúa, Borderlands La Frontera: The New Mestiza (San Francisco: Aunt Lute Books, 1999).

10. Diane C. Fujino, *Samurai Among Panthers: Richard Aoki on Race, Resistance, and a Paradoxical Life* (Minneapolis: University of Minnesota Press, 2012).

11. "Understanding AAPA," *AAPA Newspaper* I: 5 (Summer 1969), Berkeley, CA. Reproduced in *Stand Up: An Archive Collection of the Bay Area Asian American Movement 1968–1974* (Berkeley, CA: Asian Community Center Archive Group, 2009), p. 30; and in Amy Tachiki, ed., *Roots: An Asian American Reader* (Berkeley, CA: California University Press, 1971), p. 252.

12. "AAPA Perspectives," in *AAPA Newspaper* I: 6 (October 1969), reproduced in *Stand Up*, pp. 31–2.

13. Reprinted in *Gidra* 4: 3 (March 1972) p. 22.

14. Audre Lorde, "Poetry Is Not a Luxury," in *Sister Outsider* (Trumansburg, NY: Crossing, 1984).

15 Nobuko (Joanne) Miyamoto and Chris Iijima, "Something About Me Today," in *A Grain of Sand: Music for the Struggle by Asians in America*, Paredon Records, 1973. DVD available at folkways.si.edu.

16. Ibid. A download link to the album's liner notes is included on the site.

17. "Yellow" was also used as an early term of self-reference. In the 1920s, Japanese immigrants in the United States often identified themselves as *oushoku jinshu* (a member of the "yellow race") or *yushoku jinshu* (a member of a "colored race"). In a 1922 article in the Japanese American newspaper *Rafu Shimpo*, the author declared that he would rather Japanese be considered yellow (*oushoku minzoku*) rather than white (*hakujinshu*). From Fuminori Minamikawa, "Vernacular Representation of Race and the Making of an Ethnoracial Community of Japanese in Los Angeles," in Japanese and Asian Americans: Racializations and Their Resistances, a conference at Kyoto University, 2012.

18. Larry Kubota, "Yellow Power!" *Gidra* 1: 1 (April 1969), pp. 3-4.

19. Amy Uyematsu, "The Emergence of Yellow Power in America," *Gidra* 1: 7 (October 1969).

20. Scott Kurashige, "Amy Uyematsu," in King-Kok Cheung, ed., *Words Matter:*

*Conversations with Asian American Writers* (Honolulu: University of Hawaii Press, 2000).

21. Fujino, *Samurai Among Panthers: Richard Aoki on Race, Resistance, and a Paradoxical Life* (Minneapolis: University of Minnesota Press, 2012). p. 169.

22. Frantz Fanon, *The Wretched of the Earth* (New York: Grove, 1963); Vijay Prashad, *The Darker Nations: A People's History of the Third World* (New York: New Press, 2007).

23. Cynthia Ann Young, *Soul Power: Culture, Radicalism, and the Making of a US Third World Left* (Durham, NC: Duke University Press, 2006).

24. "Amerasian Power," *Gidra* 2: 4 (April 1970), p. 31.

25. Natsue, "Amerasian Culture," *Gidra* 2: 12 (December 1970), p. 4.

26. Mike Yamamoto, "Amerasia Chapter of JACL," *Gidra* 2: 12 (December 1970), p.10.

27. Amerasian Generation poster and blurb, *Gidra* 3: 1 (January 1971), p. 16; "Amerasian Generation, photo spread and poem," *Gidra* 4: 2 (February 1971), pp. 12–13.

28. The website asian-nation.org is unrelated to the political concept discussed.

29. "Asian Nation," *Gidra* 4: 10 (October 1971), pp. 16–19.

30. The "collective" mentioned was the Community Workers Collective, which was formed in 1971 as a political grouping, after which many members moved in and lived together.

31. Shinya Ono, "Finding a Home Community," in S. Louie and G. Omatsu, eds., *Asian Americans: The Movement and the Moment* (Los Angeles: UCLA Asian American Studies Center Press, 2001).

32. Laura Pulido, *Black, Brown, Yellow and Left: Radical Activism in Los Angeles* (Berkeley/Los Angeles/London: University of California Press, 2006).

33. Peter X. Feng, "Being Chinese American, Becoming Asian American: 'Chan Is Missing,'" *Cinema Journal* 35: 4 (1996), p. 90.

34. Peter X. Feng, "The Politics of the Hyphen," in "In Search of Asian American Cinema," *Cineaste* 21: 1–2 (1995). Feng added an interesting historical note: When the JACL had been founded in 1930, it had also debated whether or not to include a hyphen, "finally deciding that to identify themselves as 'Japanese-American Citizens' suggested that their allegiance was divided."

35. Feng, "Being Chinese American, Becoming Asian American," p. 93.

36. Maxine Hong Kingston, *Tripmaster Monkey: His Fake Book* (New York: Vintage International, 1990), quoted in Feng, "Being Chinese American, Becoming Asian American," p. 93.

37. Violet Rabaya, "I Am Curious (Yellow?)," *Gidra* 1: 7 (1969). Also included in Tachiki, *Roots*.

38. Dorothy Cordova's introduction to Fred Cordova, *Filipinos: Forgotten Asian Americans* (Seattle: Demonstration Project for Asian Americans, 1983), p. ix.

39. Antonio J. A. Pido, "Macro/Micro Dimensions of Pilipino Immigration," in M. P. P. Root, ed., *Filipino Americans: Transformation and Identity* (Thousand Oaks: Sage, 1997), p. 31.

40. Florante Ibanez, "The Phenomena and the Politics of the Filipino People's Far

West Convention: 1970s–1980s," unpublished student paper, University of California, Los Angeles, 2003.

41. Nobuko (Joanne) Miyamoto and Chris Iijima, "Divide and Conquer," in liner notes to *A Grain of Sand: Music for the Struggle by Asians in America* (Paradon Records, 1973).

42. C. L. R. James, "Africans and Afro-Caribbeans: A Personal View," *Ten* 8: 16 (1984).

43. Nelson Nagai, "I Came From a Yellow Seed," in Louie and Omatsu, *Asian Americans: The Movement and the Moment.*

44. Malcolm Gladwell, *The Tipping Point: How Little Things Can Make a Big Difference* (Boston: Little, Brown, 2002).

## 4. Spontaneous Arisings

1. William L. Van Deburg, *Hoodlums: Black Villains and Social Bandits in American Life* (Chicago: University of Chicago Press, 2004).

2. Glenn Suravech, "Code of Honor: Japanese American Gangs, 1950–1965," *Rafu Shimpo*, December 18, 1993, p. A8.

3. Roy Nakano, "Them Bad Cats: Past Images of Asian American Street Gangs," *Gidra* 5 (1973).

4. Ibid.

5. According to Victor Shibata, the Ministers merged from two multiracial, mostly black and Asian gangs—the "Little Gents" at Mount Vernon Junior High School and the "Internationals" at Audoban Junior High School. Tad Nakamura, "The Yellow Brotherhood: From the Past to the Present," unpublished college paper, UCLA, March 1999.

6. Calvin Toy, "A Short History of Asian Gangs in San Francisco," *Justice Quarterly* 9: 4 (1992).

7. Michael Zelenko, "The Tongs of Chinatown: A Conversation with Bill Lee," *FoundSF* (San Franicsco), n.d., at foundsf.org.

8. Stanford Lyman, "Red Guard on Grant Avenue: The Rise of Youthful Rebellion in Chinatown," in Stanley Sue, *Asian-Americans: Psychological Perspectives* (Palo Alto, CA: Science and Behavior, 1973).

9. Ibid.

10. Paul Takagi and Tony Platt, "Behind the Gilded Ghetto: An Analysis of Race, Class and Crime in Chinatown," *Crime and Social Justice* 9 (1978).

11. "Leways Invaded by Pigs," *Getting Together*, February 1971, p. 1.

12. Attorney General, State of California, "Proceedings of the Conference on Chinese Gang Problems: California Organized Crime and Criminal Intelligence Branch," March 1972. Cited in Takagi and Platt, "Behind the Gilded Ghetto."

13. Jennifer L. Thompson, "Are Chinatown Gang Wars a Cover-Up?" *San Francisco Magazine*, February 1976. Cited in Takagi and Platt, "Behind the Gilded Ghetto."

14. "Red Guard Program and Rules, 1969," reprinted in Fred Ho, ed., *Legacy to Liberation: Politics and Culture of Revolutionary Asian Pacific America* (San Francisco: Big Red Media/AK, 2000), p. 401.

15. Lyman, "Red Guard on Grant Avenue."

16. Ibid.

17. Yuji Ichioka, "Early Issei Socialists and the Japanese Community," in E. Gee, ed., *Counterpoint: Perspectives on Asian America* (Los Angeles: Asian American Studies Center, University of California Press, 1976).

18. Him Mark Lai, "A Historical Survey of Chinese Left in America" in Gee, *Counterpoint.*

19. Yen Le Espiritu, *Asian American Panethnicity: Bridging Institutions and Identities* (Philadelphia: Temple University Press, 1992), p. 34.

20. Ibid., p. 178.

21. Diane C. Fujino, *Samurai Among Panthers: Richard Aoki on Race, Resistance, and a Paradoxical Life* (Minneapolis: University of Minnesota Press, 2012), p. 169.

22. V. Wong, "Origins of the Asian American Political Alliance," in ACCA Group, ed., *Stand Up: An Archive Collection of the Bay Area Asian American Movement: 1968–1974* (Berkeley: Eastwind, 2009), pp. 23–24.

23. Floyd Huen, "The Advent and Origins of the Asian American Movement in the San Francisco Bay Area: A Personal Perspective," in S. Louie and G. Omatsu, eds., *Asian Americans: The Movement and the Moment* (Los Angeles: UCLA Asian American Studies Center Press, 2001).

24. Gary Y. Okihiro, "Introduction," in G. Y. Okihiro, S. Hune, A. A. Hansen, and J. M. Liu, eds., *Reflections on Shattered Windows: Promises and Prospects for Asian American Studies* (Pullman: Washington State University Press, 1988), p. xvii.

25. Daryl J. Maeda, *Chains of Babylon: The Rise of Asian America* (Minneapolis: University of Minnesota Press, 2009).

26. S. I. Hayakawa, "American Youth Continues to Dance to Beat Provided by Young Negroes," *Evening Outlook*, August 3, 1970.

27. "Blue Meanies" was the nickname Berkeley protestors gave to Alameda County Sheriffs, known for their blue jumpsuits and use of tear gas. The name referred originally to the Beatles' animated film *Yellow Submarine.*

28. Colin Watanabe, "Asian American Studies Conference," *Gidra* 1: 7 (October 1969), p. 2.

29. "Ethnic Studies Interim Conference 1971 Report," *Hawaii Pono Journal* I, April 1971.

30. Bob Santos, *Hum Bows, Not Hot Dogs!* (Seattle: International Examiner Press, 2002), p. 71.

31. Allison Marie O'Connor, "Jackson Street Community Council (1946–1967)," at blackpast.org.

32. Phil Hayasaka, "Seattle Oriental Communities form 'ACE': Asian Coalition for Equality," n.d., at depts.washington.edu.

33. Ray Inouye, "Should Orientals Join Blacks in Racial Protest?" *Seattle Times*, October 12, 1969, at depts.washington.edu.

34. Unpublished manuscript provided by Kazu's daughter Lynne Iijima, April 2008.

35. Yuri Kochiyama, *Passing It On: A Memoir* (Los Angeles: UCLA Asian American Studies Center Press, 2004), p. 168.

36. Yuri Kochiyama, Ericka Huggins, and Mary Uyematsu Kao, "Stirrin' Waters 'n' Buildin' Bridges: A Conversation with Erika Huggins and Yuri Kochiyama," *Amerasia Journal* 35: 1 (2009). To Yuri's comments about Triple A being dominated by older women, Ericka Huggins commented that the Black Panther Party was also run by women.

37. Perhaps the first news outlet to report on Triple A members being arrested was *Muhammad Speaks*, when Triple A and the Committee of Returned Volunteers (of the Peace Corps) picketed the UN demanding the withdrawal of US forces from Okinawa and an end to the US-Japan Security Treaty. "Asians Arrested" *Gidra* 1: 6 (September 1969), p. 2.

38. *Asian Americans for Action Newsletter* (December 1969).

39. Juk Kuk (actually Jook Hop), signifying bamboo with naturally sealed ends (meaning that culture is retained), refers to immigrant born Chinese. Juk Sing (Jook Sing)—bamboo without sealed ends, meaning culture is not retained but just flows through—refers to Americanized Chinese. Thanks to Harvey Dong for the translation.

40. Iijima, unpublished manuscript.

## 5. *Gooks*

1. Bruce Iwasaki, "You May Be a Lover but You Ain't No Dancer: Helter Skelter," *Gidra* 5: 1 (January 1973), p. 16.

2. Asian Coalition, "Why an Asian Contingent?"—flyer for Anti-War March and Rally in Washington, DC, on Saturday, April 24, 1971, New York.

3. Patsy Chan, "End Your Racist War," *Gidra* 3: 6 (June 1971), p. 5.

4. Quoted in Arundhati Roy, *An Ordinary Person's Guide to Empire* (London: Penguin, 2006), p. 181.

5. Muhammad Ali did declare: "I am not going ten thousand miles to help murder and kill and burn another poor people simply to help continue the domination of white America."

6. Agnew was forced to apologize, although he always maintained the comment was meant in good fun. Diane Fujino cites a September 27, 1996, letter from the daughter of journalist Gene Oishi to the *New York Times*, which read, "My father never accepted the comment as anything but an insulting slur." Diane Fujino, *Samurai Among Panthers: Richard Aoki on Race, Resistance and the Paradoxical Life* (Minneapolis: University of Minnesota Press, 2012), p. 362.

7. David L. Weiss, dir., *No Vietnamese Ever Called Me Nigger*, 76 minutes, United States (1968).

8. Sylvia Shin Huey Chong, *The Oriental Obscene: Violence and Racial Fantasies in the Vietnam Era* (Durham, NC: Duke University Press, 2011).

9. Chris K. Iijima, "The Era of We-Construction: Reclaiming the Politics of Asian Pacific American Identity and Reflections on the Critique of the Black/White Paradigm," *Columbia Human Rights Law Review* 29: 47 (1997).

10. Anthony Kahng, "Report on the Third World Conference on Vietnam," *Asian Americans for Action Newsletter* 4: 2 (April–May–June 1972), pp. 5–6, 9.

11. "Third World People's Anti-War Conference," *Gidra* 4: 7 (July 1972), p. 3.

12. Larry Rohter, "Dead for a Century, Twain Says What He Meant," *New York Times*, July 9, 2010.

13. Pat Sumi, "US War Crimes in the Philippines," *Gidra* 3: 6 (July 1971), p. 6.

14. Isao Fujimoto, "The High Cost of Saving Face the American Way," *Gidra* 1: 8 (November 1969), pp. 8–9.

15. Charles W. Cheng, "Hiroshima—Lest We Forget," Gidra 2: 11 (November 1970), p. 12.

16. Michio Kaku, "Hiroshima, Nagasaki, Vietnam: When It Rains, It Pours," *Gidra* 5: 10 (October 1973), p. 22.

17. "AAA Blows Peoples' Minds with Ash-Filled 'Remember Hiroshima-Nagasaki' Packets," *Asian Americans for Action Newsletter* 3: 4 (August–September 1971), p. 8.

18. Norman Nakamura, "The Nature of GI Racism," *Gidra* 2: 6 (June–July 1970).

19. Frank Orr, "GI Racism Revisited," *Gidra* 2: 8 (September 1970), p. 19.

20. Winter Soldier Investigation Testimony, Racism Panel, at wintersoldier.com.

21. The Vietnam War was not the only war in which being an Asian American fighting in a war against Asians was hazardous to your health. In the film *Looking Like the Enemy* (1996), Roy Shiraga, a corporal in the US Army, recalls that when he was injured in the Korean War, his treatment was also neglected.

22. Mike Nakayama, "Winter Soldiers," *Gidra* 3: 6 (July 1971), p. 12.

23. Ibid.

24. Nakamura, "Nature of GI Racism."

25. Phil Gailey, "Mistook for Vietcong: 2 Hitchhikers in Georgia Attacked," *Los Angeles Times*, 1970.

26. Mark Baker, *Nam: The Vietnam War in the Words of the Men and Women Who Fought There* (New York: Cooper Square, 2001).

27. Wallace Terry, *Bloods: Black Veterans of the Vietnam War: An Oral History* (New York: Presidio/Ballantine, 2006).

28. Karen L. Ishizuka and Robert A. Nakamura, *Looking Like the Enemy*, Japanese American National Museum, Los Angeles (1996)—video (52 mins.).

29. David Haward Bain, *Aftershocks: A Tale of Two Victims* (New York: Penguin, 1986).

30. Asian Coalition, "Asian Americans in Support of the Vietnam Supply Drive," handout, c. 1972.

31. Iwasaki, "You May be a Lover but You Ain't No Dancer: Helter Skelter," p. 16.

32. Thai Binh Nguyen, "Death of Peace," *Gidra* 4: 6 (August 1972), p. 2.

33. Brendan I Koerner, *The Skies Belong to Us: Love and Terror in the Golden Age of Hijacking* (New York: Broadway Books, 2013), pp. 184–85.

34. Brendan I Koerner, "Skyjacker of the Day Entry 9: This Air Pirate Picked the Wrong Plane and the Wrong Captain," June 18, 2013, slate.com.

35. Lily Eng, "Honoring a Young Life that Ended Too Soon—20 Years Later, Friends Still Saddened," *Seattle Times*, July 3, 1992.

36. *Saigon–GP Daily*, "Long An Province Pays Tribute to Hero Nguyen Thai Binh," posted May 1, 2013, at saigon-gpdaily.com.vn.

37. Iwasaki, "You May Be a Lover but You Ain't No Dancer," p. 17.

## 6. To Serve the People

1. Gary Y. Okihiro, "The Idea of Community and a 'Particular Type of History,'" in G. Y. Okihiro, S. Hune, A. A. Hansen, and J. M. Liu, eds., *Reflections on Shattered Windows: Promises and Prospects for Asian American Studies* (Pullman: Washington State University Press, 1988).

2. Larry Neal, "The Black Arts Movement," *Drama Review* 12: 4 (1968).

3. Elaine H. Kim, "Defining Asian American Realities Through Literature," *Cultural Critique* 6 (1987), p. 109.

4. Poet and musician Norman Jayo, quoted in Robynn Takayama, "Home: Fireside Chat," 2006, at nonogirl.com.

5. "International Hotel," *Paunawa*, October 1970. Reprinted in Amy Tachiki et al., eds., *Roots: An Asian American Reader* (Los Angeles: UCLA Asian American Studies Center, 1971).

6. *The East is Red* is a lavish 1965 film from mainland China dramatizing the revolutionary ideology of Mao Zedong and Chinese Communism that was screened extensively in the United States during the Asian American movement.

7. "Chinatown Co-operative Garment Factory," *Asian Community Newsletter* 1 (July 11, 1970); and "A Better Garment Factory: The Chinatown Co-op," *Wei Min Chinese Community News* 1: 1 (October 1971). Both reprinted in *Stand Up: An Archive Collection of the Bay Area Asian American Movement, 1968–1974* (Berkeley, CA: Asian Community Center Archive Group, 2009).

8. Steve Yip, "Serve the People—Yesterday and Today: The Legacy of Wei Min She," in F. Ho, ed., *Legacy to Liberation: Politics and Culture of Revolutionary Asian Pacific America* (San Francisco: Big Red Media/AK, 2000), p. 21.

9. Estella Habal, *San Francisco's International Hotel: Mobilizing the Filipino American Community in the Anti-Eviction Movement* (Philadelphia: Temple University Press, 2007), p. 58.

10. Rocky Chin, "The House that JACS Built," *Bridge: The Asian American Magazine* 2: 6 (1973).

11. Ford Hajime Kuramoto, "A History of the Shonien 1914–1972: An Account of a Program of Institutional Care of Japanese Children in Los Angeles," Doctor of Social Work thesis, University of Southern California, 1972.

12. Japanese American Community Services, "History: About Shonien," at jacsfund.org.

13. Jim Matsuoka, "A Center for Pioneers: Los Angeles' Little Tokyo During the 1960s–1970s," in *Pacific Citizen* Holiday Issue, December 2002, p. 38.
14. "Asian American Hard Core," *Gidra* 1: 9 (December 1969), p. 14.
15. After her evaluation, she was not considered a "menace to society" and never served time in jail.
16. Rocky Chin, "New York Chinatown Today: Community in Crisis," *Amerasia Journal* 1: 1 (March 1971), p. 13.
17. Ibid., p. 8
18. These building were nicknamed "dumb-bell" tenements after their design. Usually five to six stories high, the front and rear buildings, which were connected by a hallway, had seven rooms each, which had little access to daylight and fresh air, making them a "hindrance to the health and comfort of the tenants … a fire hazard [and] a receptacle for garbage and filth of all kinds." Ibid., p. 13.
19. Paul Takagi and Tony Platt, "Behind the Gilded Ghetto: An Analysis of Race, Class and Crime in Chinatown," *Crime and Social Justice* 9 (1978).
20. Chin, "New York Chinatown Today," p. 22.
21. Eleanor Yung, "On Basement Workshop (&/or Danny Yung)," at artsasiamerica: A Digital Archive of Asian/Asian American Contemporary Art History.
22. These five are thought to have been Danny Yung, Eleanor Yung, Frank Chin, Margaret Loke, and Peter Pan.
23. Eleanor Yung, "On Basement Workshop."
24. Ibid.
25. Doug Chin, *Seattle's International District: The Making of a Pan-Asian American Community* (Seattle: University of Washington Press, 2001). The majority of the information regarding the history of the ID comes from this book and from Seattle Civil Rights and Labor History Project, at depts.washington.edu.
26. Mayumi Tsutakawa, "How The Kingdome Spurred the Asian-American Community's Coming of Age," *Seattle Times*, July 8, 1999.
27. Ibid.
28. "Kingdome Protest and HUD March, Nov. 1972," Seattle Civil Rights and Labor Project, at depts.washington.edu.
29. Bob Santos, *Hum Bows, Not Hot Dogs!* (Seattle: International Examiner Press, 2002), p. 85.
30. From Chin, *Seattle's International District*, and Santos, *Hum Bows, Not Hot Dogs!*

## 7. Arts of Activism

1. Russell Leong, "Poetry Within Earshot: Notes on an Asian American Generation 1968–1978," *Amerasia Journal* 15: 1 (1989).
2. Lincoln Cushing, "Political Graphics of the 'Long 1960s,'" in K. Dubinsky, C. Krull, S. Lord, S. Mills, and S. Rutherford, eds., *New World Coming: The*

*Sixties and the Shaping of Global Consciousness* (Toronto: Between the Lines, 2009).

3. Josh MacPhee, *Celebrate People's History: The Poster Book of Resistance and Revolution* (New York: Feminist Press at the City University of New York, 2010), p. 14.

4. Robynn Takayama, "Home: Fireside Chat," August 7, 2006, at nonogirl.com.

5. Julianne P. Gavino, Nancy Hom, and Johanna Poethig, "Visions and Voices of the I-Hotel: Urban Struggles, Community Mythologies and Creativity," *MICA Community Arts Journal* III (Fall 2011).

6. During the Asian American movement, social change and community-based art often went unsigned and undated. Because the editors of *Bridge* credited each poster whenever possible, the issue also serves as critical archival evidence of who created them and their affiliate organizations.

7. C. N. Lee, "Poster Nostalgia: Ten Years of Asian American Poster Art," *Bridge: Asian American Perspectives* 8: 1 (1982), p. 3.

8. Ibid.

9. Nancy Hom, "Drinking Tea with Both Hands," in Steve Louie and Glenn Omatsu, eds., *Asian Americans: The Movement and the Moment* (Los Angeles: UCLA Asian American Studies Center Press, 2001), p. 102.

10. Claire Peeps, "Getting in History's Way," in M. Cieri and C. Peeps, eds., *Activists Speak Out* (New York: Palgrave, 2000), p. 271.

11. Ben Fong-Torres, "Cat Mother's Guitarist Only Chinese in Rock," *East/West*, June 25, 1969.

12. In attendance that night was Yoshio Kishi, a Nisei sound and film editor, who captured their performance on audiotape. Amid the swelling beat of congas and handclaps, Nobuko sang: "Every day I can hear it, like a heartbeat, the People's Beat!" Chris called out, "Who are the People?" The enthusiastic audience responded, "We are the People!" The frenetic call-and-response continued for a full fifteen minutes. Kishi, the experienced sound editor, kept the tape rolling, recording the ending walla of Charlie's unrepeatable moment of discovery. The audiotape is archived at the Asian/Pacific/American Institute at New York University. Special thanks to Janet Liao for her assistance.

13. Elizabeth Eisenstein, *The Printing Press as an Agent of Change: Communications and Cultural Transformations in Early Modern Europe* (Cambridge: Cambridge University Press, 1982).

14. A. Gabriel Meléndez, *So All Is Not Lost: The Poetics of Print in Nuevomexicano Communities, 1834–1958* (Albuquerque: University of New Mexico Press, 1997).

15. Todd Vogel, *The Black Press: New Literary and Historical Essays* (New Brunswick, NJ: Rutgers University Press, 2001).

16. John McMillan, *Smoking Typewriters: The Sixties Underground Press and the Rise of Alternative Media in America* (Oxford: Oxford University Press, 2011), p. 192.

17. Rockwell Chin, "Going Beyond Vol. 1, No. 1: Asian American Publications," in E. Gee, ed., *Counterpoint: Perspectives on Asian America* (Los Angeles: Asian American Studies Center, University of California, Los Angeles, 1976).

18. Bruce Iwasaki, "Literature: Introduction," in Gee, *Counterpoint*.
19. Serafin Malay Syquia, "Politics and Poetry," in E. Cachapero, B. Mariano, L. Syquia, S. Belale, and R. Macabasco, eds., *Liwanag: Literary and Graphic Expressions*. (San Francisco: Liwanag Publications, 1975).
20. Elaine H. Kim, *Asian American Literature: An Introduction to the Writings and Their Social Context* (Philadelphia: Temple University Press, 1982), pp. 174–75.
21. Leong, "Poetry Within Earshot.
22. Lorde, "Poetry Is Not a Luxury."
23. Leong, "Poetry Within Earshot."
24. Lawson Fusao Inada, "Amache Gate," in Janice Mirikitani et al., eds., *Time to Greez!: Incantations from the Third World*, (San Francisco: Glide Publications and Third World Communications, 1975), p. 73.
25. Lawson Fusao Inada, "Looking Back at Camp," in *Legends from Camp* (Minneapolis: Coffee House, 1992). Thanks to Lawson for permission to use his poems.
26. Lawson Fusao Inada, "On Being Asian American," in *Legends from Camp*, p. 169.
27. Inada, "Amache Gate," p. 77.
28. Victor S. Navasky, *The Art of Controversy: Political Cartoons and their Enduring Power* (New York: Knopf, 2013), p. 34.
29. Glen Iwasaki, "What *Gidra* Means to Me," *Gidra* 6: 4 (April 1974).
30. Henri Chang, "Chinatown: On Pride and Dissent," *Bridge: As Asian American Perspective* 3: 6 (1975).
31. For example, the *Rafu Shimpo* of March 9, 1970, reported the director of exhibits at UCLA's library saying the exhibit was "the most popular ever."
32. For more on the history of Visual Communications, see Ron Hirano, "Media Guerillas," *Counterpoint* (1976); Jeanne Joe, "Visual Communications: A New Asian Image on the Screen," *Neworld* 5: 6 (1979); Rene Tajima, "Lights, Camera, Affirmative Action," *Independent*, March 1984.
33. "Who or What is Chonk Moonhunter?" at chonkmoonhunter.com.
34. Ron Eyerman and Andrew Jamison, "Social Movements and Cultural Transformation: Popular Music in the 1960s," *Media, Culture and Society* 17: 3 (1995).
35. Frank Chin, Jeffrey Paul Chan, Lawson Fusao Inada, and Shawn Wong, *Aiiieeeee! An Anthology of Asian American Writers* (Garden City: Anchor/Doubleday, 1975), p. 20.
36. Ibid.
37. Salman Rushdie, "On Censorship," *New Yorker*, May 11, 2012.

## 8. *Other Wars*

1. Dolores Hayden, *The Power of Place: Urban Landscapes as Public History* (Cambridge, MA: MIT Press, 1995).
2. Evan Roberts, "Remembering the I-Hotel Evictions," KALW, San Francisco radio station, kalw.org.

3.  Helen C Toribio, "Dare to Struggle: The KDP and Filipino American Politics," in Fred Ho, ed., *Legacy to Liberation: Politics and Culture of Revolutionary Asian Pacific America*, (San Francisco: Big Red Media and AK Press, 2000), p. 40.

4.  Estella Habal, *San Francisco's International Hotel: Mobilizing the Filipino American Community in the Anti-Eviction Movement* (Philadelphia: Temple University Press, 2007).

5.  Alex Hing, "Alex Hing Interview," in Ho, *Legacy to Liberation*, p. 295.

6.  Toribio, "Dare to Struggle," in Ho, *Legacy to Liberation*, p. 40.

7.  Calvin Trillin, "U.S. Journal: Some Thoughts on the International Hotel Controversy," *New Yorker*, December 19, 1977, p. 116. Quoted in Estella Habal's *San Francisco's International Hotel*, p. 126.

8.  Habal, *San Francisco's International Hotel*.

9.  Daryl J. Maeda, *Rethinking the Asian American Movement* (New York/London: Routledge, 2011), p. 61.

10. May C. Fu, "Keeping Close to the Ground: Politics and Coalition in Asian American Community Organizing, 1969–1977," PhD dissertation, University of California, San Diego, 2005, p. 109.

11. Neela Banerjee, "Resurrection of the I-Hotel," *Asian Week* 22: 42 (2001).

12. Ibid.

13. James Sobredo, "The Battle for the International Hotel: Historical Essay," at foundsf.org. Excerpted from "From Manila Bay to Daly City: Filipinos in San Francisco," in James Brook, Chris Carlsson, and Nancy J. Peters, eds., *Reclaiming San Francisco: History, Politics, Culture* (San Francisco: City Lights, 1998).

14. From the video production, "Something's Rotten in Little Tokyo," produced by Visual Communications, 1975.

15. Little Tokyo Anti-Eviction Task Force, "Redevelopment in Los Angeles' Little Tokyo," in E. Gee, ed., *Counterpoint: Perspectives on Asian America* (Los Angeles: Asian American Studies Center, UCLA, 1976).

16. Tracy Takano, "Aloha 'Aina (Love of the Land): The Struggle for Land and Power in Hawai'i," *East Wind: Politics and Culture of Asians in the US* 1: 1 (Spring/Summer 1982).

17. "Who Owns Hawai'i's Lands?," *Aloha Voter*, 12: 9 (March 1972), http://www.lwv-hawaii.com/alohavoter/av7203-who.htm, accessed September 17, 2013.

18. Mary Choy, "Mary Choy," in R. H. Mast and A. B. Mast, eds., *Autobiography of Protest in Hawai'i* (Honolulu: University of Hawai'i Press, 1996), p. 182.

19. Soli Kihei Niheu, "Huli: Community Struggles and Ethnic Studies," *Social Process in Hawai'i* 39 (1999).

20. Ibid.

21. John Witeck, "John Witeck," in Mast and Mast, *Autobiography of Protest in Hawai'i*, p. 346.

22. Tim Ryan, "Waiahole & Wakiane: Worth the Fight," *Honolulu Star Bulletin*, July 13, 1998.

23. Ibid.

24. Bob Nakata, "The Struggles of the Waiahole-Wakiane Community Association," *Social Process in Hawai'i* 39 (1999).

25. David Palumbo-Liu, *Asian/America: Historical Crossings of a Racial Frontier* (Stanford, CA: Stanford University Press, 1999), pp. 269–79.

26. George Robertson, "Desegregating a Maritime Union: The Marine Cooks and Stewards," *Waterfront Workers History Project*, n.d., http://depts.washington.edu/dock/mcs_desegregation.shtml.

27. The information in this section is taken in large part from Ron Chew, *Remembering Silme Domingo and Gene Viernes: The Legacy of Filipino American Labor Activism* (Seattle: University of Washington Press, 2012).

28. Ibid, p. 15.

29. Toribio, "Dare to Struggle," in Ho, *Legacy to Liberation*.

30. Chew, *Remembering Silme Domingo and Gene Viernes*, p. 27.

31. Ibid, p. 48.

32. Karen M. Tani, "The House that 'Equity' Built: The Asian American Movement and the Legacy of Community Action," in A. Orleck and L. G. Hazirjian, eds., *The War on Poverty: A New Grassroots History, 1964–1980* (Athens: University of Georgia Press, 2011), p. 418.

33. William Wei, *The Asian American Movement* (Philadelphia: Temple University Press, 1993), p. 220.

34. R. Takashi Yanagida, "The AAFEE Story: Asian Americans for Equal Employment," originally published in *Bridge Magazine*, February 1974. Reprinted in Emma Gee, ed., *Counterpoint: Perspectives on Asian America* (Los Angeles: Asian American Studies Center, UCLA, 1976).

35. Karen M. Tani notes that, although Asian Americans for Equality—the group into which AAFEE morphed—prefers not to discuss its previous connection with radical organizations, the overlap with the Asian Study Group and its successors, the Workers Viewpoint Organization and the Communist Workers Party, is well documented. Tani, "House that 'Equity' Built," p. 434.

36. Yanagida, "The AAFEE Story."

37. Ibid.

38. Tani, "House that 'Equity' Built," p. 417.

39. Dean Lan, "Chinatown Sweatshops," *Amerasia Journal* 1: 3 (1971). Reprinted in Gee, *Counterpoint*

40. "Political Summation of the Jung Sai Strike," *IWK Journal: The Political Organ of I Wor Kuen* 2 (May 1975).

41. Harvey C. Dong, "The Origins and Trajectory of Asian American Political Activism in the San Francisco Bay Area, 1968–1978," PhD dissertation, University of California, Berkeley, 2002.

42. Maeda, *Rethinking the Asian American Movement*, p. 65.

43. Dong, "Origins and Trajectory of Asian American Political Activism," p. 156.

44. Ibid., p. 180.

45. "Aid to Alcatraz," *Gidra* 2: 1 (January 1970), p. 3.

46. Rockwell Chin, "Public Record, 1989: What Have We Learned from the 60s and 70s?" *Amerasia Journal* 15: 1 (1989), p. 118.

47. "Asians Support Wounded Knee," Press Release, April 27, 1973, L.A. Press Club. Contacts: Joanne (Nobuko) Miyamoto and Marc Kondo.

48. From interviews with Dorothy Cordova, April 20, 2013, and Florante Ibanez, January 29, 2014.

## 9. Self-Appraisals and Evaluations

1. Essays and personal statements by members of various revolutionary organizations are found in Ho's anthology as well as in *Asian Americans: The Movement and the Moment* (2001), edited by Steve Louie and Glenn Omatsu and *Autobiography of Protest in Hawai'i* edited by Robert H. Mast and Anne B. Mast. Excerpts from newsletters of ACC and WMS are published in *Stand Up: An Archive Collection of the Bay Area Asian American Movement 1968-1974* (2009). Secondary commentary on Asian American revolutionary organizations can be found in *Black, Brown, Yellow and Left: Radical Activism in Los Angeles* (2006), *Revolution in the Air: Sixties Radicals turn to Lenin, Mao and Che* (2002), *The Snake Dance of Asian American Activism* (2008), *Rethinking the Asian American Movement* (2012), and *Chains of Babylon: The Rise of Asian America* (2009).

2. A copy is archived in the Stanford University Libraries Special Collections in the Nelson and Beverly Nagai collection of Asian American history and culture, ca 1968-1980, at http://searchworks.stanford.edu/view/10618384

3. I Wor Kuen, "Opportunism in the Asian Movement—Wei Min She/Revolutionary Union," *I.W.K. Journal*, no. 2 (May 1975). Encyclopedia of Anti-Revision On-Line, https://www.marxists.org/history/erol/periodicals/iwk-journal/iwk-wms-ru/index.htm

4. Index to *I.W. K. Journal*, marxists.org.

5. Bruce Iwasaki, "The Final Venemous Jabberwocky: Feverish Grunts on the Movement and the Word" *Gidra* 6: 4 (1974).

6. Ibid. Emphases in original.

7. Amy Uyematsu, "The Emergence of Yellow Power in America," *Gidra* 1: 7 (1969).

8. Editorial, "Growing Pains," *Bridge: As Asian American Perspective*, 5: 2 (Summer 1977), p. 2.

9. An article titled "New York Groups Attack Each Other," by Chen Kai-fai, reported on assaults against members and the office of the Chinese American Democratic Rights Association—allegedly by members of the Workers Viewpoint Organization and Asian Americans for Equality—in the June 6, 1979, issue of the *San Francisco Journal*.

10. Former senator and activist, Reverend Bob Nakata, also recalled a young attorney involved in the Waiahole-Waikane struggle in Hawai'i saying: "'The lawyer is not here to keep you out of trouble; the lawyer is here to get you out of trouble.' He said that in order not to inhibit the action." Bob Nakata, "The Struggles of the Waiahole-Waikane Community Association," *Social Process in Hawai'i* 39 (1999).

11. From email to author from Eddie Wong, June 25, 2015.
12. Audre Lorde, "Learning from the 60s," in *Sister Outsider: Essays and Speeches* (Berkeley, CA: Crossing, 2007), p. 136.
13. Fay Chiang, "Looking Back: Basement Workshop, 1971–86," in J. Chang, ed., *Quiet Fire: A Historical Anthology of Asian American Poetry, 1982–1997* (New York: Asian American Writers Workshop, 1996).
14. Lorde, "Learning from the 60s," p. 142.
15. Davey D, "Looking Back at Huey Newton's Thoughts on Gay Rights in the Wake of Obama's Endorsement," Hip Hop and Politics blog, May 11, 2012, at hiphopandpolitics.com. Newton's speech was also published in the *Black Panther*, August 21, 1970, as "A Letter from Huey to the Revolutionary Brothers and Sisters About the Women's Liberation and Gay Liberation Movements."
16. Sherry Wolf, *Sexuality and Socialism: History, Politics, and Theory of LGBT Liberation* (Chicago: Haymarket, 2009), p. 130.
17. Daniel Tsang, "Losing Its Soul? Reflections on Gay and Asian Activism," in F. Ho, ed., *Legacy to Liberation: Politics and Culture of Revolutionary Asian Pacific America* (San Francisco: Big Red Media, 2000), p. 59.
18. Richard Fung, "The Trouble with 'Asians,'" in M. Dorenkamp and R. Henke, eds., *Negotiating Lesbian and Gay Subjects* (New York: Routledge, 1995). Originally published in *Body Politic* 58 (November 1979).
19. Quoted in Tsang, "Losing Its Soul?," p. 61. Richard Fung's article was originally published in *Body Politic* 58 (November 1979).
20. Mary Uyematsu Kao, "Three-Step Boogie in 1970s Los Angeles: Sansei Women in the Asian American Movement," *Amerasia Journal* 35: 1 (2009), p. 134.
21. The Third World Women's Alliance was a US political formation of women of color, founded in 1971.
22. Delia D. Aguilar, "Tracing the Roots of Intersectionality," in *MRZine*, December 4, 2012.
23. Evangelina Holvino, *Complicating Gender: The Simultaneity of Race, Gender, and Class in Organizing Change(ing)* (Boston: Center for Gender in Organizations, Simmons Graduate School of Management, 2001).
24. Janice Mirikitani, "Ms," in *Third World Women* (San Francisco: Third World Communications, 1972), p. 166. Thanks to Janice for permission to use her poem.
25. Editorial, *Gidra*, 3: 1 (January 1971), p. 2.
26. Mike Yamamoto, "Male Perspective," *Amerasia Journal* 3: 1 (1971), p. 13.
27. Patrick Folliard, "Getting Real: Transgender Attorneys Talk About Coming Out in the Workplace," *Diversity and The Bar*, July–August 2008.
28. Thanks to Arnold Hiura for this information.
29. Min Zhou, "Are Asian Americans Becoming White?" *CSA Academic Perspective* 3 (2007).
30. Mia Tuan, *Forever Foreigners or Honorary Whites?: The Asian Ethnic Experience Today* (New Brunswick, NJ: Rutgers University Press, 1998).
31. My personal favorite is Nicholas Lemann's quip in his *Slate* article "Jews in Second Place": "But as Asians become America's new Jews, Jews are becoming

... Episcopalians." Slate.com, June 25, 1996.

32. Michael Liu, Kim Geron, and Tracy Lai, *The Snake Dance of Asian American Activism: Community, Vision, and Power* (Lanham, MD: Lexington, 2008), p. 97.

33. Michael Liu and Kim Geron, "Changing Neighborhood: Ethnic Enclaves and the Struggle for Social Justice," *Social Justice* 35: 2/112 (2008).

34. Chalsa Loo, "The 'Middle-Aging' of Asian American Studies," in G. Y. Okihiro, S. Hune, A. A. Hansen, and J. M. Liu, eds., *Reflections on Shattered Windows: Promises and Prospects for Asian American Studies* (Pullman: Washington State University Press, 1988), p. 17.

35. Glenn Omatsu, " 'Four Prisons' and the Movements of Liberation," pp. 20–21.

36. Theodore L. Gross, "How to Kill a College: The Private Papers of a Campus Dean," *Saturday Review*, February 4, 1978, p. 18.

37. Gary Y. Okihiro, "Introduction," in Okihiro et al., *Reflections on Shattered Windows*.

## 10. *Generations to Come*

1. Al Robles, "A Manong's Language," *Bridge: An Asian American Perspective* 4: 4 (1976), p. 37. Thanks to the Robles family for permission to use Al's poems.

2. Ron Chew, *Remembering Silme Domingo and Gene Viernes: The Legacy of Filipino American Labor Activism* (Seattle: University of Washington Press, 2012), p. 2.

3. Winifred Breines, "Whose New Left?" *Journal of American History* 75: 2 (1988).

4. Kimberly K. Smith, "Mere Nostalgia: Notes on a Progressive Paratheory," *Rhetoric and Public Affairs* 3: 4 (2000), p. 523.

5. Fredric Jameson, "Periodizing the 60s," *Social Text* 9/10 (1984).

6. David S. Meyer and Nancy Whittier, "Social Movement Spillover," *Social Problems* 41: 2 (1994).

7. James M. Jasper, *The Art of Moral Protest: Culture, Biography, and Creativity in Social Movements* (Chicago/London: University of Chicago Press, 1997), p. 215.

8. Chew, *Remembering Silme Domingo and Gene Viernes*, p. 50.

9. Bea Tam, "Learning from the Garment Workers," in ACCA Group, ed., *Stand Up: An Archive Collection of the Bay Area Asian American Movement, 1968–1974* (San Francisco: Eastwind Books of Berkeley, 2009), p. 193.

10. Audio of the broadcast has been archived at the Manilatown Archives, at manilatownfindingaids.blogspot.com.

11. Robynn Takayama, "Home: Fireside Chat," August 7, 2006, at nonogirl.com.

12. Tyrone Beason, "Bob Santos, Feisty Defender of the Chinatown International District, Has Never Left Home," *Seattle Times*, June 23, 2002.

13. Gary Iwamoto, "Bob Santos: Advisor, Confidant and Drinking Buddy for a Generation," in Doug Chin, *Seattle's International District: The Making of a*

*Pan–Asian American Community*, (Seattle: International Examiner Press, 2009).

14. Ron Chew, "Introduction," in Bob Santos, *Hum Bows, Not Hot Dogs!* (Seattle: International Examiner Press, 2002).

15. This footage was used in a memorial video of Chris, which eventually became the documentary *A Song for Ourselves* (dir. Tadashi Nakamura, 2009).

16. Him Mark Lai, Genny Lim, and Judy Yung, *Island: Poetry and History of Chinese Immigrants on Angel Island 1910–1940* (Seattle: University of Washington Press, 1991).

17. *Wei Min Bao* 2: 6 (April 1973), p. 9. Reprinted in ACCA Group, *Stand Up*.

18. Constance Hayashi and Keiho Yamanaka, "Footprints: Poetry of the Japanese American Relocation Camp Experience," *Amerasia Journal* 3: 2 (1976).

19. Carlos Bulosan, *America Is in the Heart: A Personal History* (New York: Harcourt, Brace, 1946).

20. Xiaojian Zhao and Edward J. W. Park, eds., *Asian Americans: An Encyclopedia of Social, Cultural, Economic, and Political History* (Santa Barbara, CA: Greenwood, 2014).

21. Karen L. Ishizuka, *Lost and Found: Reclaiming the Japanese American Incarceration* (Urbana: University of Illinois Press, 2006), p. 83.

22. Gregory Rodriguez, "New Wave of Immigrants—A New Target Too?" *Los Angeles Times*, June 25, 2012.

23. Belvin Louie and Miriam Ching Yoon Louie, "Damn It, Richard, What the F***?!" *San Francisco Bay View*, August 29, 2012. See also Belvin Louie and Miriam Ching Yoon Louie, "The A-Files: Richard Aoki & the FBI," November 5, 2012, http://afiles2012.blogspot.com/2012/11/damn-it-richard-a-files.html.

24. Ibid.

25. "Transcript for Becoming Detroit: Grace Lee Boggs on Reimagining Work, Food, and Community," July 18, 2013, http://www.onbeing.org/program/becoming-detroit/transcript/5836.

26. Diane C. Fujino, "Who Studies the Asian American Movement? A Historiographical Analysis," *Journal of Asian American Studies* 11: 2 (2008).

27. Mike Murase, "Toward Barefoot Journalism," *Gidra* 6: 4 (1974).

28. Harvey C. Dong, "The Origins and Trajectory of Asian American Political Activism in the San Francisco Bay Area, 1968–1978," PhD dissertation, University of California, Berkeley, 2002, p. 235.

29. Karl Marx, "Preface" to *A Contribution to the Critique of Political Economy* (1859, marxists.org).

30. Grace Lee Boggs, "Asian-Americans and the US Movement," closing speech at Asian American Reality Conference, Pace College, New York City, reproduced by Asian Americans for Action, 1973.

31. Grace Lee Boggs, *The Next American Revolution: Sustainable Activism for the Twenty-First Century* (Berkeley: University of California Press, 2012), p. 72.

32. Glenn Omatsu, "Listening to the Small Voice Speaking the Truth: Grassroots Organizing and the Legacy of Our Movement," in Louie and Omatsu, *Asian Americans*, p. 309.

33. Ibid.

34. Jim Hougan, *Decadence: Radical Nostalgia, Narcissism, and Decline in the Seventies* (New York: Morrow, 1975).

35. Maureen McKnight, "'Scarcely in the Twilight of Liberty': Empathetic Resettlement in Charles Chestnutt's *The Conjure Woman*," in *Iowa Journal of Cultural Studies* 5, 2004.

36. In "Editor's Note," *Bridge Magazine* 4: 4 (October 1976), p. 6.

# Index

Abita, Luis, 170
activism, 4–5; and arts, 161–3; careers in, 212–5; fun with, 217–9; personalities of, 215–6; wide ranging, 182–5
adults, established, 88–95; Asian Americans for Action (AAA), 91–4; Asian Coalition for Equality (ACE), 89–91
African Americans *See* blacks/blackness
Agnew, Spiro, 100
Aguilar, Delia D., 200
Aihara, Chris, 48
Aihara, Doug, 28, 31
*Aiiieeeee! An Anthology of Asian American Writers* (Frank Chin, et al.), 144, 162
Alaska Cannery Workers, 177–9
Alcatraz, 73, 182
Alfonzo, Susan, 130
Alien Land Laws, 19, 34
alienation: definition of, 35. *See also* concentration camps; discrimination; isolation; racism; segregation
aliens: and Asian America, 34–6; definition of, 34; "enemy aliens," 103; ineligible for citizenship, 2, 17, 19, 34–5
*Amerasia Journal*, 67, 87–8, 127; "New York Chinatown Today: Community in Crisis," 127
Amerasian, 66–7
"Amerasian Generation" (conference), 67
*America Is in the Heart* (Carlos Bulosan), 20, 128, 220
American: and black, 35; and Chinese, 15–6; and white, 40
American Indian movement, 4
Americanism, 40–1; Hughes on, 48–9
Anti-Coolie Act (1862), 18
Anti-Imperialist Women's Conference, 111
anti-war *See* Vietnam War
Anzaldúa, Gloria, 9, 61
Aoki, Richard, 61–2, 65, 72, 83, 221–2
Arai, Shoshana, 84
Arai, Tomie, 67, 138–9; and poster arts, 135, 138
Araki, George, 8
Araki, Nancy, 8
"Are You Yellow, Curious?" (conference), 66, 88
Ariyoshi, Koji, 95
arts, 214–5; and activism, 161–3; Amerasia Creative Arts, 127, 138; Black Arts Movement, 116; and black power, 141; and capitalism,

197; and culture, 197; film, 159–61;
    illustration, 151–2; literature, 128,
    143–6, 162–3; music, 139–41, 161–
    2; newspapers, 141–3; photography,
    154–9; poetry, 63, 104, 133, 144–6;
    political cartoons, 146–53; posters,
    134–8
Asian–African Conference (1955), 43,
    66
Asian America: and aliens, 34–6; and
    Basement Workshop, 125; and
    counterculture, ix-x; creation of,
    1–2; demographics of (1970), 21–2;
    ethnic ambiguity of, 68; multiplicity
    of, 210; revolution gave birth to, 163
Asian American Draft Resistance, 72
Asian American movement, 2, 11–2,
    63; awakening to, 7, 209–10;
    beginning of, 6, 9; development
    of, 70–4; end of, 189–90, 194–7;
    established adults in, 88–95; goals of,
    205; literature on, 4–6; principles of,
    65; social bandits, 76–82; talented
    tenth, 82–8; and Third World, 65,
    73, 84, 182; widespread awakening
    of, 75; and yellow power, 64–6
The Asian American Movement (Wei), 5
Asian American Political Alliance
    (AAPA), 62, 76, 83–5, 95
Asian American Resource Center, 124,
    127–8
Asian American Studies, 30, 87–8,
    117, 204–6; and community, 116;
    conferences, 88. See also names of
    individual conferences
Asian American Studies Center
    (UCLA), 15, 63, 87–8
Asian American Vietnam Veterans
    Organization, 106
Asian Americans: birth of, 209; and
    blackness, 41–7, 66, 90–1, 161, 177,
    183;
    definition of, 3, 61–2; language
        before, 64–8; neutralization of, 3;
        struggle over, ix

ethnic makeup, 1; good & bad, 53;
    and Hawai'i, 31–4; isolation of,
    23–9; neither black nor white,
    47–55; nurturing of, 30–1; and
    whites, 51–2
Asian Americans: The Movement and the
    Moment (S. Louie and G. Omatsu),
    5
Asian Americans for Action (AAA), 8,
    91–5, 104, 221
Asian Americans for Equal Employment
    (AAFEE), 135, 179–80, 204
Asian Americans for Peace, 99
Asian Coalition for Equality (ACE),
    89–91, 95, 129
Asian Community Center (ACC), 117,
    191; and International Hotel, 169
Asian Community Center Archive
    Group, Stand Up: An Archive
    Collection of the Bay Area Asian
    American Movement, 5
Asian Exclusion Act, 19, 23
Asian Movement for Military Outreach,
    106, 111
Asian nation (term), 67
Asian Study Group, 180, 191
Asian War Brides Act, 82
Asiatic Exclusion League, 18
atomic destruction See Hiroshima-
    Nagasaki
The Autobiography of Malcolm X
    (Malcolm X), 81

Bacho, Norris, 130
Bacho, Reme, 130
Baez, Joan, 98
Bain, David Haward, Aftershocks: A Tale
    of Two Victims, 109
Baker, Mark, Nam: The Vietnam War in
    the Words of the Men and Women Who
    Fought There, 108
Baraka, Amiri, 197
Basement Workshop (group), 124–8,
    196–7; and Bridge Magazine, 143,
    146; and political cartoons, 146;

"Yellow Pearl," 66, 124, 127, 138–9, 146, 197
Beauvoir, Simone de, 3
Benjamin, Walter, 152
Betserai, Tarabu, 217
Black Juans, 77, 123
Black Liberation, 2–3, 212; Mao on, 43
*Black Panther* (newspaper), 43, 141
Black Panther Party, 72–3, 81–2, 127, 129, 183, 218; and "Serve the People," 115
black power, 52, 61, 91; and arts, 141
*Black Power: The Politics of Liberation* (Kwame Ture and Charles V. Hamilton), 61
blacks/blackness: and American, 35; and Asian Americans, 41–7, 66, 90–1, 161, 177, 183; neither black nor white, 47–55
Black Arts Movement, 116; definition of, 41; newspapers, 43, 47; and racism, 41; and Vietnam War, 100–1, 109; and whiteness, 41; and yellow, 46. *See also* whites; yellow
*Blade Runner* (film), 151, 173
Boggs, Grace Lee, xi, 84, 95, 223–4
*Bridge Magazine*, 120, 125, 127, 142–3, 146, 198; on end of movement, 194; and political cartoons, 148–9; and poster art, 135–7
Brienes, Winifred, 210
Brodkin, Karen, 9, 40
Brown, H. Rap, 91
Bruce, Lenny, 60
Buck, Pearl, 221
Bulosan, Carlos, *America is in the Heart*, 20, 128, 220

*California Eagle* (newspaper), 43
capitalism, 151, 195; and arts, 197; and imperialism, 191; and sexism, 201
Carlin, George, 60
Carmichael, Stokely, 61, 91, 100
*Catcher in the Rye* (J. D. Salinger), 25

Census, 125–6
*Chains of Babylon: The Rise of Asian America* (Maeda), 5
Chan, Jeffrey Paul, 53–4, 144, 161–2
Chan, Kenyon, 159
Chang, Henri, 155
Cheng, Charles, 104
Chew, Ron, 178–9, 209
Chiang, Fay, 49–50, 67, 87, 207; and Basement Workshop, 124–5, 128; breakdown of, 196; and women, 200
*Chicago Defender* (newspaper), 43
Chin, Charlie, 3, 63, 92; and Basement Workshop, 125, 127; and music, 139
Chin, Frank, 53–4, 144, 161–2
Chin, Mike, 134
Chin, Rocky, 28, 183, 216; and Basement Workshop, 124, 127; on JACS, 120; "New York Chinatown Today: Community in Crisis," 127
Chinatown Cooperative Garment Factory, 118, 217; advertisement for, 119
Chinese, and American, 15–6
Chinese Exclusion Act, 18, 25, 47, 49
Chinese Socialist Club, 83
*Chinese Times* (newspaper), 182
Chinese War Brides Act, 85
Ching, Frank, 143
Chink (term), 48, 100
Chinn, Sherrie, 130
Chong, Sylvia Shin Huey, 100
chop suey, 16–7, 27
Chow, Carmen, 88
Chow, Peter, 143
Choy, Christine, 138
Choy, Curtis, 160; *The Fall of the I Hotel* (film), 161, 167
Choy, Mary, 174
Christian, Barbara, 9
Chu, Grace Zia, 16
Chun-Hoon, Lowell, 87–8, 127
citizenship: aliens ineligible for, 2, 17, 19, 34–5; finally available, 20;

US nationals without, 68–9; and whiteness, 40
civil rights, 2–4, 45, 89–90, 154, 216
Civil Rights Act of 1964, 179
class, and racism, 26, 49
Clearwater, Frank, 184
Cleaver, Eldridge, 81, 91
Cleaver, Kathleen, 8
Coleman, Ornette, 44
college *See* Asian American Studies; ethnic studies; "Talented Tenth"
comics *See* political cartoons
communism, 176, 198, 221
community, 115–6, 120; and poster arts, 135
concentration camps (WWII), 23, 28–9, 37, 44, 48, 50, 73, 87, 89, 95, 107, 120–1, 176, 182, 206, 220; black newspapers on, 43; and Internal Security Act, 7; and Japanese Americans, 50–1; Manzanar Pilgrimage, 154, 156–7; and photography, 159; and racism, 28, 103; and Vietnam War, 103
Confucius Plaza: labor struggles at, 179–80; and poster arts, 135
Cordova, Fred, 70, 185; *Filipino: Forgotten Asian Americans*, 68
counterculture, ix-x, 4. *See also* activism
*Counterpoint: Perspectives on Asian America* (Bruce Iwasaki), 143
Crow Dog, Henry, 183
Crow Dog, Leonard, 183
cultural revolution, 4
Cushing, Lincoln, 134

Dane, Barbara, 64
dialectical materialism, 224
difference, 61
disassociation, 40
discrimination, 27, 129; in Hawai'i, 34; in housing, 25–6, 37, 44; in labor, 178–80
diversity, protests for, 84

Dixon, Aaron, 218
Dixon, Elmer, 218
*Do the Right Thing* (film), 42
Domingo, Silme, 178–9, 212
Dong, Harvey, 98–9, 117, 132, 185, 217, 224; on labor struggles, 181–2
Dong, Jim, 134
Dorhn, Bernardine, 6, 221
double consciousness, 35
Douglas, Emory, 141
Douglass, Frederick, 47, 225; *North Star* (newspaper), 141
drugs, 79, 124
Du Bois, W. E. B., 35, 42; on black/ Asian solidarity, 66; on "Talented Tenth," 75, 82
dual domination, 49–51, 82

*The East Is Red*, 118
*Ebony* (magazine), 37
Eisenstein, Elizabeth, 141
El Centro de la Raza, 129
Embrey, Sue Kunitomi, 95
Emergency Detention Act, 95
"The Emergency Summit Conference," 101
Eng, Lincoln, 91
English (language) *See* language
Enlai, Chou, 95
Enomoto, Jerry, 124
*Esquire* (magazine), "The New Yellow Peril," 60
ethnic studies, 84–5, 95, 116, 174, 205–6
Everybody's Book Store, 118
Eyerman, Ron, 161

Fanon, Frantz, 11, 24, 66; on color, 38
Farmer, James, 91
fascism, 183
FBI, 98, 221–2
fear, 165, 181
Feng, Peter, 67–8
*Filipino: Forgotten Asian Americans* (Cordova), 68

Filipino People's Far West Convention (conference), 70
Filipino Youth Activities (FYA), 70
Filipinos, 68–70; *Liwanag: Literary and Graphic Expressions by Filipinos in America*, 143–4
film, 159–61
film group, 117–8
Fong, Joe, 80
Fong-Torres, Ben, 140
Foo, Lora, 134
*Freedom's Journal* (newspaper), 141
Freire, Paulo, 1, 9–10
Fujimoto, Isao, 99, 103
Fujino, Diane C., 4, 6, 11, 61, 224
Fukuda, Greg, 147
Fung, Richard, 198
Furumura, Jeff, 32–3
Furutani, Warren, 8, 75, 123; photograph of, 73; and public speaking, 71; on self-appraisals, 193; and Vietnam War, 99

García, David, 183
Gavino, Julieanne P., 134
Gee, Emma, 83
Gee, Zand, 135
gender, 200–2
Geron, Kim, 5, 204
*Getting Together* (newspaper), 81
GI Bill, 25, 98
*Gidra: The Monthly of the Asian American Experience* (newspaper), 7, 87, 97, 111, 142–4, 154; description of, 63; on Hiroshima & Vietnam, 103; images of, 105, 122, 150; last issue, 189–90, 192; and Little Tokyo, 171–2; and political cartoons, 147, 150–2; and "Serve the People," 131–2; on women, 201, 203; "Amerasian Culture," 67; "Amerasian Power," 66; "Asians Throughout America," 21–2; "The Emergence of Yellow Power," 65; "I Am Curious (Yellow?)," 68; "Kill that Gook, You Gook!," 104–5,

147; "Little Tokyo 1984?," 151, 172; "Manzanar Pilgrimage," 156–7; "The Nature of GI Racism," 104–6; "Where Do We Go From Here?," 190; "Yellow Power!," 64–5
Gladwell, Malcolm, 72
Glazer, Nathan, 20
González, Juan, 88
González, N. V. M., 145
Gooks (term), 104
Gossett, Larry, 218
Gotanda, Neil, 72
Gotanda, Philip, 8
*A Grain of Sand: Music for the Struggle by Asian Americans* (music), 64
graphic novel, 147
Gross, Theodore L., 205–6
Guzman, Emil De, 167, 170

Habal, Estella, 119, 167–9
Hall, Stuart, 41
Hama, Larry, 125; and political cartoons, 146, 148
Hamada, Miles, 135
Hamilton, Charles, 61
Hampton, Lionel, 44
haole (term), 204
Hardcore (group), 7, 72, 78, 121, 123
Hawai'i, 203–4, 221; and Asian Americans, 31–4; Asian population of, 22; and rural removal, 174–6
Hayakawa, S. I., 85, 121
Hayasaka, Lois, 90
Hayasaka, Phil, 89–90, 129
Hayden, Delores, 166
Hayden, Tom, 6
Herzig-Yoshinaga, Aiko, 8
*The Hidden 1970s: Histories of Radicalism* (Dan Berger), 5
Higa, Kaz, 159
Hing, Alex, 72–3, 81, 168, 193
Hirabayashi, Jim, 8
Hirabayashi, Lane, 8
Hirano, Ron, 8, 159
Hirano, Tatsuo, 183–4

Hiroshima (band), 72

Hiroshima-Nagasaki, 94, 102–4; and poster arts, 135

history, 222–4; and nostalgia, 225; oral, 210, 212; recovery of, 219–20

Ho, Fred, 161; *Legacy to Liberation: Politics and Culture of Revolutionary Asian Pacific America*, 5, 191

Hobsbawm, Eric, 75–6

Holvino, Evangelina, 200

Hom, Nancy, 135, 139–40, 155, 197, 214–5

homosexuality, 198–9

Hoover, J. Edgar, 93, 126

Hougan, Jim, 225

housing, 26, 37, 44; and immigration, 121; Rumford Fair Housing Act, 25

Hsia, Bea, 8

Hsiang, Bob, 154

Hu, Arthur, 54

Huang, Arlan, 104, 125, 197

Huen, Floyd, 84

Huggins, Erica, 183

Hughes, Langston, 42; on Americanism, 48–9; on concentration camps, 43

*I Am Curious (Yellow)* (film), 64, 147

I Wor Kuen (IWK), 81, 88, 94, 118, 191–2; and International Hotel, 168–9; and Jung Sai strike, 181–2

*I Work Kuen's Reactionary Line on May Day and the Worker's Movement* (booklet), 191–2

Ibanez, Florante, 69, 185

Ichioka, Yuji, 62, 83

identity, 30, 34; and Asian American movement, 65, 205; and disassociation, 40; double consciousness, 35; and imperialism, 109–13; and language, 61; national identification buttons, 40; personal as political, 35–6, 65, 93; and political cartoons, 147; and racism, 62; as resistance, 161–2; and "Serve

the People," 115, 127; and Third World, 209; and Vietnam War, 97. *See also* alienation

Ijima, Chris, 3, 8, 63, 66, 92–3, 101, 109, 154, 211, 218; and Basement Workshop, 125, 127; *A Grain of Sand* (music), 161; on Hawai'i, 33; on identity, 161; and music, 139–41; photograph of, 158; and Vietnam War, 101; "Yellow Pearl" (song), 66

Ijima, Kazu, 8, 33, 91–4, 221; on Vietnam War, 97

Iki, Darcie, 32

illustration, 151–2

immigration: aliens ineligible for, 2, 17, 19, 34–5; Chinese, 17–8, 21; and "enemy aliens," 103; Filipino, 19–21; and housing, 121; Japanese, 18–9, 21; and labor, 177; and language, 50; and New York, 125; policy, 17–21, 82; quotas for, 18–20, 69, 85, 125, 155, 181; and whites, 17. *See also* names of individual Acts

Immigration Act of 1924, 19

Immigration and Nationality Act of 1965, 20–1, 125, 177

Immigration and Nationality (McCarran-Walter) Act (1952), 20

imperialism, 163, 184–5; and capitalism, 191; and identity, 109–13; and racism, 189

Inada, Lawson, 46, 144–5, 160, 162, 225; *Before the War*, 145

Internal Security Act, 7, 94; and concentration camps (WWII), 7; and photography, 159

International District (Seattle), 128–31; International District Improvement Association, 129; and Kingdome, 129–30

International Hotel (I-Hotel), 117–9, 217; and arts, 134; *The Fall of the I Hotel* (film), 161; police raid, 167–9; rebuilding of, 169–70; and urban renewal, 166–70

International Ladies Garment Workers' Union, 94

intersectionality, 200–2

isolation, 23–9; Filipino, 68. *See also* alienation

Itliong, Larry, 70, 95

Iwasaki, Bruce, 97, 113, 192; and graphic novel, 147; on literature, 143–4; "A Separate Peace: War," 151

Iwasaki, Glen, 147, 151–2

Iwataki, Miya, 121

Izumi, Lance, 54

James, C. L. R., 71

James, Clive, 12

Jameson, Fredric, 4, 212

Jamison, Andrew, 161

Japanese American, 28–30, 53; and concentration camps, 50–1; and disassociation, 40; gangs, 76–8. *See also* concentration camps

Japanese American Citizens' League (JACL), 8, 67, 120–1, 140, 159, 182

Japanese American Community Services (JACS), 120–4; and Little Tokyo, 171

Japanese Community Youth Council, 72

Jasper, James M., 6

Jayo, Norman, 116, 217

Joe Boys (group), 80

Joint Communications, 123

Jordan, June, 61

*Joy Luck Club* (film), 214

Jun, Helen J., 41, 47

Jung Sai Garment Workers, 165, 180–2, 217

Kagawa, Paul, 135

Kahan, Louis, 109

Kahng, Anthony, 102

Kaku, Michio, 103

Kalayaan Collective, 70, 191

*Kalayaan International* (magazine), 110, 118, 142

Kanno, Hiroshi, 95

Kao, Don, 48, 198

Kao, John, 155

Kao, Mary Uyematsu, 200

Katagiri, Mineo, 91

Kazama, Don, 95

Kearny Street (San Francisco), 116–9, 214–5, 217; and poster art, 134–5, 140

Kelly, John, 175

Kim, Claire Jean, 39, 54

Kim, Elaine, 39, 116, 144

Kim, Nami, 47

King, Martin Luther, Jr., 43, 116

Kingdome (Seattle), 129–30

Kingston, Maxine Hong, 68

Kipling, Rudyard, "The White Man's Burden," 19

Klineberg, Stephen, 21

Kobata, Dennis, 184

Kochiyama, Aichi, 8

Kochiyama, Bill, 8, 45

Kochiyama, Yuri, 8, 84, 92, 102; and Malcolm X, 45–6, 179

Kodani, Masao, 45

Koerner, Brendan I., *The Skies Belong to Us: Love and Terror in the Golden Age of Hijacking*, 112

Kōkua, 174–5

Kondo, Alan, 38, 159; *I Told You So* (film), 160; photograph of, 160

Kubo, Duane, 154, 159, 183; *Cruisin' J-Town* (film), 160

Kubota, Larry, 65

Kurashige, Scott, 44, 65

Kusumoto, Rokuichi, 120

labor, 176–82, 218, 221; and activism, 182; Alaska Cannery Workers, 177–9; cheap, 17–9, 53, 69; Chinatown Cooperative Garment Factory, 118–9; at Confucius Plaza, 179–80; for immigrants, 24, 26, 50; and immigration, 177; International Ladies Garment Workers' Union,

94; International Longshore and
Warehouse Union (ILWU), 32; Jung
Sai Garment Workers, 165, 180–2;
strikes, 83, 117; struggles, 166;
United Farm Workers, 95, 129; and
women, 181–2
Lai, Denny, 80
Lai, Tracy, 5, 204
Lamont, Buddy, 184
land ownership, 174
language: before "Asian American," 64–
8; black English, 45; and emergence,
60–4; and Filipinos, 68–70; and
identity, 61; and immigration, 50;
and music, 140; and self-definition,
61; and whiteness, 40, 45; yellow,
64–6
Lawrence, Chuck, 44, 52
Lee, Bill, 80, 127, 183
Lee, C. N., 135
Lee, Chuck, 135
Lee, Corky, 155
Lee, Gordon, 155
Lee, Robert G., 34
Lee, Spike, *Do the Right Thing*, 42
*Legacy to Liberation: Politics and Culture
of Revolutionary Asian Pacific America*
(F. Ho), 5
legislation, 17–8. *See also* names of
individual Acts
Lennon, John, 141
Leong, George, 160
Leong, Russell C., 144–5, 161, 225;
"Poetry Within Earshot: Notes on an
Asian American Generation," 133
Lester, Julius, 54
Leways (group), 80–2, 118
LGBTQ, 198–202
Li, David Leiwei, 39
liberation, 205–6
*Library Journal* (magazine), 63
*Life* (magazine), 46
Lim, Happy, 220
literature, 128, 143–6; graphic novel,
147; illustration, 151–2; minority,

162–3; and Third World, 143. *See
also* names of individual authors and
works; newspapers; poetry
Little Tokyo, 170–3; "Little Tokyo
1984?," 151, 172
Liu, Eric, 39
Liu, Michael, 5, 204
*Liwanag: Literary and Graphic
Expressions by Filipinos in America*,
143–4
Loke, Margaret, 143
Long, Edward, 15–6
Loo, Chalsa, 205
*Looking Like the Enemy* (film), 108
Lorde, Audre, 63, 133, 144, 195, 225;
on doing our enemies' work, 196
*The Los Angeles Free Press* (newspaper),
64, 193; "The Emergence of Yellow
Power," 65; "Yellow Power Arrives!,"
59, 193
*Los Angeles Times* (newspaper), 103,
108, 183, 221
Louie, Adna, 98
Louie, Belvin, 82, 85–7, 98, 222
Louie, Miriam Ching Yoon, 222
Louie, Paul, 7, 216
Louie, Steve, 2, 72, 215–6; *Asian
Americans: The Movement and the
Moment*, 5; isolation of, 25, 35; on
sexism, 202
Lowe, Lisa, 5
Lu, Xun, 42, 115
Lyman, Stanford, 81–2

Macias, Ysidro, 88
MacPhee, Josh, 134
Maeda, Daryl, 85; *Chains of Babylon:
The Rise of Asian America*, 5; on
International Hotel, 169; on Jung
Sai, 181; *Rethinking the Asian
American Movement*, 5
Maeda, Sharon, 37
Maestas, Roberto, 218
Malkin, Michele,  x
*Manzanar Free Press*, 95

Manzanar Pilgrimage, 154, 156–7, 159
Mao Zedong, 53, 95, 192, 206–7;
    on black liberation, 43; "Serve the
    People," 42, 115
Mar, Warren, 169
Marcos, Ferdinand, 178–9, 185
Martínez, Elizabeth, 4
Marwick, Arthur, 4
Marx, Karl, 10
Masaoka, Kathy Nishimoto, 184
Masaoka, Mark, 173
Masuda, Minn, 91
Matsuda, Mari, 44, 46, 222
Matsui, Jeffrey, 8, 121
Matsuoka, Jim, 78, 121
Matsushita, Karl, 104
McCarthyism, 23
McIntosh, Peggy, 38
McKnight, Maureen, 225
McWilliams, Carey, 28, 221
Meléndez, Gabriel A., 141
melting pot, 20; as metaphor, 17
The Melting Pot (play), 17
memory, 210; and history, 225; and
    nostalgia, 226
Meyerhoff, Barbara, 10
Mills, C. Wright, 35
Minami, Dale, 194
Mirikitani, Janice, 200
Miyamoto, Nobuko, 63, 92, 155; and
    Basement Workshop, 125, 127; A
    Grain of Sand (music), 161; and
    music, 139–41; photograph of, 158;
    "Yellow Pearl" (song), 66
Miyano, Jim, 121
model minority, 10, 16, 29, 51–2, 55,
    60, 221–2; success stories, 52–3; and
    white supremacy, 52
Modood, Tariq, 61
Monkawa, David, 147, 150–1, 214;
    and combat analogy, 165; "Little
    Tokyo 1984?," 151, 172–3
Moraga, Cherrie, 9
Morales, "Uncle" Royal, 69–70
Morita, Walter, 193

Moses, Bob, 109
Moynihan, Daniel, 20
Muhammad Speaks (newspaper), 45
Mullen, Bill V., 41–2
Murase, Mike, 41, 73, 173, 189,
    192, 207, 224; and Gidra, 143;
    and political cartoons, 151–2; and
    Vietnam War, 101
Museum of the Chinese in America,
    128
music, 139–41; and activism, 161–2; A
    Grain of Sand, 64; and language, 140

Nagai, Nelson, 72
Nagatani, Nick, 106; and graphic novel,
    147; photograph of, 122
Nakagawa, Scot, 52
Nakamura, Norman, 159; "The Nature
    of GI Racism," 104–6, 108
Nakamura, Robert A., 7–8, 23–4, 27,
    30, 54, 108, 115, 132, 154, 159;
    isolation of, 23–4; Looking Like
    the Enemy (film), 108; Manzanar
    (film), 160; photograph of, 160;
    as photographer, 154, 159; and
    segregation, 54; and "serve the
    people," 115, 132
Nakanishi, Don, 87–8, 127
Nakano, George, 78, 211
Nakasako, Spencer, 205, 223
Nakata, Bob, 175
Nakayama, Mike, 106–9, 111;
    photograph of, 110
Nash, Phil Taijitsu, 8
National Coalition for Redress and
    Reparations, 78
national identification buttons, 40
National Origins Act, 19
Native Americans, and Wounded Knee,
    183–4
Naturalization Act of 1790, 17
Naturalization Act of 1870, 17
Neal, Larry, 116
Nee, Roy, 102
New York Times, 93

*New York Times Magazine*, 52
*New Yorker* (magazine), 169
newspapers, 141–3. *See also* names of
    individual publications
*Newsweek* (magazine), 52
Newton, Huey P., 73, 198
Ngo, Vinh Long, 104
Nguyen, Thai Binh, 9, 112
Niheu, Soli, 174–5
Nisei, Doug, 28
Nishida, Mo, 121, 123, 184; on end of
    movement, 190; photograph of, 131;
    and "Serve the People," 131–2
Nishio, Alan, 7, 88, 121
Nixon, Richard, 151
"No Vietnamese Ever Called Me
    Nigger!" (film), 100
Noguchi, Thomas, 121
*North Star* (newspaper), 141
*Northwestern Enterprise* (newspaper), 43
nostalgia, 211; and history, 225; and
    memory, 226
Nunberg, Geoffrey, 60

Oba, Ron, 47
Ohashi, Alan, 8, 154, 159; *Kites and
    Other Tales* (film), 160; photograph
    of, 160
Ohelo, Kalani, 88
Okada, Alan, 125
Okada, John, *No-No Boy*, 128
Okamura, Jonathan, 33
Okamura, Ray, 7, 94
Okihiro, Gary, 37, 46, 84, 206; on
    community, 116
Okura, Pat, 95
Omatsu, Glenn, 127, 205, 224–5;
    *Asian Americans: The Movement and
    the Moment*, 5
Ono, Shinya, 8, 67, 99, 123
oral history, 210, 212
Orientals, 3, 9, 15–7, 35, 45; definition
    of, 61; Said on, 41; vs Amerasian, 67
Orr, Frank, 105
Orwell, George, *1984*, 151, 172

Pajaud, Bill, 147
Palumbo-Liu, David, 176
personal, and political, 35–6, 65, 93
Petersen, William, 52
Pew Research, 221–2
Philippine-American War (1899-1902),
    102
Philippine Independence Act, 69
Philippines, 68–70; "US War Crimes in
    the Philippines," 102
photography, 154–9
Pido, Antonio J. A., 69
Pioneer Project, 78
Platt, Tony, 53, 81
poetry, 63, 104, 133, 144–6, 200, 220
police, 82; brutality, 155, 158;
    harassment, 81; International Hotel
    raid, 167–9
political, and personal, 35–6, 65, 93
political cartoons, 146–53; graphic
    novel, 147; and identity, 147;
    illustration, 151–2
political correctness, 195, 197
politicization, 6
Poor People's Campaign, 81
post-traumatic stress disorder (PTSD),
    86–7
poster arts, 134–8; and *Bridge
    Magazine*, 135–7
Powell, Adam Clayton, 221
power, 205–6
Prashad, Vijay, 52, 66
prison, 123–4
protest *See* activism; labor
Prowler, David, 167

Rabaya, Violet, 68
racism, x, 19–20, 32, 91–2; and
    blacks, 41; and class, 26, 49; and
    conentration camps, 28, 103;
    double consciousness, 35; and
    identity, 62; and imperialism, 189;
    national identification buttons,
    40; as race extermination, 103;
    racial profiling, 206; racist love,

53–4; and sexism, 200–2; struggle against, 43; and Vietnam war, 97, 99–102, 104–8, 104–9, 147. *See also* blacks/blackness; discrimination; segregation; white standards; white supremacy; whites/whiteness; yellow

rape, 108–9, 111

Reagan, Ronald, 85–6

Reagon, Bernice Johnson, 139

Red Guard (group), 81–2, 118

*Red Star Over China* (Edgar Snow), 81

*Rethinking the Asian American Movement* (Maeda), 5

Revolutionary Communist Party, 175

Robles, Al, 3, 133, 170, 225, 229

Rock, Chris, 36

*Rodan* (newspaper), 72, 142

Rohmer, Sax, 18

*Rolling Stone* (magazine), 140

*Roots: An Asian American Reader* (Amy Tachiki, et al.), 87, 105

Rosenfeld, Seth, 222

Rumford Fair Housing Act, 25

Rumi (poet), 60, 133

Rushdie, Salman, 163

Said, Edward, 16; on Orient, 41

Saika, Peggy, 29–30, 215

Saito, John, 121

Salazar, Rubén, 183

*San Francisco Chronicle* (newspaper), 181

San Francisco Japanese Socialist Party, 83

*San Francisco Magazine*, 81

Sanada, Kikyo, 220

Santos, Bob, 7, 40, 89, 129, 165, 177, 218; on ACE, 89; and combat analogy, 165; and International District, 129–31; and labor, 177; and national identification buttons, 40; photograph of, 130

Santos, George, 174

Sato, Wilbur, 87

Schlesinger, Arthur, 20

Seale, Bobby, 183

Search to Involve Pilipino Americans (SIPA), 69–70

*Seattle Times* (newspaper), 90

segregation, 24, 27; acceptance of, 78; and bathrooms, 49; and public pools, 54–5, 60; and whiteness, 48

self-determination, 1–2, 113

Serikaku, Seisuke, 175

"Serve the People," 79, 115, 120, 131–2; Basement Workshop (New York), 124–8; and Black Panthers, 115; end of, 168, 190–1; International District (Seattle), 128–31; Japanese American Community Services (JACS), 120–4; Kearny Street (San Francisco), 116–9; and Mao, 42, 115; and Nakamura, 115; and poster arts, 135

sexism, and racism, 200–2

Shabazz, James, 46

Shibata, Victor, 7–8

Shimabukuro, Scott, 106–8

Sixties, 4, 6, 211, 226; and Asian American Studies, 206; *The Los Angeles Free Press*, 59; skyjacking epidemic, 112

*The Sixties: A Journal of History, Politics and Culture* (journal), 4

skyjacking, 112

slavery, 41, 47

Smith, Kimberly K., 211

*The Snake Dance of Asian American Activism: Community, Vision and Power* (Michael Liu, Kim Geron, and Tracy Lai), 5

social bandits, 75–82; Japanese American gangs, 76–8; Joe Boys, 80; Leways, 80–1; Red Guard, 81–2; Yellow Brotherhood, 79; Yow Yee, 79–80

social change, 219

social movements, 6, 11, 212

socialism, 178, 195, 221

Sone, Monica, *Nisei Daughter*, 128

Sorro, Bill, 170
speech *See* language
St. John de Crèvecoeur, J. Hector, 17
*Stand Up: An Archive Collection of the
    Bay Area Asian American Movement*
    (Bea Tam), 5
Steele, Claude, 54
suburbanization, 23
Sugiyama, Al, 130
suicide, 117
Sumi, Pat, 7, 73, 94, 99, 102, 111; "US
    War Crimes in the Philippines," 102
Sun, Yat-sen, 42
surveillance, 194; FBI, 98, 221–2
Syquia, Serafin Malay, 144

Takagi, Mary Ann, 94–5
Takagi, Paul, 53, 81
Takano, Tracy, 174
Takemoto, Alan, 105, 150, 160; "Kill
    that Gook, You Gook!," 104–5, 147
"Talented Tenth," 75, 82–8; Asian
    American Political Alliance, 83;
    Asian American Studies, 87–8; Third
    World Liberation Front, 84–6
Tam, Bea, 217
Tani, Karen, 179
Tara, Bill, 147
Tasaki, Ray, 7, 78, 123
Tchen, Jack, 194, 197
Terry, Wallace, *Bloods: An Oral History
    of the Vietnam War by Black Veterans*,
    108
theater, 44
theory, 193
Third World, 1, 3, 212; and Asian
    American movement, 65, 73, 84,
    182; and black/Asian solidarity, 43;
    definition of, 66; and identity, 209;
    and literature, 143; and poster arts,
    135; strike, 117; and urban renewal,
    176; and Vietnam War, 101; and
    yellow power, 65
Third World Liberation Front (TWLF),
    84–6, 98, 165

*Third World Women* (Janice Mirikitani),
    200
Togawa, Paul, 44
Toguchi, Richard, 121
Toji, Dean, 147
Tokeshi, Rich, 135
Tokunaga, Mike, 32
Toribio, Helen C., 168, 190
*Tri-Continental*, 134
Trillin, Calvin, 169
Tsang, Daniel, 198
Tsang, Jim, 104
Tsutakawa, Mayumi, 129
Ture, Kwame *See* Carmichael, Stokely
Twain, Mark, 18, 102
Tydings-McDuffie Act (1934), 19, 69

Union of Democratic Filipinos (KDP),
    78, 118, 178, 191; and International
    Hotel, 168–9
unions *See* labor
United Farm Workers, 95, 129
United Indians of All Tribes, 129
Uno, Edison, 95
urban renewal, 166–76; and Hawai'i,
    174–6; and International Hotel,
    166–70; and Little Tokyo, 170–3;
    and Third World, 176
US-Japan Security Pact (1970), 73,
    185
*US News & World Report* (magazine),
    52
Uyematsu, Amy, 65

Valparaiso, Russell, 7, 102; photograph
    of, 77
Van Deburg, William, 76
Vaughn, Eugene, 112
Vera Cruz, Philip, 70, 95
Viernes, Gene, 177–9, 212
Vietnam Veterans Against the War, 106
Vietnam War, 2–3, 94, 97–113, 151,
    212; and blacks, 100–1, 109; and
    concentration camps (WWII), 103;
    costs of, 98; end of, 189–90; and

identity, 97, 155; Mai Lai massacre, 102–3; "The Nature of GI Racism" (report), 104–6, 108; as race extermination, 103; and racism, 97, 99–102, 104–8, 104–9, 147; and Third World, 101; Winter Soldier Investigation, 106, 108; and women, 108–9

Visual Communications (VC), 159–60, 171

Vogel, Todd, 141

Wakabayashi, Ron, 8

Wang, L. Ling Chi, 6, 82, 209; on dual domination, 49–51

War Brides Act, 98

*Washington Post*, 93

Watson, Cathryn, 42

Weathermen (group), 8, 67, 99, 123

Weglyn, Michi, 8

Wei Min She (WMS), 118–9, 142, 191–2; and International Hotel, 168–9; and Jung Sai strike, 181–2

Wei, William, *The Asian American Movement*, 5

West, Cornel, 35, 41

Westmoreland, William, 97

*Westside Story* (film), 139

White, Charles, 147

"The White Man's Burden" (Kipling), 19

white standards, 2, 24, 27

white supremacy, 211; and Asian American movement, 65; and black/Asian solidarity, 46–7; and double consciousness, 35; and dual domination, 49; and model minority, 52; opposition to, 43; and racist love, 54

Whitebear, Bernie, 218

whites/whiteness, 1, 38–41; and blackness, 41; and citizenship, 40; as good as, 51–2; and immigration, 17; and language, 40, 45; neither black nor white, 47–55; and segregation,

48; and "Serve the People," 115. *See also* blacks/blackness; racism; yellow

Widener, Daniel, 44

Williams, Robert F., 43

Witeck, John, 175

Wittgenstein, Ludwig, 60

Wolf, Sherry, 198

Wolfe, Tom, "The New Yellow Peril," 60

women, 49–50, 200–2; Anti-Imperialist Women's Conference, 111; and labor, 181–2; rape, 108–9, 111; and Vietnam War, 108–9, 111

Wong, Eddie, 154, 159, 195; photograph of, 160; *Wong Singsaang* (film), 160

Wong, Legan, 125

Wong, Leland, 134–5, 162

Wong, Shawn, 144, 162

Woo, George, 60

Wood, Natalie, 139

Wounded Knee, 225; and Native Americans, 183–4

X, Malcolm, 4, 8, 78, 154–5, 179, 205; *The Autobiography of Malcolm X*, 81; death of, 46; and Kochiyama, 45–6, 179

xenophobia, 23

Yamamoto, Mike, 201–2

Yamashita, Karen Tei, *I Hotel: A Novel*, 166

Yamashita, Qris, 30–1; and poster arts, 135

Yanagida, Takashi, 125, 180, 185, 197

Yanagita, Mike, 28

Yasui, Min, 95

yellow: and activism, 163; and black, 46; and political cartoons, 146–7; use of, 64–6

Yellow Brotherhood (group), 7, 66, 72, 79

Yellow Identity (conference), 66

"Yellow Pearl," 66, 124, 127, 146, 197; poster for, 138–9

"Yellow Peril," 18
"Yellow Power Arrives!" (*Los Angeles Free Press*), 59, 193
Yellow Symposium, 88
Yew, Peter, 155
Yip, Steve, 119
yogores (term), 76, 124
Yoneda, Goso, 95
Yoshimura, Evelyn, 2, 44, 124; as

"Asian sister," 45
Young Communist League, 91
Yow Yee (group), 79–80
Yung, Danny, 125–7, 143

Zhou, Min, 39
Zia, Helen, 198–9; black or white, 48; isolation of, 26–7; on women, 49–50